FOURTH EDITION

DRUGS: A FACTUAL ACCOUNT

Dorothy E. Dusek

and

Daniel A. Girdano

UNIVERSITY OF UTAH

**RANDOM HOUSE
NEW YORK**

Fourth Edition
98765432
Copyright © 1987 by Newbery Award Records, Inc.

Library of Congress Cataloging in Publication Data

Dusek, Dorothy.
  Drugs, a factual account.

  Includes bibliographies and index.
  1. Drug abuse. 2. Drug abuse—Physiological aspects. 3. Drug abuse—Treatment. I. Girdano,
Daniel A. II. Title

HV5801.D88   1986   613.8   86-1309   1
ISBN 0-394-35577-6

Manufactured in the United States of America

Designer: Susan Phillips

Cover Design: Nadja Furlan-Lorbek

PREFACE

In a recent national survey on what students want to know about drugs, it was found that students seek information about what to expect from the drug they use, that is, how the drug is absorbed and metabolized, what are its effects and its related behavioral changes. The students surveyed were concerned with the problems related to drug abuse, such as drunken driving and antisocial or destructive behavior, as well as the positive aspects of drug use. They were primarily interested in alcohol and marijuana, but also expressed a need for a basic understanding of all drugs and the reasons leading to drug use.

We mention the results of this survey not only because we believe in the validity of the survey, but also because it supports our contention that what most students want and need is a factual overview of the total drug scene that zeros in on up-to-date findings on specific topics.

Drugs: A Factual Account, Fourth Edition, was designed to meet these student needs. It gives the reader a basic understanding of the drug problem by first presenting physiological knowledge of the nervous system, and then discussing the pharmacology of particular drugs and their active ingredients, and how they relate to behavior modifications. This knowledge helps dispel the mystery about the cause of behaviors such as sleepiness, alertness, anorexia, physical dependence, and tolerance resulting from drug consumption; the absence of such material in many of the current books on drugs seemed to us a serious omission. It is our contention that we should attempt to understand the drug user at all levels—from microscopic nerve cells, through brain functions, to psychological and social interaction. This basic information should enable the reader to make the transition more easily from the current drug scene to future patterns of drug use.

To illustrate the influence of history and society's acceptance of drugs, we have included a brief historical perspective on drugs combined with some basic definitions needed for a full understanding of the drug problem. We have attempted to summarize some of the more popular reasons for drug use and abuse early in the book and to continually relate the social and cultural factors to the medical and pharmacological aspects throughout the text. Because each of the drugs of current use and interest is unique in action and effects, we have devoted a separate chapter to each drug or group of related drugs. Each chapter discusses the psychophysiological effects of the drug(s), use patterns, individual and societal problems that are arising from abuse, the medicinal or beneficial uses, and where pertinent, the historical and legal perspective. In this edition, alcohol and tobacco smoking have been given extended coverage due to their widespread use and the dangers involved therein. Driving and drinking, the female alcoholic, fetal alcohol syndrome, and motivation for safe, moderate use of alcohol are emphasized in the Alcohol chapter. The chapter on Smoking includes a smoking cessation program that can be self-initiated so that readers may use it for themselves or to help others in their effort to become a nonsmoker. The issue of "stemming the tide" of drug misuse and abuse in the 1980s is addressed in a new Chapter 12 of this edition. This chapter gives a broad look at the nation's attempt, from Federal legislation to local education, to stop the growth, production, import, sale, and use of dangerous drugs. Particular emphasis is placed on educational interventions and personal coping skills that can help individuals develop drug-free life styles.

Drugs: A Factual Account, Fourth Edition, was written to fill the needs of a wide range of individuals with different backgrounds and interests. Fully realizing that each reader may desire further specific knowledge, we have included references to original scientific studies which serve both as verification of factual information and as guides to further research on each topic. Additional references at the end of each chapter should also help the reader to branch out into more specific informational areas.

We hope the basic information we have supplied in this book will serve as a catalyst for continued research and will promote greater understanding of the drug problem and its possible solutions.

D.E.D.
D.A.G.

CONTENTS

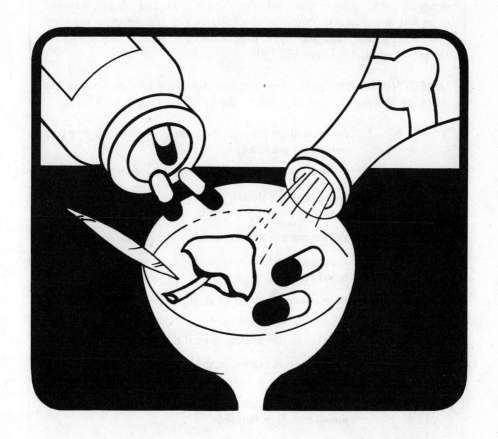

CHAPTER 1

DRUG
PERSPECTIVES

Self-Test: YOUR DRUG BELIEF SYSTEM

The first two chapters of this book discuss current trends in drug use and perspectives on why people use drugs. Drug use can be interpreted as positive or negative depending on one's belief or value system. Thus, before you read these first two chapters, complete this exercise which is designed to help you understand a little more about your drug belief or value system (Centers for Disease Control, 1983, pp. 178-180).

DIRECTIONS: *Circle the letter that best expresses your position on the following statements (Y = Yes   M = Maybe   N = No).*

Y   M   N   1.   People will not get addicted to drugs or alcohol if they take only small amounts.

Y   M   N   2.   Using drugs or alcohol can be bad for your health.

Y   M   N   3.   Using drugs or alcohol can cause people to have problems in getting along with their families.

Y   M   N   4.   People can use drugs or alcohol and still get good grades.

Y   M   N   5.   People who use drugs or alcohol have an easy time making new friends.

Y   M   N   6.   People who use drugs or alcohol can get into trouble with the law.

Y   M   N   7.   People can stay healthy even if they use drugs or alcohol.

Y   M   N   8.   People who use drugs or alcohol have a hard time making new friends.

Y   M   N   9.   Using drugs or alcohol does not affect how well people get along with their families.

Y   M   N   10.   It is hard to keep good friends if you use drugs or alcohol.

Y   M   N   11.   People who use drugs or alcohol can become addicted to them.

Y   M   N   12.   Using drugs or alcohol can cause you to get lower grades in school.

Y   M   N   13.   People who use drugs or alcohol have more friends than people who don't use drugs or alcohol.

Y   M   N   14.   Most people who use drugs or alcohol don't get into trouble with the law.

Self-Test: YOUR DRUG BELIEF SYSTEM (continued)

SCORING: Point values are assigned to responses according to the following key:

Question:	1	2	3	4	5	6	7	8	9	10	11	12	13	14
YES	0	2	2	0	0	2	0	2	0	2	2	2	0	0
MAYBE	1	1	1	1	1	1	1	1	1	1	1	1	1	1
NO	2	0	0	2	2	0	2	0	2	0	0	0	2	2

Add the point value of every response and divide by the number of responses (14). The maximum score attainable (2) indicates a strong belief in the negative effects of drugs or alcohol on one's health, family, grades, ability to make and keep friends, as well as the legal dangers associated with addiction.

INTRODUCTION

The basic scientific definition of a drug is that it is a substance that, by its chemical nature, affects the structure or function of a living organism. This definition covers almost everything that people ingest, inhale, inject, or absorb. It includes medicines, over-the-counter drugs, illegal drugs, beverage drugs, cigarettes, food additives, industrial chemicals, even food. Therefore, any discussion of drugs must be somehow limited, and that limitation is dependent upon a particular point of view of the world.

For this discussion the emphasis will be on psychoactive drugs that alter behavior. This will necessitate not only taking a look at the pharmacology of drugs for their effect, but also looking at the characteristics of the substance and the way it interacts with the living organism. There is no such thing as a single effect of a drug. All drugs have multiple effects, and these vary from dose level to dose level, from person to person, and are greatly influenced by time and setting. Drug effects are a function of the interaction between the drug and the individual's physical, psychological, and social milieu.

All drugs are dangerous for some individuals at some dosage level under some circumstances; some drugs are more dangerous than others, some individuals are more susceptible to drugs than others. The use of any drug involves risks. To some extent, the purpose of the discussion of drug use and abuse is to come up with a more informed assessment of that risk.

The choice of risk depends on the cost versus worth equation constructed by each individual. The elements that must be considered are the substance, the individual, and the social-cultural milieu. Action based exclusively on any one element increases the risk.

Very often, the flow of information designed to influence drug use decisions focuses on one element more than others, often excluding one element completely. This usually results from a personal or philosophical bias. There are four major points of view or models of drug use, and each has a bias. None by itself provides complete understanding of the world of drug use and abuse. However, knowing the boundaries of the type of information being received can be useful, for at least one knows that some dimension is missing. The four models are: (1) the moral-legal model, (2) the disease or public health model, (3) the psychosocial model, and (4) the sociocultural model.

The first two models of drug use operate from the premise that the answer to drug abuse problems is to keep drugs away from man. In these two models drugs are classified as either safe or dangerous. "Dangerous" includes not only drugs that are physically dangerous but also those that are not socially or legally sanctioned. Drugs are the active ingredient, people are the deviant victims who must be protected. Protection comes in the form of legal controls on cultivation, manufacture, distribution, or possession. The deterrents are punishment or fear of harm. The major difference between the legal-moral and the disease or public health model is that the latter dwells less on the legality of the substance and more on its potential harm.

The other two models, the psychosocial model and the sociocultural model, operate from the premise that the object is to keep man away from drugs. The psychosocial model tends to put major emphasis on the individual rather than on the substance as the active agent. Drug use is seen as another behavior that persists in order to serve some purpose for the individual. This model makes important distinctions among different use patterns, attitudes, and behaviors.

The fourth model is the sociocultural model, which views drug use and the problems associated with drug abuse from the social context, emphasizing environmental and socioeconomic conditions. Poverty, poor housing, discrimination, lack of opportunity, urbanization, etc., all are seen as the breeding ground of the personal factors which ultimately lead to drug use.

In each model, the tactics or information designed to reduce drug use are slanted toward the specific philosophical bias of the model. The tactic may be punishment, control, threat, reduction of need, or restructuring of the environment. Each model defines the goals of specific attempts to influence drug use. While the recognized bias in this book is toward the psychosocial approach, the other models do receive attention so that the reader can realize the place and importance of each, and put together a composite picture of drug use and abuse.

TRENDS AND TERMINOLOGY

Drug use and abuse are factors in the everyday lives of all Americans. Therefore, everyone should become aware of drug terminology, facts, and trends that pertain to this topic. This chapter first outlines some current trends in the use and abuse of common licit and illicit drugs, then presents the definition of terms that will be useful in reading this book and other drug literature.

The National Survey on Drug Abuse conducted by the NIDA (National Institute of Drug Abuse), along with other hospital records and general survey reports, give us the following information about drug taking in the United States (Cohen, 1981; Hollister, 1983; Miller & Cisin, 1983; Miller et al., 1983).

Alcohol

This is the most widely used drug in America. More than one-half the adult population drinks. More than nine million Americans are believed to have definite problems associated with drinking. Six percent of high school seniors report that they consume alcohol daily; however, from 1979 to 1982 there was a slight drop in the number of current users of alcohol (i.e., those who have used alcohol within the month prior to the survey).

It is estimated that 50,000 deaths occur each year from motor vehicle accidents, and about 50 percent are alcohol-related. Cirrhosis of the liver remains the fourth leading cause of death for middle-aged men and fifth for women. The number of homicides and suicides committed under the influence of alcohol is difficult to assess, but is believed to be considerable. A greater awareness among pregnant women of the effects of alcohol on the fetus shows promise in reducing the incidence of fetal alcohol syndrome.

With the possible exception of the teenage drinking problem, the number of drinkers and the severity of their problem as well as deaths attributed to alcohol have remained fairly constant over the last decade. In addition, little progress has been made in the understanding of the factors that cause alcoholism. As might be expected, little progress has been made in alcohol treatment techniques, and little new information has been uncovered on how alcohol affects the human organism (Hollister, 1983).

Tobacco

Nicotine is the second most widely used drug in the United States. Approximately 55 million Americans smoke daily, and more than 485,000 Americans die prematurely from tobacco-related illnesses. Smoking annually causes 147,000 cancer deaths, 240,000 deaths from diseases of the circulatory system, 61,000 non-cancer deaths from diseases of the respiratory system, 14,000 from diseases of the digestive system, 4,000 infant deaths due to mother's smoking, 4,000 deaths due to fires and accidents, and nearly 15,000 deaths from miscellaneous and ill-defined diseases. Add to that the deaths caused by the smoking of pipes and cigars, the passive inhalation of environmental tobacco smoke, and the chewing and snuffing of tobacco, which probably raises the total United States tobacco death toll to more than a half million—more than one-fourth of all deaths from all causes (Center for Health and Safety Studies, 1985).

There has been a slight drop since 1979 in current users of cigarettes. In a breakdown by age group, it is seen that 22 percent of youth and 40 percent of adults are regular smokers. By age twelve, one out of five youngsters smoke. One alarming increase in smoking patterns is that of young girls—the smoking pattern of high school girls now approximates that of high school boys.

Marijuana

Over 40 million persons have experienced cannabis. The number of regular users is estimated to be ten to fifteen million and seems to be decreasing. Four million are between the ages of twelve and seventeen, and 8.5 million are between eighteen and twenty-five. Ten percent of high school seniors are daily users. Along with the downward trend in the number of current users of alcohol and tobacco, there appears to be as well a diminishing percentage of youth and young adults using marijuana.

The health hazards of cannabis are of great concern, and this remains an area of interest for researchers, as does the possibility of positive therapeutic use of cannabis. The legal attempt to control the supply of this drug in the United States has been unsuccessful (Hollister, 1983).

Stimulants

The 1982 NIDA survey showed that 6.7 percent of youth, 18 percent of young adults, and 6.2 percent of older adults had used stimulants for nonmedical reasons at least once. Additionally, 2.9 percent of youth, 4.3 percent of young adults, and 12 percent of older adults reported using stimulants for medical reasons at some time in their lives.

There has been a remarkable increase in the use of cocaine over the last decade. While there is widespread support for the notion that cocaine is a relatively harmless drug, recent experience suggests the opposite. Cocaine is one of the most reinforcing drugs known, and dependence on the drug is very difficult to break. Heavy users can experience psychosis when high for prolonged periods and severe depression when the drug is withdrawn. The flow of cocaine into the United States seems to be increasing with its demand. Even though the Federal government has greatly increased its efforts to stem the tide of cocaine importation, the monetary rewards for this expensive drug are so large that many people are willing to take the risk of dealing in cocaine.

Treatment centers that specialize in cocaine dependence are springing up throughout the country, but to date little research has been done on the efficacy of treatment programs.

Sedatives

Although illicit supplies of sedatives do reach the market, these drugs are largely prescribed. The benzodiazepines are the most widely prescribed class of sedative-hypnotics. One recent concern has been the problem of low-dose dependence. This occurs when long-term treatment with therapeutic doses seems to create a type of dependence that is difficult to distinguish from symptoms of anxiety. It is now known that receptors for benzodiazepines, as well as barbiturates, occur naturally in the brain, and the reaction of these receptors to long-term benzodiazepine treatment may bring about dependence (Hollister, 1983).

In 1982, nearly 6 percent of youth, 18.7 percent of young adults, and 4.8

percent of older adults reported that they had used sedatives nonmedically at least once in their lives. For medical use, the corresponding figures were 5.6 percent of youth, 9.7 percent of young adults, and 21.4 percent of older adults.

Similarly, tranquilizers have been used illegally and also medically by all age groups at some point in their lives; the 1982 figures are as follows:

	Nonmedical (in percent)	Medical (in percent)
Youth (12–17)	4.9	9.3
Young adults (18–25)	15.1	19.3
Older adults (26+)	3.6	41.3

Hallucinogens

Phencyclidine (PCP) has replaced lysergic acid (LSD) as the preferred hallucinogen, but unlike LSD, phencyclidine can cause death directly from overdose. The illegal manufacture of PCP is lucrative and relatively easy, its chemical precursors being substances widely used commercially and impossible to control. Although there is an encouraging trend toward decreased use of PCP, it remains to be seen as to whether it will be sustained (Hollister, 1983).

As of 1982, 21 percent of the 18–25-year-olds and 19 percent of the 26-34 group had tried hallucinogens. Only about 5 percent of the youth and only 2 percent of those over 35 reported having "ever used." Since 1979, the current hallucinogen use has dropped from 4.4 percent to below 2 percent. Among youth and young adults, there has been a drop in PCP use during the last five years. It appears that current users of hallucinogens are a small minority of "ever-users."

The appearance of MDMA, a synthetic hallucinogen that was billed as the ideal hallucinogenic drug, will no doubt add to the incidence of drug taking in this category—especially because it was not illegal when it made its media appearance in *Time* and *Newsweek*. Since that time, it has been placed under legal control, making it difficult to determine its impact until further research is done.

Heroin

It appears that there has been a stabilization of the number of heroin-dependent persons in the last few years, with estimates given at approximately one-half million people. After the tenfold increase from 1960-1969, there was a slow decline in the number of dependents, and a final leveling off during the mid-1970s. Rather than being primarily a problem of minorities, it now affects the white, native-born majority to a great degree. The ills associated with opiate abuse continue to be more social than medical; thievery and prostitution are the most common consequences of having a habit that is expensive while at the same time debilitating and precludes useful employment (Hollister, 1983).

About 80,000 opiate-dependent persons are in treatment at any given time in the United States. Some centers advocate drug programs, such as methadone maintenance, and some advocate social programs of the self-help variety, such as Synanon. There is more proof for the efficacy of methadone programs than for any other modality, but this should not negate the advocacy of other types of programs.

Definition of Drug Terminology

As the social and medical impact of drug taking increased in America, new terms were added to the drug literature. Medicine was denoted as a kind of drug taken into the body to prevent or cure a disease or disabling condition. The taking of drugs to an extent that they caused social or medical harm to the taker was soon termed "drug abuse." Opiate dependence was one of the earliest problems with drug abuse in the United States, and much of the early drug terminology came from defining and treating that problem. The World Health Organization (WHO) defined the addict and addiction, but with the increased use of other euphoric drugs, new terminology evolved. For instance, chronic users of some of the newer psychotropic drugs did not fit the WHO description of the "addict." The WHO described *addiction* as a condition in which the addict was committed to a drug physically and mentally, had progressed steadily along the tolerance ladder, and was a societal problem. It was learned, however, that many of the new drugs did not produce physical dependence, but the mental drive to take them was still overpowering. Hence, the term *psychological dependence* (or psychic dependence) was coined. This took up where the old term *habituation* left off. It was defined as a strong desire or compulsion to continue the use of a psychoactive drug, a craving for repetition of the pleasurable, euphoric effects of the substance. As a WHO drug table shows, however, there are no commonly used psychoactive drugs that are not capable of producing psychological dependence. This inadequacy of term challenges the concept of discarding the older, but more meaningful term *addiction*, a process that may have exacerbated our current problem in understanding and dealing with the seriousness and depth of the condition. The term *dependency* shifted us out of the human realm somewhat and into the medical realm, rather than the opposite. This is paradoxical, since discouragement of the use of the term *addiction* was meant to help change society's stereotyped picture of the addict as a criminal so that we would begin to treat dependence on drugs as a disease.

Stanley Peele, in *Love and Addiction* (1975), gives an in-depth description of addiction to help develop an understanding of this condition. He describes addiction as a human reaction to drugs and many other experiences as well, such as love, marriage, home, medicine, psychiatry, school, and religion. It is an attachment to an object, person, or sensation that is so strong that the person diminishes appreciation of and ability to attend to other things in the environment or within the self to such a degree that he or she becomes dependent on that experience as the sole source of gratification.

The bottom line of addiction *is* dependency, but not necessarily on a drug. Dependency in addiction is a descriptor of character, one that denotes that a person is not independent and therefore must rely on someone else for care. Blum et al. (1969) pointed out that drug users are trained early in childhood to accept the sick role and to exploit it. This readiness for submission to others is the basis for addiction, since it appears that addiction occurs in those who have little resource to stabilize their own lives. And addicts are those who do not possess the ability or desire to meet life head-on, to experience new things and grow with those experiences, whether they be positive or negative. Addiction stems from unresolved childhood conflicts about autonomy and dependence (Peele, 1975).

Drug addiction offers a dulling of sensibility so that for some it protects against new and demanding situations. This reduces the user's ability to learn and to grow, and creates a situation in which the individual becomes less and less prepared to confront life. It is a downward spiral. Becoming a depressant addict in adolescence helps a young person avoid decision making. For all young people the decision is made at some time either to gather experiences to gain maturity or to become dependent on something or someone.

Once the mental form of dependence was designated, the term *physical dependence* also came into being. This denoted that the body developed a cellular demand for a specific drug. (Physical dependence can be discovered only if the drug is taken away from the user. If the user then develops withdrawal symptoms or the abstinence syndrome, he or she has become physically dependent on the drug.) Recently, these terms have been replaced by two clinical terms: *harmful abuse* and *chemical dependency*. Harmful abuse has been described by three characteristics: (1) a pattern of pathological use, (2) impairment in social or occupational functioning due to substance use, and (3) minimal duration of disturbance of at least one month.

Chemical dependency to any substance is a more severe form of substance abuse because it includes evidence of either tolerance or withdrawal. Both harmful abuse and chemical dependency are possible with alcohol, barbiturates, and other similar sedatives or hypnotics, opiates, amphetamines, and cannabis. Besides these five classes of substances, three others are related to abuse: cocaine, phencyclidine (PCP) or others with similar actions, and hallucinogens. Tobacco is associated with dependence only. Abuse or dependency for each substance is professionally determined by applying specific diagnostic criteria for each drug using the APA's *Diagnostic and Statistical Manual of Mental Disorders, third edition* (1980).

Some of the other terms that are useful in understanding the drug education literature are as follows:

Minimal dose: the smallest dose that is sufficient to produce an effect
Maximal dose: the largest dose that produces an effect without producing a toxic reaction
Average dose: the dose used successfully by the majority of the people. The average response in the average person who is not sensitive or allergic to the drug. There are numerous factors that alter the response to drugs and must be considered when using drugs. Some of the most important factors are:

  age: children show significant differences in absorption, distribution, metabolism sensitivity, and excretion of most drugs. Likewise persons over sixty require lower dosages of most drugs.
  size: underweight and overweight adults also show differences in drug effect. The average effects are often measured on a 70-kg (154-lb) adult. The same dose consumed by a 100-pound and a 200-pound person will produce marked

differences in effect. Body composition is also important as those individuals with a higher percentage of adipose tissue will have less body water, therefore, smaller amounts of the drug will be bound and larger amounts of the drug will be free to act on sensitive tissue.

disease: renal disease is an important factor in that elimination of the drug or its harmful metabolites will be slowed.

Liver disease will also slow the biotransformation of most drugs allowing for increased concentrations to act on sensitive tissue. Other conditions that will affect an individual's response to drugs are: heart disease, electrolyte imbalance, hypoproteinemia, thyroid disease, and gastrointestinal disorders.

Genetic determinants: much of the physical variation in response to drugs may be due to biological differences influenced by genetics. Such factors as drug metabolism, drug receptor synthesis, and activity which affects response may differ in individuals and may be predominant in specific races of people. Specific genetic differences in response to alcohol consumption is currently a very active area of research.

Concomitant drug use: simultaneous use of several drugs can influence the absorption, distribution, metabolism, or excretion of a drug. This may take the form of a competition for protein binding sites or a depletion of enzymes necessary for biotransformation.

Environmental factors; food and/or alcohol consumption, cigarette smoking, food additives, exposure to household or occupational chemicals, and physical activity can alter the effect of drugs.

Route of administration: when a drug is injected intravenously, a high level in the blood is achieved almost immediately but the concentration remains high for a relatively short period of time. Intramuscular (into muscles) or subcutaneous (under the skin) injections provide for a slower rise in plasma drug levels. Oral administration produces an even slower rise in plasma drug level because of the slower rate of absorption from the digestive tract. Inhalation results in a rapid onset of the drug effect.

Loading dose: "filling" the body with a drug quickly to obtain maximal effects instead of waiting for drug accumulation to take place. Once this concentration is achieved an effective dose can be maintained by smaller maintenance doses given at regular intervals (Wartak, 1983).

Tolerance: A reduction in response to repeated administration. Traditionally, tolerance has been explained as a reduced physiological or behavioral response to the same dose of a drug with a need to increase the dose to obtain a constant effect. One important mechanism of tolerance that is understood is that the presence of a particular drug, such as a barbiturate, stimulates an increase in drug-metabolizing enzymes. As the rate of metabolism of the drug increases, the activity of the drug diminishes. This is known as *metabolic tolerance*. Another phenomenon, *cellular tolerance*, has also been observed. This is due to some unknown cellular adaptation in the brain whereby the receptors responsible for the drug action become less sensitive to the drug. Still another theory of tolerance has been advanced, the concept of *learned tolerance*, also referred to as *behavioral tolerance*. This theory stresses the importance of the corollary processes, such as environmental cues, associated with consumption of any particular drug (Cornfield-Sumner & Stolerman, 1978). *Cross tolerance* has been observed between drugs of the same general class of action. That is, consumption of one depressant drug often produces a tolerance to another depressant drug. Although learning or adaptation on a cognitive level is undoubtedly part of the tolerance phenomenon, researchers have found evidence of physical changes as well. One such change is in the activity of the liver's drug-metabolizing enzymes. As the intake of barbiturates increases, so does the activity of the liver enzymes that break down the drug. As time goes on, increasing quantities of the drug must be ingested in order to have the same amount of the drug circulating in the system (Stevenson & Turnbull, 1968).

Another enzymatic theory was proposed by Shuster (1961), who indicated that initial depression of neurohormone-producing systems (that is, systems for production of norepinephrine, serotonin, etc.) caused the body to overproduce these hormones so that the natural, normal (predrug) levels could be maintained. Therefore, increased drug dosage would be necessary to overcome the increased levels of neurohormones. Withdrawal symptoms, then, are due to the high level of neurohormones that would be present when the depressant drug was no longer there to counteract them. As the neurohormone level diminished—or returned to normal, preaddiction levels—withdrawal symptoms would also diminish.

Other interesting theories of tolerance currently being studied include the possible interaction of the depressants with the neurohormone serotonin. It has been found that animals that are tolerant to depressants use more serotonin than do control animals or withdrawn animals. This, along with the hypothesis that tolerance resembles an immune reaction, has revived interest in an old theory that there are actually two forms of tolerance: one form persisting up to eight hours, called short-term tolerance, and one lasting up to three weeks, known as long-term tolerance (Cochin, 1970). In summary, one can only say that tolerance is basically a phenomenon of biochemical and biophysical cellular adaptation to external stimuli.

Physical dependence is more abstract and not so easily demonstrated or studied as tolerance. A unique biological phenomenon characterized by a *metabolic demand* for a *particular substance,* it has been described as a state of pseudo-homeostasis—a hyperexcitability that develops in the cells of the central nervous system after prolonged use of depressants such as heroin, alcohol, or barbiturate-like substances. However, this phenomenon can be seen only when the depressant is withheld, and symptoms known as the *abstinence* or *withdrawal syndrome* emerge.

Theories presented to explain physical dependence generally center on (a) the production, release, and/or destruction of neurohormones (such as norepinephrine), (b) neuronal sensitivity, and (c) depression of endocrine function.

Because of similarities in the abstinence syndrome caused by such chemically dissimilar agents as alcohol, barbiturates, meprobamate, paraldehyde, chlordiazepoxide, and others—and because these substances have the capacity to stave off signs of withdrawal in users of other depressants, including heroin, due to cross-tolerance—one mechanism for physical dependence seems to be depression of nervous activity in similar central nervous system pathways. This may be initial depression at the synapse followed by a gradual limiting of the production of neurohormones. As one pathway becomes depressed, other parallel, or redundant, pathways may enlarge their function and continue body processes on a somewhat depressed level (Martin, 1970). The body's amazing homeostasis or equilibrium-maintaining mechanisms (centered primarily in the hypothalamus) allow for continued functioning without triggering stress reactions. This results in a sort of disease of adaptation (theories of tolerance here interact with the theory of physical dependence.) This adaptation affects the endocrine glands, which are depressed and therefore do not produce the stress reactions that usually accompany altered homeostatic conditions.

Upon withdrawal of the depressant there is extreme hyperexcitability, due in part to release of depressed stress reactions and in part to restoration of depressed neutral pathways. In essence, the body is now able to realize to what extent its homeostasis or equilibrium has been altered, and violent stress reactions (the classic withdrawal symptoms) are now felt. This first appears as a sense of apprehension and general weakness, which soon develops into muscle fasciculations, tremors of the hands, hyperactive reflexes, insomnia, abdominal cramps, nausea, and vomiting. There is an extreme dehydration and rapid loss of weight accompanied by increases in heart rate, blood pressure, and respiratory rate. Disorientation in time and space, hallucinations, and death are not uncommon.

REFERENCES

American Psychiatric Association. *Diagnostic and Statistical Manual of Mental Disorders.* 3rd ed. Washington, D.C.: APA, 1980.

Blum, R. H., et al. *Drugs I: Society and Drugs.* San Francisco: Jossey-Bass, 1969.

Center for Health and Safety Studies. *Smoking and Health Reporter* 2(3):8, 1985.

Cochin, J. "Possible mechanisms in development of tolerance." *Federation Proceedings, Federation of American Societies for Experimental Biology* 29:19–27, 1970.

Cohen, Sidney. *The Substance Abuse Problems.* New York: Haworth Press, 1981.

Cornfield-Sumner, P. K., and J. Stolerman. "Behavioral tolerance," in D. E. Blackman and D. J. Sangel, eds. *Contemporary Research in Behavioral Pharmacology.* New York: Plenum Press, 1978.

Hollister, Leo. "Drug abuse in the United States: the past decade." *Drug and Alcohol Dependence* 11:49–55, 1983.

Martin, W. R. "Pharmacological redundancy as an adaptive mechanism in the central nervous system." *Federation Proceedings, Federation of American Societies for Experimental Biology* 29:13–18, 1970.

Miller, J. D., and I. H. Cisin. *Highlights from the National Survey on Drug Abuse: 1982.* Rockville, Md.: NIDA, 1983.

Miller, J. D., et al. *National Survey on Drug Abuse: 1982.* Rockville, Md.: NIDA, 1983.

Peele, Stanley. *Love and Addiction.* New York: Signet, 1975.

Shuster, L. "Repression and de-repression of enzyme synthesis as a possible explanation of some aspects of drug action." *Nature* 189:314–315, 1961.

Stevenson, J. H., and M. J. Turnbull. "Hepatic drug-metabolism enzyme activity and duration of hexobarbitone anaesthesia." *Biochemical Pharmacology* 17:2297–2305, 1968.

Wartak, J. *Clinical Pharmacokinetics.* New York, Praeger, 1983.

SUGGESTED READINGS

Cohen, Sidney. *The Substance Abuse Problems.* New York: Haworth Press, 1981.

Duncan, David, and R. Gold. *Drugs and the Whole Person.* New York: Wiley, 1982.

Inciardi, J. A., ed. *The Drugs-Crime Connection.* Beverly Hills, Calif.: Sage, 1981.

Krivanek, J. A. *Drug Problems, People Problems.* Sydney, Australia: George Allen & Unwin, 1982.

Walker, William. *Drug Control in the Americas.* Albuquerque: University of New Mexico Press, 1981.

CHAPTER 2

WHY DRUGS?

From the earliest of times, natives identified and used indigenous plants and other substances that would alter their health and their states of consciousness. The shaman, medicine person, priest, or other central person of high authority knew how to use these special substances to unify and balance energy in the human body and to help the earthling commune with the spirits. This art of substance use slowly evolved into the taking of substances for altered states but without the spiritual connotation. In recent decades, the name that has been given to this experience is "getting high."

GETTING HIGH

Being high is considered an altered state of consciousness, which usually implies a state of mind or consciousness that is different from the normal state. Simple enough, but there is a catch. What is "normal"? In this case, the term *normal* is used to mean that one is in control of the environment. This is characterized by rational, cause-and-effect, goal-directed and reflective thinking—in other words, a "taking-care-of-business" state.

According to Tart (1975), normal consciousness is "consensus reality," an enculturated state tailored to show reality in terms of what is good for society. It is society's prejudice that classifies this state as normal, because it is this state of consciousness that turns the wheels of industry: the state in which we converse, write checks, and make comparisons . . . a state developed as a specialized tool for coping with society.

To change from the normal ego-consciousness, one must steer the normal thought processes away from the "planning-doing" state to a "feeling-experiencing" state, sometimes described as an egoless state. In this egoless state of consciousness the environment is perceived as nonthreatening: The proper clothes, cars, colleges, and vacation spots are not important; impressions do not have to be made, images protected, or feelings guarded. It is no wonder that a work-ethic society frowns on a state of consciousness that departs from "normal."

Another reason why altered states are difficult to understand is that we are not *taught* to understand them. As we benefit from the part of our cultural development that enables us to make a living, we are diminished by the limited visions of reality and are not taught how to enjoy quiet and tranquility and the spiritual search, or, in general, how to live. We are not taught to understand and to use the other natural states of consciousness that differ from the "normal" waking-doing state. This is not to diminish the importance of waking consciousness, because it is a naturally developed coping state. The importance of exploring the other-than-normal states of consciousness is to give greater recognition to the need to understand, express, and develop the other natural states as well.

As yet we have not developed communicative words or phrases that can accurately describe our varied states of consciousness, and so we use the symbols of the normal state and apply scientific methodology to probe and describe the workings of the mind. Science explains that the brain conserves energy in attending to the environment so that it can most efficiently assure psychological and physiological survival (see Fig. 2.1).

Under special conditions of dysfunction, such as in cases of acute psychosis, some drugged states, or some meditative states, the system of automatic thought processing breaks down and permits a less efficient mode of processing to take over, in which everyday activities, feelings, or events are perceived differently or shifted more toward perceptual than cognitive functioning. When this breakdown of automatic, protective processing occurs, one shifts from the normal state to an altered state (Deikman, 1969).

THE ALTERED STATE OF CONSCIOUSNESS

Being in an altered state of consciousness means that one has shifted from the normal, taking-care-of-business state to some other level of consciousness. This other level may be as basic as daydreaming or as spiritual as cosmic consciousness, but be assured that we all wander in and out of normal consciousness many times throughout the day and night. The frequency of these occurrences depends a great deal on our external and internal environment, especially on the level of stimulation around us; but the frequency can also be planned or allowed by one's own mind.

Environmental levels of stimulation that are above or below the accustomed

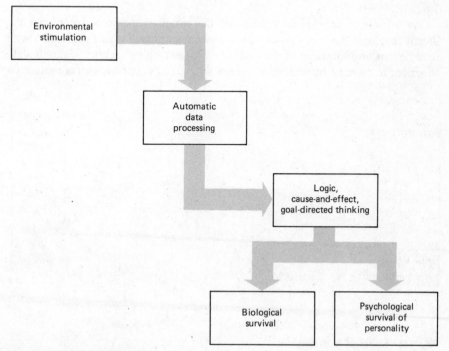

Fig. 2.1 The normal state.

range may produce an altered state. For instance, decreasing external stimulation to the point of social deprivation may trigger an altered state. Other low-stimulus activities, in which incoming information is monotonous and nonspecific, may allow one to slip from the normal state. These conditions might develop during solitary confinement, when flying at high altitudes in cloudless skies, or when driving for extended periods on a straight, open highway in the early morning hours. Other conditions, such as religious or spiritual states, passive meditation, floating in water, extreme muscle relaxation, the use of depressant drugs, application of deep pressure as in massage, or tightly holding a frightened child, may reduce the intensity and rate of stimulation, hence inducing the altered state.

Just as reduced stimulation may bring about an altered state, so may increased stimulation. Examples of such hyperaroused states include activities that involve sharp, loud, and everchanging noise or light, as with some revivalistic meetings, ecstatic trances, and brainwashing techniques. Other activities or conditions that have been known to cause altered states of consciousness are the quickening beat of a drum or mounting applause, prolonged vigilance during sentry duty, intense mental absorption (as in many tasks of reading, writing, or problem solving), light tactile touch as in tickling, and the use of certain psychedelic or stimulant drugs.

In addition to these predominantly external factors, there are certain somatopsychological factors or alterations in body chemistry caused by hypoglycemia, dehydration, sleep deprivation, or the administration of anesthetics, psychedelics, stimulants, or sedative drugs, that can induce an altered state of consciousness (Ludwig, 1969).

As one might surmise from knowing the various conditions that trigger the altered state, our states of consciousness can range through a vast continuum with extreme hypoarousal states on one end, in which awareness occurs without thought or action, to extreme hyperarousal, manic states, and ecstatic mystical rapture on

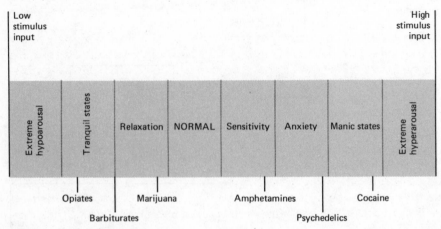

Fig. 2.2   States of consciousness.

the other end (see Fig. 2.2). The normal state is somewhere in the middle. The altered states produced in these two areas beyond the normal are behaviorally quite different, yet they exhibit some characteristics that are common to both and serve to distinguish the altered from the normal state of consciousness.

One of the factors central to most altered states is the shift in the level of attention and concentration away from ego-centered consciousness. Memory of an altered state is usually poor since the usual pattern of thinking and laying down of memory patterns is changed during that state. One does not think in terms of cause and effect; thus the significance or meaning attached to subjective experiences or ideas is also changed. In many altered states, one loses the feeling that he or she is in control of the environment or of the relationship of the self to the environment; thus, self-centered daydreams diminish, a sense of depersonalization occurs, and inhibitions are lessened. The sense of time changes with the reduction of attention to time-dictated events. Most often, there is a feeling of timelessness or of time coming to a standstill. The perception of body, self, and reality often changes and often, visual imagery occurs.

Most of us have experienced some or all of these characteristic events of the altered state by daydreaming, by becoming completely immersed in an enjoyable activity, or perhaps by meditating. And after the state has been experienced, it is difficult to describe it in everyday ego-consciousness language. Thus, we can, and do, experience dozens of different states of consciousness throughout the day, but have little recollection of those changes.

It is beyond the scope of this discussion to describe in detail the twenty or more different states of consciousness that have been analyzed in the literature, but one should be familiar with the five that are most often recognized and discussed. These are:

Level 1   Deep sleep without dreams
Level 2   Sleep with dreams
Level 3   Waking sleep or identification (I-Coping)
Level 4   Self-transcendence
Level 5   Objective or cosmic consciousness

Robert DeRopp (1968) discussed these five basic levels in terms of where people are now, and to which level they must go to obtain ego- or self-transcendence and enlightenment. According to DeRopp, the highest level of consciousness is attainable only by those who can relieve themselves of ego involvement and the need for power over others.

To DeRopp, what is classified as the waking ego consciousness is little better than Level 2 (sleep with dreams), because we do not know where we are going or what we are doing. In fact, we live in a dream, inhabit a world of delusions, and become puppets manipulated by external forces. But, since that is all we have ever known, it is reality. Being surrounded by others just like us and never experiencing the freedom of spirit of the fourth level, we become complacent and live out our lives without ever entering into the struggle to develop our expanded consciousness.

Self-Transcendence

The fourth level in DeRopp's schema has been defined as a state of relative egolessness, free from anxiety and defenses, which allows for expansion of experiences and feelings and for increased knowledge of self. Ego, time, and space are transcended, giving rise to peace and tranquility. It is a state of awareness without thought.

Once you have experienced this state, you realize that the feeling is not new; you have been there before, and we all have, but only for brief glimpses, since it is an experience difficult to sustain. These glimpses were described by Maslow (1968) as "peak experiences" and "the greatest attainment of identity, autonomy, or selfhood." Peak experiences happen more often for those whose aim is inner awareness but seldom occur for most people. To Maslow, a person in a peak experience takes on, at least temporarily, some of the characteristics of his often-described, "self-actualized" individual. In this context, self-actualization is not an "all-or-none" phenomenon, but a spurt in which the powers of a person are unified and integrated. The various parts of the self are functioning harmoniously and not laboring in restraint. A reduction in inhibition allows a more spontaneous natural expression and an emancipation of the true nature of self.

Cosmic Consciousness

Many philosophers believe that at the pinnacle of the hierarchy of consciousness states lies a fifth level of consciousness—"cosmic consciousness" or a state of oneness with the universe. Cosmic consciousness, according to the Tao, is impossible to explain or define since it is a pure feeling state, and those who enter it are not in a thinking state (which is needed to relate and form memory and explanations). It is a state of universal consciousness where ego boundaries are completely obliterated. It is a oneness with all other living organisms, including the highest spirit or divine being. Nature is laid bare and the spirit exists in harmony with the spirit of all things.

Picture every organism as a circle with ego consciousness, inner or subconsciousness, and cosmic consciousness as layers within the circle. Most of us experience occasional glimpses of universal or cosmic consciousness, the larger circle. After intense training and complete attainment of the fourth state, some share consciousness with the universal consciousness and enter the largest circle (Fig. 2.3).

As society has become more complex, so has our pattern of coping behavior. The masks we wear, the roles we play, the plans, the schemes, and the worrying are all "I-centered" activities. We have been taught to fight fire with fire or to fight complexity with complexity, developing a vicious cycle. With the rebirth of popularity of the ancient Eastern philosophies, we are learning that often it is better to fight fire with water or increased complexity with increased simplicity.

The search for self-transcendence is an interesting phenomenon in that those who do not understand its true nature continue to use complex and unnatural methods to obtain it. An analogy might be that of digging at an archeological site with a steam shovel. To one group of individuals, the steam shovel represents the

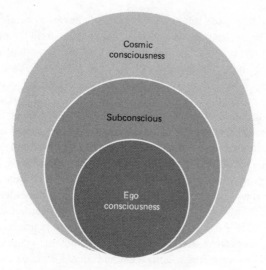

Fig. 2.3   Levels of consciousness.

easiest, most effortless way of seeing what is buried at the site. This analogy is applied to those individuals who seek self-transcendence through the use of mind-altering chemicals.

THE DRUG HIGH

A drug-induced altered state of consciousness is often a pleasant experience, but its relationship to the transcendent state is tenuous. The intensity or quality of the experience depends on such factors as when and even where one takes the drug. The quantity and quality of the drug are important, as are one's mood when taking the drug, one's motivation for taking it, and one's general state of health, especially emotional well-being, learned drug skills, and personality and expectations. Frustration and disappointment may develop when expectations are not met; and fear, apprehension, and injury can result if the drug is too strong or dangerously adulterated. Either way, one is not really in control of the experience and is in a sense imprisoned in an altered state of consciousness until the drug has been metabolized. More important, drugs change but do not stop the flood of sporadic thoughts that bombard the consciousness; thus, quieting the mind is almost an impossibility.

Herein lies the crux of the problem, a lack of understanding of what constitutes self-transcendence. Psychoactive drugs can induce an altered state of consciousness through either the alteration of incoming sensory stimuli or the deautomatization of the thought processes previously discussed. This change from the normal state of consciousness is made manifest by changes in awareness, memory, emotions, and mood. Such alterations lend an air of novelty to everyday occurrences, thus changing their significance and one's interest in them. Motivations become obscure and one may begin pondering the significance of an object, feeling, or idea, forgetting that it was previously rendered insignificant, and thus canceling some of one's adaptive habituation process. Obligations and goals become obscure and somewhat meaningless, as experiencing the moment becomes extremely pleasurable. The anxiety of passing time is diminished. What is real and important is making sense of the impulses that have the attention of the consciousness. Awareness is heightened, and imagery becomes more stimulating and significant. Touch, taste, and smell are not just stimulators of the senses—their origins almost seem to become part of the body or mind. The sense of unreality and lack of ego involvement is calming, but the learned tendency of the mind to create logic and order often gains awareness, creating alterations in moods that oscillate between pleasure and apprehension. At times, goal-directed activity seems alien and the body is only intermittently disturbed by sporadic arousal. Most often the stress of time, goals, and ego is reduced, as are the pressures of everyday existence. The drug creates a temporary block in that one is not actively thinking about the problem. Unfortunately, the problem still exists; it is stored in parts of the brain, and is producing feelings and other body alterations that continue to exist even though one is not actively thinking about it. The psychoactive drugs, both legal and illegal, that we typically consume to promote relaxation do not change body physiology. The problem is still present and continues to stress the system. The only difference is that we have temporarily blocked the situation from active, here-and-now thoughts.

In order to gain inner awareness—an active process from within—one must have control of one's thoughts, feelings, and thinking processes. But all drugs are uncontrollable to a lesser or greater degree, and drugs promote the feeling that the experience is a passive process, externally induced. In *The Master Game*, DeRopp (1968) writes that although some transcendence of self is experienced, the drug consciousness is but a glimpse of transcendence.

The passivity of the drug experience is in itself an often-mentioned drawback to drug use. Passive experiences in which the individual just rides along, seeing, feeling, and experiencing are somehow not as satisfying as those in which the individual is the active, creative center of the experience. Creative activities increase one's feelings of self-esteem, and in a circular pattern increase motivation and readiness for future unknown ventures.

SOCIAL ASPECTS OF THE ALTERED STATE: MOTIVATIONS FOR DRUG USE

Most drug users experience an altered state of consciousness from the drug they take, especially if they enter the experience with that expectation. From the initial experience of an altered state the person may or may not choose to seek that experience again. If the end of initial drug use is "just to see what it's like," the person's motivation is likely to be explained as curiosity. As the altered state is repeatedly sought, the motivation changes—it may be for pleasure or to "be like the other kids," or perhaps to escape from a world that seems unfriendly. Between the one-time user whose motivation is curiosity to the daily user is a continuum that can be described in terms of motivation and frequency of use. Figure 2.4 shows that continuum.

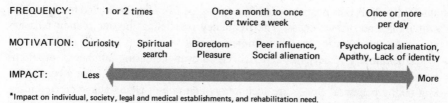

FREQUENCY:	1 or 2 times		Once a month to once or twice a week		Once or more per day
MOTIVATION:	Curiosity	Spiritual search	Boredom-Pleasure	Peer influence, Social alienation	Psychological alienation, Apathy, Lack of identity
IMPACT:	Less				More

*Impact on individual, society, legal and medical establishments, and rehabilitation need.

Fig. 2.4   Continuum of drug users according to motivation, frequency of use, and impact.*

Curiosity

The left side of the continuum represents those who report that they have used drugs once or twice and have not engaged in any further drug experimentation. The motivation for this abbreviated drug behavior is probably curiosity and requires no rehabilitative thrust. There exists in all of us an intrinsic desire to experience the unknown, and this desire is especially pronounced during the ages of strong peer influence, when many of a youngster's friends are experiencing drugs. Contradictions regarding psychological effects and medical hazards that are constantly seen in news reports also enhance the desire to discover something of the unknown.

Just as curiosity is a short-term motivation in the majority of this population, it can also be an initial factor exposing vulnerable individuals to effects that will meet other motivational needs. These individuals will continue to take drugs, but with a reason more profound than that of mere curiosity. Although curiosity is placed on the side of least impact, drug abuse prevention measures should be aimed especially at the left side of the continuum.

Spiritual Search

Moving toward the right of curiosity in Figure 2.4, spiritual search appears as the next motivation. The search for self-transcendence, the meaning of life, and one's reason for existence is as old as time. No one individual or group may be credited with the idea that drugs might help in this search; mystics and people such as the Aztecs and the Indians of the Native American Church have, for years, used mind-altering chemicals to communicate with their Ultimate Power. Chapter 6 deals with this subject in depth, providing historical background to the upsurge in the use of psychedelic drugs as a religious sacrament.

As would be expected, rehabilitative efforts are not often directed toward those who take drugs for spiritual purposes. The exception might be those zealots who surrender themselves to drugs and become lost in a fantasy world that bears no relation to ongoing society. Again, these are the drug-vulnerable, whose motivation has gone from spiritualism to one reflecting deeper psychological maladjustment.

Pleasure

The next motivation for drug taking as shown in Figure 2.4 is that of pleasure or recreation, which can be viewed as the antithesis of boredom. One could say that these individuals take drugs to have fun, to escape from boredom, and to experience a different kind of awareness. The frequency paralleling this motivation falls between once a month to one or two times a week.

Contemporary society has experienced an ever-increasing number of problems created by affluence, population growth, and related factors that have a bearing on drug-taking behavior. Space-age technology and rate of change have created more leisure time, which has led in turn to an apparent lack of meaningful activity and disinterest in the things about us. Instant foods, instant energy, and prepackaging have eroded the ability to endure boredom and consequently many Americans learn to expect the excitement of the "instant high."

Although our culture is expected to shoulder some of the responsibility because it creates stresses and provides forms of instant relief, individuals must learn how to deal with monotony within themselves. As Bertrand Russell in his work *The Conquest of Happiness* (1958) suggests, one should learn in childhood to endure a monotonous life because no great achievement is possible without persistent work. An effective antidote for monotony is meaningful activity—activity that challenges creativity.

The further we progress from the day-to-day fight for survival of our pioneer forebears, the more time we have for less essential activity. This activity can be creative, but the problem is that far too many individuals have had increasing amounts of free time thrust on them without proper direction for the creative use of this time. Passive forms of entertainment and excitement, devised to fill the vast time void, create the misconception that fulfillment can be realized through activities not requiring any input. This passivity contributes to the pleasure motivation for drug taking.

Pleasure motivation can be viewed in two ways:

1. Drugs *for* pleasure—the use of drugs at a social affair as refreshments or for the purpose of augmenting sociability. In this situation, social interaction is the main goal or pleasure being sought, that is, the drug is a means to an end. One would no longer be able to enjoy the party when a disabling high developed.
2. Drugs *as* pleasure—the effect of the drug being the pleasure sought and an end in itself, such as the heightened sensitivity one might experience from smoking marijuana.

If either pleasure-motivation form were to become compulsive, it would depart from the realm of recreation.

Maslow's (1968) ideas on deficiency-need gratification offer insight into the pleasure motivation. If one takes a drug to overcome boredom or seek excitement and pleasure, the drug may produce that end. However, when the high is over, one returns to the same base-line level from which the high ascended; hence no personal growth has occurred (Fig. 2.5).

The antithesis of Maslow's deficiency-need gratification as a motivator is growth motivation, which substitutes creative activity for a drug (or its parallel), and establishes a new, higher base line, with the area between base lines called personal growth (Fig. 2.6).

There is little question that America has and will continue to regard drugs as a form of pleasure. Nearly 70 percent of our adult population drink alcohol, nearly 50

Fig. 2.5   Motivation model based on Maslow's deficiency-need gratification theory.

percent smoke cigarettes, and about 60 percent have tried marijuana at least once (Miller, 1983).

Neither the mainstream culture nor the various subcultures have chosen to live without the pleasure derived from drugs, and there is little chance that this will come about. Because of this, many drug programs in the United States have been doomed to failure. They attempt to eradicate all drug taking rather than concentrate on drug-use patterns likely to result in drug dependence, which is the real drug problem (Louria, 1975).

True pleasure motivation is not seen here to be of serious consequence unless it is an initial step to increased motivation in susceptible individuals (i.e., social drinking is not the cause of alcoholism).

Social Alienation

The two remaining sections of Fig. 2.4 deal with alienation and are closely related, although we will discuss them separately. The term *alienation* has been used to describe two different phenomena related to motivation for drug use. One is *social alienation,* which is closely tied to peer influence and is further explained by theories of conformity. The other is termed *psychological alienation,* an intense feeling of estrangement and separation not only from society's established values but also from any subculture and often from individual goals and life meaning.

Social alienation is the alienation of an individual or a whole group from the dominant society. In theorizing about the cause and effect of contemporary social alienation of American youth, one might consider that many of those involved in the

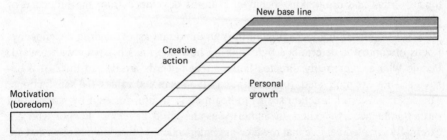

Fig. 2.6   Motivation model based on Maslow's growth-motivation theory.

counterculture were reared to live out the fantasies of their parents who, while always working hard, were frustrated with the assembly line, big organizations, and bureaucracy. Being unable to "talk back to the boss," they gave more freedom to their children to dissent without being thrown out in the cold. This is part of a system of permissive childrearing, which Theodore Roszak in *The Making of a Counter Culture* (1969) says equips youth with an anemic superego. The carrying into adulthood of childhood fantasies and dependence usually results in an abrupt and harsh awakening, leading to unfulfilled expectations, frustration, and anger, as well as disappointment in the dominant social structure. In the counterculture movement of the 1960s, these thoughts and feelings served to widen the generation gap, and in a roundabout way they were responsible for certain patterns of drug behavior. As these young adults threw off the establishment's values, guidance, and identity, they became more dependent on the subculture, which in a cyclical pattern increased social alienation. Clothing, vocabulary, hair styles, and patterns of drug use all became part of belonging. These helped to define a group that was set apart from the established society.

Some groups are as loosely defined as the members of a student body, or those who are young, or even those who like a particular politician (we somehow feel that if someone believes as we do, we ought to like him or her). Other groups are small and sharply delineated, such as fraternity or therapy groups. In order to be accepted in a group, an individual must adhere to the belief system of the group. The more attractive the group appears to the individual, the more influence the group exerts over him or her. Members of the group influence others and are influenced by them until attitudes and actions become uniform.

A group of people who use the same drug tend to assign their experience a collective interpretation; thus, a naive person entering the group learns what to expect and what not to expect from the particular drug that the group uses. The group is not concerned with discrepancies between their experience and that of others because group approval is all they need. Members of such a group can become increasingly dependent on one another.

According to theories of social conformity, *peer pressure* or *influence* is the degree to which persons or groups influence the behavior or attitudes of others. This may take the form of mere compliance, which is outward action without consideration of private conviction; or it may take the form of private acceptance, which is change of attitude in the direction of group attitudes (Kiesler & Kiesler, 1970). The formation of private acceptance resulting from group compliance is subtle and not readily discerned, nor is it readily admitted by the individual that his or her attitude toward drugs and drug-taking behavior patterns developed from the influence of peers.

It is recognized that locus of control is an important aspect in drug dependency. Locus of control is determined by exploring how one links behavior with reward. People who are internally directed believe that rewards are due to their own behavior. They are motivated from within, based on personal values and satisfactions. The source of inner direction seems to begin early in life, fostered by parents and further influenced by others in authority as the child develops. People who are externally directed believe that rewards are independent of their own actions and are controlled by forces outside themselves, so they are motivated by the drive to perform to meet the needs, expectations, and values of others in the hope of being rewarded. Approval by others becomes their highest goal, and their primary method of obtaining it is by manipulation.

In analyzing the use of drugs that is a reflection of peer pressure, it should be noted that the weaker the ego structure of the individual, the more externally motivated he or she becomes. In this case, motivation may subtly shift from social alienation to a deeper problem of self-identity; hence, treatment becomes necessary for that individual.

Psychological Alienation

Nearing the right side of the continuum in Figure 2.4 are the motivations that reflect serious psychological problems when human needs are not met. Drugs may be taken at abusive levels in an attempt to meet some of these needs. There is agreement among psychologists, philosophers, and anthropologists that some of the most basic human needs are food, clothing, and shelter. But we also need psychological and emotional fulfillment in the form of acceptance and love by others in order to gain self-esteem; we need to become competent in some social, intellectual, and physical skills; and we must fulfill the need for power over our own destiny through wealth, achievement, and/or respect from others. When these needs for emotional good health are met, one can say with confidence, "I'm an OK person!" At the right end of the continuum are those individuals who cannot say this with any confidence; they require the most difficult rehabilitation because personality structuring is necessary.

Increasingly, we see a lack of self-identity in the young people of today's complex, rapidly changing society; some of the economic, political, and technological forces in the United States are at the root of this problem. There has been a decline in family nurturing in the last three decades. In addition to the absence of the father in the home due to divorce, in recent years there has been a drastic increase in the number of working mothers. In 1948, only 26 percent of married women with school-age children worked outside the home, whereas in 1976, that figure had risen to 54 percent, the majority of whom worked full time. Thirty-seven percent of mothers with children of preschool age had joined the labor force by 1976—an increase from 13 percent in 1948. Because many parents have less time to spend with their children, increasing responsibility for nurturing these children has been placed on other institutions, such as schools and day-care centers.

Apathy

Another pressure of our time that defies meeting basic needs of the individual is the sense of powerlessness arising from race, sex, age, and social-class discrimination. Discrimination may be the overwhelming response of the outside world to the handicapped, to poor children, and to minority children; it can initiate the endless self-fulfilling prophecy of defeat and powerlessness.

There has also been a decline in tradition, in the sense of community and culture, especially in large cities. Americans are extremely mobile—the American family moves, on the average, every five years! And commuting long distances to work tends to make the home a virtual bedroom and the community just a town in which to park the car.

Another phenomenon of our American culture is a prolonged adolescence; young people growing up in our society do not take the opportunity to assume adult roles when, biologically and emotionally, they are ready to leave childhood behind. Whereas the grandparents of many of these children took responsibility for job and family by the age of sixteen, the modern young adult is virtually forced to stay in school until becoming sufficiently prepared (that is, with a college or vocational school degree) to compete on the job market. Until they can test their earning power, the financial destiny of young adults is in the hands of their parents.

These are but a few of the cultural maladies that may form the backdrop for the deep-seated psychological problems we see in drug abusers. The motivations shown at the extreme right of the continuum in Fig. 2.4 may or may not have been the original reason for drug experimentation, but they persist as the motivation for abuse once a susceptible individual has experimented with various types of drugs. Drug takers who reach this stage have turned to the use of depressant drugs—they generally follow a pattern of alcohol and/or marijuana, then speed and/or psychedelics, and then the strong depressants such as barbiturates and nonbarbiturate sedatives, alcohol, and/or opiates. Dosages that will produce the needed high move closer and closer toward the lethal level. The psychological motivators that are involved here are of serious consequence and deserve further exploration.

In *Love and Will*, Rollo May (1969) demonstrated his insight into the prophetic nature of his neurotic patients with several examples, two of which have particular bearing on this discussion. These problems were brought to his attention in the 1940s and 1950s by his patients, people who were consciously living out what the remainder of the population was capable of controlling or keeping at a subconscious level, at least for the time being. One of these problems was *lack of identity,* and the other was the *inability of his patients to "feel,"* which May simply called *apathy*. Both of these problems reflect psychological alienation. Since the time when psychiatrists first began diagnosing these problems at an increasing rate, the endemic explosion of these symptoms has occurred just as May proposed that it would, and the shrapnel still lies imbedded in American culture.

The problem of lack of identity seems to be based on changes in American society in the last several decades. Institutions such as church, school, family, marriage, and the work place have all undergone radical change. In May's words, "the cultural values by which people had gotten their sense of identity had been wiped away" (p. 26). The role of formal religion as an authoritarian moral anchor has been altered to passive preaching. The family as a centralized unit has moved toward decentralization. Sexual identity that was clearly defined in the 1950s has become much less so. Since the advent of the assembly line, fewer people than ever before see a project through from beginning to end. Impersonal mass communication and the computer have replaced much of our face-to-face contact. Thus, it is not astounding that the nation has seen a rash of identity seekers, especially among the young. The institutions that had been the underpinnings of cultural values from which a sense of identity could be gained eluded not only the drug generation of the 1960s, but the parents of these young people as well. It was during the parents' generation that Willy Loman's search for identity helped to trigger a realization of emptiness. This inheritance plus a popular laissez-faire mode of childrearing, the space-age technology explosion, and the war in Vietnam all spawned disdain, if not frank disrespect, for authority in a new generation. Heroes were hard to come by and identity was difficult to build from scratch even though Maslow, Rogers, and other humanistic psychologists insisted that a positive self-identity could be formed by anyone truly seeking to do so, in spite of social calamity.

Drug rehabilitation research throughout the country has clearly documented the lack of self-identity as a deep-seated aspect of drug abuse, and many rehabilitation programs, such as Synanon, are aimed specifically at the formation of a positive identity within the individual.

Another psychological problem, also prophesied by May, erupted in the middle 1960s and emerged time and again in drug rehabilitation centers. This was the problem that May identified as apathy—call it alienation, estrangement, indifference, anomie, or what you will. This was not the social alienation of a hopeful group of flower children, but rather the withdrawal of an individual into a lonely, hopeless inner world. To the psychologically alienated, drugs became a suicide equivalent, and unless society somehow intervened, these individuals would eventually subject themselves to a lethal overdose.

Whether looking at these two psychological problems (apathy and lack of identity) from a prophetic or from a hindsight stance, it is clear that they dominate the drug-rehabilitation treatment efforts. They are the most difficult of drug-taking motivations to treat because therapy involves the reshaping of a personality that is as old as the individual being treated. Rehabilitation seems a misnomer in such a case, because it is hard to prove that "habilitation" preceded this state.

John Atkinson (1964) summarized motivation on a continuum between achievement motivation at one pole and fear-of-failure motivation at the other. Achievement motivation is parallel to Maslow's growth motivation, which represents a positive desire to challenge a situation in expectation of the satisfaction that we can derive from successfully completing a job. From repeated challenging and experiencing, we grow and learn to be independent. On the other hand, when we are motivated out of fear of failure, we isolate ourselves from experiencing and growing because we do not see new situations as opportunities to succeed and accomplish— we see them, instead, as threats and as the disgrace that will befall us when we fail. This motivation feeds on itself because the more we withdraw from growth experiences, the less capable we become in handling new situations. Peele (1975) points out that drugs are not addictive when they serve as a means of fulfilling a larger purpose in life, such as increased self-awareness, expanding consciousness, or just plain enjoyment. But drugs are addictive when they are taken in order to hide from life or to remain untouched by the social order, and they become the sole source of gratification for that person who has chosen not to grow and to control his or her own destiny.

LIVING WITH DRUGS

The motivations presented here may raise more questions than they answer. Perhaps drug abuse is symptomatic of an underlying pathology with which our society is stricken, or perhaps it is an offshoot of a new social consciousness or a backlash against bigness, depersonalization, and technology. Whatever the "social" reason given for drug use, it is apparent that each drug user seeks to alter his or her normal state by using drugs. Society is undergoing change, and we would like to think that the current drug-abuse problem is just a phase or cultural lag that we are going through until we learn to live harmoniously with chemical substances, just as we must learn to live with technology.

If drug use is a barometer of social ills, then we must accept the challenge by analyzing the reasons for drug abuse that have been presented here and throughout the remainder of this text. We must also educate young people toward the proper use of chemical substances and begin to move toward eradication of the dehumanizing patterns of our lives.

REFERENCES

Atkinson, J. W. *An Introduction to Motivation*. Princeton, N.J.: Van Nostrand, 1964.

Deikman, A. J. "Deautomatization and the mystic experience," in C. T. Tart, ed. *Altered States of Consciousness*. New York: Doubleday, 1969.

DeRopp, R. X. *The Master Game*. New York: Dell, 1968.

Kiesler, C. A., and S. B. Kiesler. *Conformity*. Reading, Mass.: Addison-Wesley, 1970.

Louria, D. B. "A critique of some current approaches to the problem of drug abuse." *American Journal of Public Health* 65(6): 581–584, 1975.

Ludwig, A. M. "Altered states of consciousness," in C. T. Tart, ed. *Altered States of Consciousness*. New York: Doubleday, 1969.

Maslow, A. H. *Toward a Psychology of Being*. New York: Van Nostrand Reinhold, 1968.

May, Rollo. *Love and Will*. New York: Dell, 1969.

Miller, J. D., et al., *National Survey on Drug Abuse*. Rockville, Md.: NIDA, 1983.

Peele, S. *Love and Addiction*. New York: Signet, 1975.

Roszak, T. *The Making of a Counter Culture*. New York: Doubleday, 1969.

Russell, B. *The Conquest of Happiness*. New York: Bantam Books, 1958.

Tart, C. T. *States of Consciousness*. New York: E. P. Dutton, 1975.

SUGGESTED READINGS

Atwater, E. *The Psychology of Adjustment*. Englewood Cliffs, N.J.: Prentice-Hall, 1983.

Blum, Kenneth. *Handbook of Abusable Drugs*. New York: Gardner Press, 1984.

DeCatanzaro, Denys. *Suicide and Self-Damaging Behavior*. Orlando, Fla.: Academic Press, 1981.

Golas, Thaddeus. *The Lazy Man's Guide to Enlightenment*. New York: Bantam, 1972.

Rathus, S., and J. Nevid. *Adjustment and Growth*. New York: Holt, Rinehart and Winston, 1983.

Rogers, Carl. *A Way of Being*. Boston: Houghton Mifflin, 1981.

Toffler, A. *The Third Wave*. New York: Morrow, 1980.

Walsh, P. *Growing Through Time*. Monterey, Calif.: Brooks/Cole, 1983.

Warga, R. *Personal Awareness*. Boston: Houghton Mifflin, 1983.

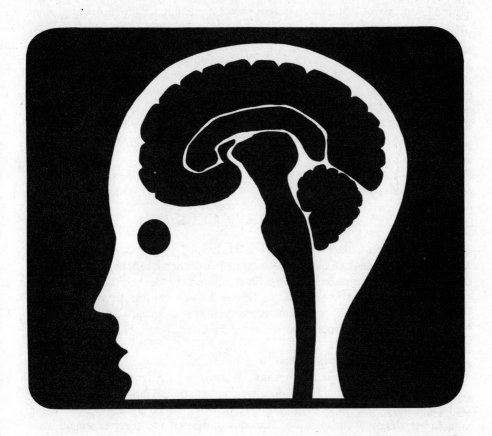

CHAPTER 3

PHYSIOLOGICAL BASIS OF DRUG ACTION ON THE CENTRAL NERVOUS SYSTEM

Normal function of the nervous system makes it possible for the reader to pick up this book, maneuver its pages, coordinate eyesight, be aware of the book's weight, and, most important, decipher the meaning of the words, which have been arranged in statements and ideas. Were it not for the integrative function of the brain, controlling the action of the billions of nerve cells throughout the body, neither action nor thought would be possible. One's behavior is the result of the brain's interpretation of all incoming nerve impulses. These impulses can be depressed, intensified, or distorted by chemical substances—substances known as *drugs*. A basic facet of the study of drugs is the action of these substances on the central nervous system.

THE NERVE CELL

The nervous system, like every other system in the body, is composed of specialized cells. The specialized cell of the nervous system is the nerve cell, or the *neuron*. The neuron is as an electrochemical unit with its action dependent on the constant flow of chemical-carrying electrical charges. The action of many drugs can be explained merely by their presence inside the nerve cell. The chemical similarity between some of the currently popular drugs and natural body chemicals may explain how drugs get inside the nerve cell.

To better understand how these foreign chemicals alter nerve cell function, consider the basic structure and function of nerve cells. Although these cells vary in shape and size according to their location and basic neural function, they typically consist of a number of impulse-receiving branches called *dendrites* and of one impulse-sending branch, the *axon*. The body of the cell also receives stimuli from other axons (Fig. 3.1). One nerve cell may receive impulses from hundreds of different axons, some of them *excitatory* and some of them *inhibitory*. Summation of like impulses (excitatory or inhibitory) then causes the nerve cell to "fire" or remain inactive.

Transmission of the Nerve Impulse

A unique feature of nerve cells is that they do not come into direct physical contact with one another. They are separated by a microscopic space. This space, known as the *synapse*, prevents the continuous flow of impulses and becomes the focal point of the discussion of drug action on the nervous system (Fig. 3.2) (Eccles, 1963a; 1963b; 1965).

By analogy, the synapse serves as a switch for electric current. If conditions at the synapse are biochemically correct for the regular propagation of the nerve impulse, the switch is "on." Some drugs turn this switch on themselves and extra nerve impulses are emitted. If conditions are not normal—for example, because of the presence of a depressant drug or of fatigue—the switch is "off."

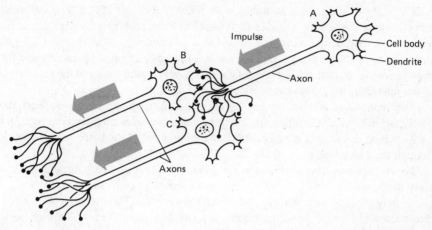

Fig. 3.1 Nerve Cell A receives an impulse through its dendrites and/or cell body and sends it on through the axon. The axon of Cell A sends its impulses to Cell B via a dendrite, and to Cell C via the cell body. Cells B and C send impulses via their axons to other cells.

At the end of the axon (the *bouton*) there are certain chemicals located in small pockets called *vesicles*, which appear to be all-important in transmitting the nerve impulse to the next nerve cell. These chemicals are called *neurohormonal transmitter substances*. Some of these substances that have been identified to date are *acetylcholine, norepinephrine, serotonin, dopamine,* and *gamma amino butyric acid,* or *GABA.* In addition to these neurotransmitters, there are a number of CNS (central nervous system) hormones that may act as neurohormonal transmitters as well as carry out their roles as hormones. Walker (1978) suggests that the hypothalamic-based hormones *thyrotropin, luteinizing hormone releasing factor,* and *growth hormone inhibiting factor* and the *antidiuretic hormone* may function as central transmitters. It is also suggested that various polypeptides (groups of amino acids) called *endorphins, enkephalins,* and *Substance P* may function in the brain as neurotransmitters.

Each nerve axon contains one of these transmitter substances, and the hypoth-

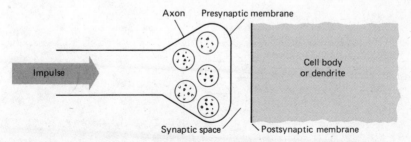

Fig. 3.2 The synapse is a microscopic space between the axon and the next nerve cell. The nerve impulse coming down the axon must jump the synaptic space if the impulse is to be carried on.

esized action of the neurotransmitter is as follows (Eccles, 1963). The incoming nerve impulse causes the vesicles of transmitter substance to join with the membrane at the end of the axon (the *pre*synaptic membrane), as shown in Fig. 3.3. Upon fusing with the presynaptic membrane, the vesicles open up and release the neurohormone into the space between the presynaptic membrane and the membrane of the next cell, the *post*synaptic membrane (Fig. 3.4).

The neurohormone has within its chemical makeup the ability to alter the postsynaptic membrane. When this alteration takes place, electrochemical reactions occur, which re-create a nerve impulse of the same intensity as the one that came through the preceding axon.

Nerve impulses, then, are due to *electric* current that proceeds through the cell body to the axon, where it causes *chemical* events to occur due to movement of electrically charged ions such as sodium and potassium. These chemical events at the synapse in turn re-create the electric activity necessary to carry the impulse to the next cell.

Proper function of the CNS may depend on the interaction of the various peptides and neurotransmitter systems that control pituitary secretion, functions of the limbic system and motor centers, and other parts of the brain that govern the overt responses that we call "behavior" (Verebey et al. 1978).

Drugs and Nerve Transmission

Even though we generally understand that each part of the brain serves a specific function and we are beginning to understand what some of those functions are, there are two large pieces of the puzzle that need to be in place in order to understand CNS functioning. One is how these various parts of the brain relate or communicate, and two is how they are activated or inhibited. The latter is of primary interest to the study of the behavioral effect of drugs. Generally speaking, drugs act on the CNS because of their ability to mimic or displace the naturally occurring neurotransmitters. Understanding the presence, nature, and action of neurotransmitters and the "look-alike" drugs should help in understanding the behavioral effects of taking specific drugs.

Since the synaptic events are chemical in nature, they are vulnerable to foreign chemicals, such as drugs. Looking at the synapse, consider what would happen if

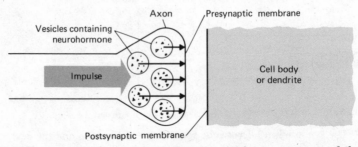

Fig. 3.3   The electrical nerve impulse causes the vesicles to move toward the presynaptic membrane.

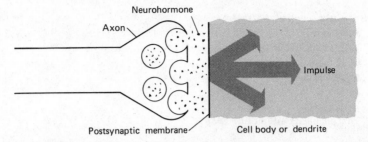

Fig. 3.4   Neurohormonal transmitter substance is released into the synaptic space and alters the postsynaptic membrane, allowing electrochemical events to occur which re-create the nerve impulse.

a drug could (a) inhibit the production of the neurohormone, (b) cause the neurohormone to be broken down more rapidly than normal, or (c) alter the postsynaptic membrane so that neurohormones would not affect it. In any of these cases, it is apparent that the nerve cell action would be depressed because either there was no neurohormone or it was not allowed to work normally (Grodsky, 1973; Harper, 1985). It appears that this is the action of the depressant drugs (such as alcohol, narcotics, barbiturates) when they come in contact with nerve cells in special parts of the brain (Caldwell, 1974; Woolley & Shaw, 1957).

On the other hand, consider the drugs that cause *excess* production and release of neurohormonal transmitter substances, or have the ability to *mimic* the action of the neurohormone or not allow its reuptake. In these cases, the neurons involved would be stimulated at a greater than normal rate. This is the action of the stimulatory drugs on nerve cells within the brain (Sjoerdsma et. al., 1955).

Neurotransmitters

Neurotransmitters are those substances that act with immediate effect on synaptic receptors to produce excitatory or inhibitory postsynaptic potentials. Another class of substances are called *neuromodulators*. These are substances that act along with the more direct-acting neurotransmitters to modify a specific response.

The following are the neurotransmitters and neuromodulators thought to be most important in those parts of the CNS that are especially reactive to drugs.

1. Acetylcholine: especially active in the Hippocampus, Neocortex, and Caudate nucleus
2. Biogenic Monoamines
   norepinephrine
   epinephrine
   dopamine
   serotonin
3. Amino Acids
   glutamute
   aspartate
   GABA
   glycine

4. Neuroactive peptides
   Substance P
   VIP (vasoactive intestinal polypeptide)
   CCK (cholecystokinin)
   Neurotensin
   Somatostatin
   B-endorphin
   Enkephalins (Lane et al., 1983)

It should be noted that recent studies have found large concentrations of more than one neurotransmitter at many sites, which leads to the hypothesis that in many brain structures, perhaps in all of them, there exists a concurrent modulation by more than one neurotransmitter. Such a system of multiple neurotransmitters acting in combination, which questions the one-neuron-one-transmitter theory known as Dale's Principle, gives further evidence of the versatility of the CNS. It also adds credence to the idea that the CNS possesses many redundant pathways (Chronister & DeFrance, 1981).

The reason for this multiplicity of neurotransmitters is not known; however, one hypothesis is that it represents a mechanism for increasing the fine control over thoughts and actions. The synaptic junction is more than an on-off switch. It is more like a dimmer switch that has hundreds of potential setpoints. Some neurotransmitters are degraded rapidly while others stay at the site longer. Thus, excitatory or inhibitory responses evoked by neurotransmitters can vary from fractions of a millisecond to hundreds of milliseconds. The result is the flexibility and precision exhibited by the CNS (Iversen & Iversen, 1981).

Neuromodulators are small peptides present in the neuronal system that act as local hormones or act to "aid" neurotransmitters, thus giving a finer level of control.

The list of neurotransmitters and modulator substances is constantly being updated as methods of identification become more sophisticated. Examples of some recent additions are: *aspartic acid*, which has an excitatory action similar to that of glutamute; the *amine histamine*, which exists in small amounts in specific locations in the CNS; *Substance P* and *Somatostatin*, found in the primary sensory fibers; and the *Enkephalins* and *B-endorphin*, widely distributed in the CNS areas associated with the control of pain (Emson, 1983; Hughes, 1978).

ORGANIZATION OF THE NERVOUS SYSTEM

Every system of the body is involved in behavior, and every system is at least partially regulated by the brain. Sometimes this regulation is direct, through nervous innervation of an organ; other times it is indirect, through neural stimulation of the endocrine glands. But the brain is always involved, and thus becomes the logical starting point in the analysis of the effect of drugs on behavior.

To understand the brain, it may help to use the analogy developed by noted NIMH researcher Dr. Paul Maclean, who likens the brain to an archeological site revealing three distinct layers. Each of these layers not only indicates a stage in evolutionary development but also describes units of functional differentiation, each of which demonstrates a distinctly different type of behavior that the body is capable of exhibiting.

Phylogenetically, the oldest part of the brain is found in the lower centers, nearest the spinal cord. For simplicity's sake, these will be referred to as the *brainstem* or *hindbrain*, although this discussion refers more to functional units, which transcend the anatomical boundaries typically found in anatomy textbooks. These are simple structures (if there is such a thing in the brain) in the sense that they are reflex in nature, with the primary function of preserving the self and the species. We are referring here to structures such as the spinal cord, the coordination centers of the cerebellum, the medulla oblongata with its cardiovascular, respiratory, and vasomotor centers, the transmitting network of the pons, the integrating interconnecting network of the thalamus, and the visceral regulating centers for hunger, thirst, body temperature, rage, pain, and pleasure of the hypothalamus.

If humans resemble any other animal species, it is due to basic programs stored within these lower centers. The actions or behavior governed by these centers are natural, direct, and open, without learned inhibition. Activities centered on keeping alive, procreating, preparing a home site, establishing and defending territory, hunting, hoarding, forming of simple social groups, and performing daily activities are instinctive and exist in lower animals as well as in humans.

Perhaps to ensure survival, a new layer of brain tissue that enabled a modification or refinement of the basic instincts evolved or appeared in so-called higher animals. This new layer, called the *limbic system* (Latin for ''border''), is wrapped around the old layer and is often referred to as the *interbrain*, since it has structures that communicate with both the higher and lower brains.

Animals evolved to the second layer, or limbic system, were further ensured of survival, for not only did they have basic survival instincts, but now they added a measure of freedom from ancestral stereotyped behavior. They could think and act on emotions and approach new situations with additional abilities. Primarily, the limbic system added feeling and emotion, which further assured attendance to basic survival activities, ostensibly by making some activities pleasurable and others unpleasurable. Feelings such as fear, anger, and love attached to external situations guided behavior *toward* that which protected and *away from* that which was threatening. Understandably, two of our major neural pathways (those governing oral and genital behaviors) have intricate connections to the pleasure and unpleasure centers of the limbic system. The concepts of reward-pleasure and punishment-unpleasure are important to drug-related behavior and seem, to a large extent, to be centered in this area. Numerous researchers have been able to stimulate electrically various parts of the limbic system and elicit both the pleasure and unpleasure responses.

The brain continued to develop with the addition of a third layer called the *cortex, neocortex,* or *forebrain,* and reached the zenith of development in humans. The addition of the vast number of cortical cells allowed the development and storage of analytical skills, verbal communication, writing ability, empathy, fine motor control, additional emotion, memory, learning, and rational thought, and gave a new dimension to problem solving and survival abilities. New dimensions were added to basic oral and sexual behaviors, and vision replaced olfaction as the primary sense. Reactions could be more than reflex and, for better or for worse, reality could be determined by perception, which is unique to each individual. Behavior could be measured in relation to possible outcomes. Symbolism, goals, motivation, and anticipation became part of the functioning human being.

Drugs and the Brain

The brain controls and integrates all human movement and behavior, and nearly all drugs of abuse modify behavior by their action on the brain and brainstem. Behavior modifications caused by drugs, resulting in uncontrollable emotions, restricted information storage, limited capability for decision making, and other uncontrolled behavior, have led us to the study of how the various areas of the brain react to drugs. If one understands what events are taking place at the cellular level and at higher, more sophisticated levels, one can understand more easily why certain behavior occurs.

The brain and brainstem consist of a number of different structures concerned with the control of specific actions, thought, and emotions. Figure 3.5 depicts the brain and brainstem down to the spinal cord. Alteration of the nerve cell transmissions within these areas affects both mental and physical behavior. Drugs are known to affect these areas, but many drugs are specific to certain structures; thus, each drug causes its own behavioral characteristics. Drug dosage is an important consideration; light doses of a drug may cause little or no behavioral change, whereas very large doses may cause death.

Drugs reach the central nervous system by way of the circulating blood. In general (depending on the physical properties of the drug itself), the faster the drug enters the bloodstream, the more rapidly its effects are felt. Drugs injected into a vein travel directly to the heart and are circulated throughout the system immediately; inhaled drugs enter the bloodstream a little less rapidly, since the chemicals involved must enter capillaries in the lungs; in general, ingested drugs take even longer, because they must first dissolve and are often mixed with food products, thus slowing absorption into the blood supplying the digestive area.

Once the drug enters the nervous tissue of the brain, various reactions may

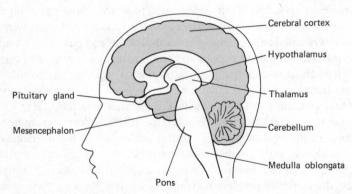

Fig. 3.5 The brain and brainstem.

occur, because different drugs appear to have different target areas. Because of this specificity of drug action on the various parts of the central nervous system, the following paragraphs are designed to elaborate on the main functions of each major area of the brain and brainstem. Once the normal function is known, it becomes easier to determine logically what would happen if the action of a specific area were depressed by alcohol or a barbiturate, or if the cell action of that area were stimulated with cocaine or an amphetamine.

The Brainstem (Vital Centers)

Medulla oblongata, pons, and mesencephalon. These three structures are mainly nerve fiber bundles, or tracts, that carry messages between the spinal cord and the brain.

The *medulla* is of special interest since it contains the respiratory, cardiac, and vasomotor centers. When drugs completely depress this area, death occurs as a result of respiratory failure.

The Thalamus (Stimulus Relay)

The thalamus is the "switchboard" of the brain, since all "incoming" and "outgoing" calls pass through this area.

The thalamus serves four important "switchboard" functions.

1. It serves as a transmitter of sensory impulses from other parts of the body to the sensory areas of the brain (Fig. 3.6). Specialized groups of cells do this work; these cells are analogous to switchboard operators who take incoming calls and know to what specific department (or specific sensory brain cells) to transfer the calls.
2. Another special task of the thalamus is much like the first except that the "incoming calls" are put through to the association areas of the brain. Again,

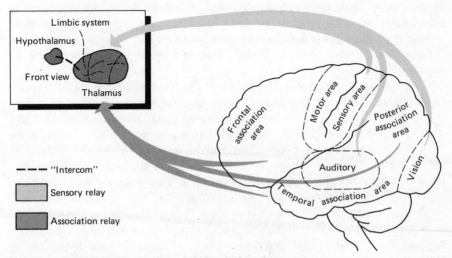

Fig. 3.6 Schematic illustration of thalamic function.

specialized cell groups (called *nuclei*) send specific messages to specific brain areas (Fig. 3.6).

3. The third function is communication among subcortical areas—in our analogy this is the "intercom system." In reality, these specialized cells communicate with other thalamic areas, the hypothalamus, and the limbic system (Fig. 3.6).

4. In addition to these three functions, the thalamus serves as a relay of motor impulses back to the body.

Because of the nerve tracts, or bundles of nerve fibers, that serve as direct connections between the thalamus and the cerebral cortex, it is thought that the neocortex is the evolutionary outgrowth of the thalamus.

The Hypothalamus (Homeostasis)

This interesting structure may hold the answers to many of the mysteries concerning behavior. The hypothalamus is continuously maintaining body temperature, regulating the production of hormones, maintaining water balance in the body, and gauging nutritional needs, sexual needs, and countless other bodily functions. Exciting investigations regarding the endorphins and enkephalins, morphinelike substances of the brain, lead us to believe that this portion of the CNS produces its own analgesic (Hughes, 1975; Pasternak et al. 1955). The level of these naturally occurring pain killers appears to be exceptionally high in the hypothalamus and limbic structures—areas involved in emotionality and stress responses (Smith et al., 1976). These substances appear to produce the same pharmacologic responses in animals as do various opiates and hold promise in the treatment of mental illness (Verebey et al., 1978).

Perhaps the two most important areas of interest concerning the hypothalamus in relation to drug abuse are those of (a) pleasure and pain, and (b) hunger and satiety. It has been found through experimental studies that there are specific areas of the hypothalamus that elicit a quite distinctive pleasure sensation when experimentally stimulated, and there are cells that elicit pain when stimulated. These pleasure and pain areas are all-important in drug use and abuse, for some drugs elicit an intense euphoria that is thought to be the result of the stimulation of cells in these hypothalamic pleasure areas or the depression of cells in the corresponding pain centers.

Just as there are pleasure and pain areas in the hypothalamus, it has been found that there are also hunger and satiety centers. As one would expect, when hunger cells are stimulated, the body feels the desire for food. When electrodes are implanted in these areas in experimental animals, repeated electrical stimulation causes the animal to eat itself into obesity. Conversely, if this area is destroyed, the animal starves itself to death. It appears that amphetamine diet pills work on the hypothalamic satiety centers plus the pleasure areas, because they depress hunger and pep up the individual (Teitelbaum & Epstein, 1962).

Integrated emotional behavior is controlled to some extent by the hypothalamus; in fact, it has been shown through animal experimentation that unless the hypothalamus is intact, fully developed rage cannot be elicited. Electrical stimulation of the medial portion of the hypothalamus provokes affective defense reactions, including direct attack on the object closest at hand; upon termination of the stimulation, this action ceases immediately (Bard & Macht, 1958). In addition to controlling the emotional reaction of rage, the anterior hypothalamus appears to produce fear behavior, and stimulation of the posterior area yields alertness and curiosity.

Whereas stimulation of some areas of the hypothalamus has been found to bring about fear, pain, defense, and escape reactions, it is of great interest and importance to discover that stimulation of other areas soothes an animal. Stimulation of these areas brings about reactions akin to pleasure in experimental animals; hence, these areas have been dubbed the "pleasure" or "reward" centers. Experimentation has shown that when animals are allowed to self-stimulate this center, they often choose this self-stimulation over various delectable rewards. Experimental animals have been known to repeat self-stimulation of the pleasure center up to 4,000 times an hour! However, experimental stimulation of pain centers can inhibit the pleasure centers; indeed, prolonged stimulation of pain centers may cause severe illness and may eventually lead to the death of the animal (Olds & Milner, 1954).

In relating the hypothalamic pleasure-pain control centers with the hypothalamic autonomic control centers (control over blood pressure, hydrochloric acid secretion, etc.), it becomes apparent how so-called psychosomatic diseases might be brought about. Chronic stimulation of pain centers in monkeys has produced ulcers in those animals.

The scientific study of drug action on the pleasure center could be very important in studying psychological dependence on certain drugs. For example, amphetamine action on the pleasure center has been found to facilitate the self-stimulation responsiveness of rats. Control studies showed that facilitation was due to the greater reinforcement value of the stimulus rather than just heightened bodily activity, which is known to occur as a result of amphetamine administration. It has been hypothesized that the amphetamine mimicked the action of (or affected the release of) norepinephrine, the chemical transmitter susbstance of nerve endings in this hypothalamic area. This illustrates that amphetamines do excite the pleasure area and thus makes it easier to understand why individuals may desire to take this type of drug repeatedly (Stein, 1964).

It is difficult to summarize the function of this underrated structure, the hypothalamus, because it is so all-encompassing, controlling such aspects of bodily behavior as homeostasis, feeding and drinking behavior, emotional behavior, wakefulness, sexual behavior, combinations of these, and perhaps many unknown aspects. It is beyond anyone's ability to specify detailed hypothalamic reactions to the various drugs of abuse and the human behavior resulting from these reactions, because science has not yet provided much information. However, if one applies his or her knowledge of the action of depressant drugs, stimulants, or hallucinogens to the general knowledge of hypothalamic function presented here, greater insight into drug-induced behavior is possible.

The Limbic System (Emotional Memory and Behavior)

The limbic system (Fig. 3.7) is a rim of cortical tissue associated with deep rhinencephalic structures. It is phylogenetically the oldest portion of the cerebral cortex, with few direct connections with the neocortex, the newest portion of the

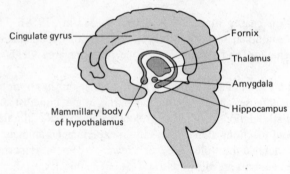

Fig. 3.7 The limbic system (amygdala, hippocampus, cingulate gyrus, and fornix). This system is made up of large groups of nuclei in and around the temporal areas of the cortex.

brain. In drug studies, the areas comprising the limbic system have often shown a high concentration of the drug and thus are thought to be effective in altering behavior. This system is in direct neural contact with the thalamus and the hypothalamus, and they are often included in discussions as parts of the limbic system.

Early scientific investigation of the limbic system showed that electrode stimulation in various areas of the system would elicit changes in blood pressure, heart rate, sexual behavior, eating patterns, and many other physiological responses. This information led to a belief that the limbic system also possessed (along with the hypothalamus and other old-brain structures) specific autonomic nervous system nuclei. It is now believed that excitation of limbic areas causes efferent stimulation of lower brain centers, especially the hypothalamus, which control the various physiological responses that accompany emotion (Stroebel, 1972).

It has become apparent in only the last decade that the limbic system is the memory area of emotions. As certain situations evoke particular emotions, it is this system that provides the memory and synchronization of feelings with physiological response. If a child is afraid of the dark, this memory pattern of fear takes form in the limbic cortex, and thereafter (perhaps even into adulthood), a dark house or dark street, for example, may trigger this memory, complete with rapid heartbeat, increased breathing rate, and feelings of fear or anxiety.

As the hypothalamus is involved when one uses pleasure-producing drugs, so too is the limbic system. If one takes a drug in a pleasurable setting or receives pleasurable feelings from the experience, its emotional content is stored in the limbic system and may become a stimulus to repeat the experience.

The Cerebral Cortex (Thought Processes)

The cerebral cortex, the most recent evolutionary development of the vertebrate nervous system, is divided into a number of areas according to function (Fig. 3.8).

The two association areas are responsible for responding logically to time, environment, and social climate. The temporal association area is involved in learning processes and memory; the frontal association area is especially implicated in drug use, since this area is the first to be depressed by alcohol and other depressant drugs, thus removing social inhibitions.

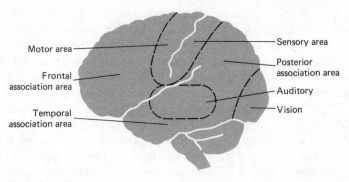

Motor area

Frontal
association area

Temporal
association area

Sensory area

Posterior
association area

Auditory

Vision

Fig. 3.8   Function of cerebral areas.

The sensory area receives impulses from the body via the thalamus, and responds via the motor cortex. The visual and auditory areas integrate sight and sound into meaningful images.

Ornstein (1973) has studied the role of the right cerebral hemisphere versus that of the left side and has found that a unique control is elicited by each side. The functions of the right and left are dichotomized into automatization and time-space orientation, respectively. That is, the left hemisphere is highly active (and the right hemisphere inactive) when one is writing, thinking through logic or math problems, conducting scientific ventures, or translating and speaking a particular language. The reverse neurological situation occurs (that is, the right hemisphere is active and the left side inactive) when one is involved in fantasy, art, dance, and music or art appreciation. It has been suggested that drugs, meditation, and other such highs erode the automatization through which we protect our physical and mental being and shift us into time-space orientation. The newness of this experience and the extension of one's ego boundaries make right-brain dominance pleasurable and a sought-after state.

It is obvious that drugs alter behavior, thought processes, and other reactions controlled by cortical cells. However, one general question that comes to mind is whether drugs work directly on the cortical cells, on the thalamic areas that supply information to and relay information from the cortex, or even perhaps on other brain structures that may control cerebral function, such as the hypothalamus. This must remain pure conjecture until we have sufficient scientific understanding of drug action on the brain.

The Reticular Activating System (Arousal)

Even though the brain developed in three stages phylogenetically, the three areas do not function independently. Although the lower centers do attend primarily to biological survival and the higher centers permit the existence of complex society, one cannot view the lower centers as primitive or negative, requiring control by the higher consciousness thought centers. While it is difficult to understand drug-altered behavior without knowledge of the function of each specific structure, it is impossible to conceptualize that behavior as anything but total brain integration.

The concept of upper-center-lower-center integration may be perceived best by understanding the action of the reticular system. The reticular system, often referred to as the reticular activating system or RAS because it generally controls attention and wakefulness of the brain, consists of two neural pathways. These pathways should not be conceptualized as nerve tracts, since the boundaries are not delineated in the usual anatomical sense. Functionally, the RAS is part of the neutral transmitter network, which is neither sensory nor motor but internuncial, and thus is a two-way street, transmitting impulses from brain to body and from body to brain (Fig. 3.9). Nearly all signals coming to the cortex travel into the RAS; that is, impulses come into the reticular formation, synapse there, and are sent on or damped out. The function of the lower two-thirds of this system is that of arousal only. Like an alarm clock, it awakens the brain (or if awake, the brain is alerted), but gives no explanation of why it has done so. Most of us have awakened at night to find our covers off—sensations of chilliness synapse in the RAS and this wakes up the brain. Upon first awakening, we are not sure what is wrong. Then we assess the situation for meaning and pull the covers back on. The RAS has said "Wake up," not "Wake up; your covers are off."

In the upper third of the RAS, called the thalamic portion, the decision to send on the impulse is conditional, according to whether the message is new, different, or threatening. The ability of this portion of the RAS to damp out monotonous stimuli is extremely important to our ability to concentrate on one thing at a time. Theoretically, hyperkinetic activity denotes that the neurologic function of the hyperactive person is not up to par, that is, unimportant signals are not damped out so that every sight, sound, smell, or other sensory input is sent on to the brain for attention. This produces an individual with a limited attention span who continually reacts to all new stimuli. It surprises many that stimulant drugs such as amphetamines or Ritalin are given to the hyperactive, but they are given in order to stimulate underactive cells of this area to produce this damping or selectivity function.

In addition to using amphetamines for this medical purpose, many take these drugs to keep themselves awake, since the RAS is aroused by their action. The continuous activation of cells in this area by impulses from muscles, sense receptors, or stimulatory drugs will keep an individual awake and alert. This is why muscle tension due to anxiety or fear may cause insomnia—the tension of the muscles neurologically stimulates the RAS, which in turn arouses the brain. Since

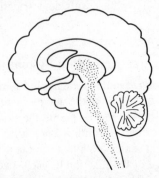

Fig. 3.9 **The reticular activating system (dotted area).**

the brain can arouse the RAS, worrying or thinking about what tomorrow may bring can also cause insomnia. The theories on neuromuscular relaxation are based on the importance of damping out RAS activity. Likewise, this is naturally the target of the sedative-hypnotics (Caldwell et al., 1974; Moruzzi & Magoun, 1949).

The Cerebellum (Coordination)

The cerebellum controls balance and coordination of body movements by integrating the incoming messages from the motor area of the cortex, the spinal sensory nerves, the balance system of the ear, and the auditory and visual systems. Removal of the cerebellum will not cause paralysis, but rather uncoordinated movement.

DRUG ACTION: A SYNTHESIS

To summarize the hypothesized action of various drugs on the central nervous system, it is helpful to categorize some representative drugs by the action they produce. These are as follows:

1. *Drugs affecting arousal*

    a. *Amphetamines and cocaine.* These drugs probably mimic the effects of norepinephrine (NE) by displacing this amine from peripheral adrenergic nerve endings. In the brain they act to release both NE and dopamine (DA) from nerves containing these amines. These drugs may also act by displacing catecholamines from storage sites. Dopamine release is correlated with rewarding stimulation, and since these drugs release dopamine, their use can be self-rewarding.

    b. *Barbiturates and nonbarbiturate sedative-hypnotics.* These drugs probably act by slowing oxidative metabolism and depression of synaptic transmission. They generally act throughout the brain with a specific inhibition of synaptic action of the neurohormone GABA. In large dosages, they suppress ongoing behavior and induce sleep. In small doses, they may increase behavioral output due to improved discriminative behavior in certain activities by blocking the overstimulation of the reticular activating system.

    c. *Alcohol.* Ethanol, as a depressant capable of interacting with nerve cell membranes, can profoundly alter central nervous system function. When administered acutely, ethanol acts in a biphasic, dose-dependent manner such that very low doses of ethanol increase neural excitability in many brain regions, while higher doses produce the more well-known sedative effects. Many laboratory studies, attempting to define the primary sites of ethanol's acute effects within the brain, have supported a regional hierarchy of susceptibility ranging from primary sensory neurons as least affected to association cortex and reticular formation as most affected. However, a general disruptive effect at synapses throughout the brain has not been ruled out. Data from experiments using several physical/chemical techniques agree that ethanol causes membrane disorder, making them more fluid and increasing the mobility of their components. The phase transition temperature is lowered. Alcohol may increase the proportion of the lipid that is fluid rather than in a gel state. Membrane proteins depend on the lipid for an appropriate environment, and their function may be affected by slight changes in membrane fluidity. Disruption of membrane protein function by changes in the enveloping lipid may be the mechanism for intoxication.

2. *Drugs affecting mood*

a. *Antianxiety drugs.* The tranquilizers (i.e., the benzodiazepines) are thought to affect the brain at various levels due to their action on the inhibitory neurotransmitter, GABA. Tranquilizers narrow the range of behavioral responses to adverse stimuli.

b. *Antidepressants (e.g., the MAO inhibitors).* These drugs probably act by producing a long-lasting rise in the concentration of NE, DA, and 5 HT. While the presence of more neurohormone in storage does not necessarily mean more will be released, it is known that the MAO inhibitors result in a potentiation of NE and/or 5 HT on the synapse.

3. *Drugs affecting perception*

a. *Psychedelics (e.g., LSD, mescaline, cannabis).* LSD may mimic the effect of 5 HT at certain synapses in the brain or slow the rate of 5 HT turnover in the brain. Psychedelics can replace the present world reality with an alternative that is equally real but different. Both the drug-induced, and nondrug world can be attended to at the same time and there is memory for the drug-induced reality after the drug effect diminishes.

   Other drugs in this class, such as mescaline, bear a structural resemblance to the catecholamine transmitters.

   Cannabis, in addition to producing its own effects, can potentiate the depressant effects of barbiturates or the excitatory action of amphetamines. Less is known about the physiological action of cannabis itself, but it is believed that the subjective feeling of being stoned is the result of the direct action of THC on brain cells having a special affinity or chemical attraction for cannabinoids.

Self-Test: PHYSIOLOGY OF DRUGS

The concepts contained in this chapter are some of the most difficult for nonbiological science-oriented readers, so we offer here a self-test that is designed to allow you to ascertain if you have retained some of the more important concepts in the chapter. Circle the correct response (T = True   F = False).

T   F   1.   The nerve cell, or neuron, transmits messages in one direction only: from the cell body out the axon.

T   F   2.   There is a space between the axon and the next neuron that can be affected by various kinds of drugs.

T   F   3.   A neuron "fires" only when there are enough excitatory messages stimulating that cell.

T   F   4.   Drugs work on the neuronal synapses by mimicking or altering the activity of naturally occurring neurohormones in the central nervous system.

T   F   5.   Two of the main brain centers affected by amphetamine-like drugs are the cerebrum and cerebellum.

T   F   6.   The vital centers (cardiac, respiratory, and vasomotor) that are fatally affected by alcohol intoxication are located in the hypothalamus.

T   F   7.   The thalamus serves as a main "switchboard" for nearly all impulses coming into and leaving the brain.

T   F   8.   The pleasure centers are found in the hypothalamus.

T   F   9.   Emotional memories of pleasant or painful past experiences are stored in the limbic area of the brain.

T   F   10.   The Reticular Activating System (RAS) has two main functions: arousal of the central nervous system and storing basic social inhibitions learned early in life, such as control of bladder.

ANSWER KEY: 1. T   2. T   3. T   4. T   5. F (the centers most affected are the RAS and the hypothalamus) **6. F** (the vital centers are found in the medulla) **7. T   8. T   9. T   10. F** (the main functions are arousal of the c.n.s. and habituation to or inhibition of nonthreatening signals coming into the c.n.s.). After answering these questions, go back and see if you understand the drug implications of each.

A score of 8 or higher indicates a good understanding of the basics presented here. A score lower than 8 may motivate you to reread the chapter and perhaps do some outside reading in this area as well.

REFERENCES

Bard, P., and M. B. Macht. "The behavior of chronically decerebrate cats," in *CIBA Foundation Symposium, Neurological Basis of Behavior*. London: Churchill, 1958, pp. 55–71.

Caldwell, J., et al. "The biochemical pharmacology of abused drugs iii. Cannabis, opiates and synthetic narcotics." *Clinical Pharmacology and Therapy* 16(6):989–1013, 1974.

Chronister, R. B., and J. F. DeFrance. "Functional organization of monoamines," in G. C. Palmer, ed. *Neuropharmacology of Central Nervous System and Behavioral Disorders*. Orlando, Fla.: Academic Press, 1981.

Eccles, J. C. *The Physiology of Synapses*. Orlando, Fla.: Academic Press, 1963.

Eccles, J. C., et al. "The mode of operation of the synaptic mechanism producing presynaptic inhibition." *Journal of Neurophysiology* 26:523–531, 1963b.

Eccles, J. C. "The synapse." *Scientific American* 212:56–59, 1965.

Emson, P. "Peptides as neurotransmitter candidates in the mammalian CNS." *Progress in Neurobiology* 13:61–116, 1983.

Grodsky, G. M. "The chemistry and functions of the hormones," in H. A. Harper, ed. *Review of Physiological Chemistry*. Los Altos, Calif.: Lange Medical Publications, 1973, pp. 426–481.

Harper, H. A. "Protein and amino acid metabolism," in H. A. Harper, ed. *Review of Physiological Chemistry*. Los Altos, Calif.: Lange Medical Publications, 1985, pp. 311–360.

Hughes, J. "Isolation of an endogenous compound from the brain with pharmacological properties similar to morphine." *Brain Research* 88:295–308, 1975.

Hughes, J., ed. *Centrally Acting Peptides*. London: Macmillan, 1978.

Iversen, Susan D., and Leslie L. Iversen. *Behavioral Pharmacology*. Oxford: Oxford University Press, 1981.

Lane, John, James E. Smith, and Graham E. Fagg. "The origin and termination of neuronal pathways in mammalian brain and their putatic neurohumors," in T. E. Smith and J. D. Lane, eds. *The Neurobiology of Opiate Reward Processes*. Amsterdam: Elsevier Biomedical Press, 1983.

Moruzzi, G., and H. W. Magoun. "Brain stem reticular formation and activation of the EEG." *Electroencephalography and Clinical Neurophysiology* 1:455–473, 1949.

Olds, J., and P. Milner. "Positive reinforcement produced by electrical stimulation of the septal area and other regions of the rat brain." *Journal of Comparative and Physiological Psychology* 47:419–427, 1954.

Ornstein, R. E. "Right and left thinking." *Psychology Today*, May, 1973, pp. 87–93.

Pasternak, G. W., R. Goodman, and S. H. Snyder. "Endogenous morphine-like factor in mammalian brain." *Life Science* 16:1765–1769, 1975.

Sjoerdsma, A., et al. "Metabolism of 5-HT by monoamine oxidase." *Proceedings of the Society for Experimental Biology and Medicine* 89:35–38, 1955.

Smith, T. W., et al. "Enkephalins: isolation, distribution and function," in H. W. Kosterlitz, ed. *Opiates and Endogenous Opiod Peptides*. Amsterdam: North Holland, 1976, pp. 57–62.

Stein, L. "Self-stimulation of the brain and the central stimulant action of amphetamines." *Federation Proceedings, Federation of American Societies for Experimental Biology* 23:836–849, 1964.

Stroebel, C. F. "Psychophysiology pharmacology," in N. S. Greenfield and R. A. Sternbach, eds. *Handbook of Psychophysiology*. New York: Holt, Rinehart and Winston, 1972, pp. 787–838.

Teitelbaum, P., and A. W. Epstein. "The lateral hypothalamic syndrome." *Psychological Review* 69:74–90, 1962.

Verebey, K., J. Volavka, and D. Clouet. "Endorphins in psychiatry." *Archives of General Psychiatry* 35(7):877–888, 1978.

Walker, R. J. "Polypeptides as central transmitters." *General Pharmacology* 9(3):129–138, 1978.

Woolley, D. W., and E. L. Shaw. "Evidence for the participation of serotonin in mental processes." *Annals of the New York Academy of Sciences* 66:649–665, 1957.

SUGGESTED READINGS

Eccles, J. C. *The Understanding of the Brain*. New York: McGraw-Hill, 1977.

Goodman, L. S., and A. Gilman, eds. *The Pharmacologic Basis of Therapeutics*. New York: Macmillan, 1975.

Haber, Bernard, José Regino Perez-Polo, and Joe Dan Coulter, eds. *Proteins in the Nervous System*. New York: Alan R. Liss, 1982.

Hughes, J., ed. *Centrally Acting Peptides*. Baltimore, Md.: University Park Press, 1978.

Levine, R. R. *Pharmacology: Drug Actions and Reactions*. Boston: Little, Brown, 1978.

Lipton, M. A., R. DiMascio, and K. F. Killam, eds. *Psychopharmacology: A Generation of Progress*. New York: Raven Press, 1982.

Mogenson, G. J. *The Neurobiology of Behavior: An Introduction*. New York: Halsted Press, 1977.

Ornstein, R. E. *The Psychology of Consciousness*. Orlando, Fla.: Harcourt Brace Jovanovich, 1977.

Pincus, J. H., and G. J. Tucker. *Behavioral Neurology*. New York: Oxford University Press, 1978.

Rainer, Sinz, and Mark R. Rosensweig, eds. *Psychophysiology: Memory, Motivation and Event-Related Potentials in Mental Operations*. Amsterdam: Elsevier Biomedical Press, 1983.

Schmidt, R. F., ed. *Fundamentals of Neurophysiology*. New York: Springer-Verlag, 1978.

Schwartz, M. *Physiological Psychology*. Englewood Cliffs, N.J.: Prentice-Hall, 1978.

Seiden, L. S., and L. A. Dykstra. *Psychopharmacology: A Biochemical and Behavioral Approach*. New York: Van Nostrand Reinhold, 1977.

Thompson, T., and P. B. Dews. *Advances in Behavioral Pharmacology*. Orlando, Fla.: Academic Press, 1977.

Wartak, J. *Clinical Pharmacokinetics*. New York: Praeger, 1983.

CHAPTER 4

ALCOHOL

Self-Test: ALCOHOL QUIZ

Although alcohol is the most commonly used psychoactive drug in the world, there are many misconceptions that surround its use and abuse. Before reading this chapter, test your knowledge about alcohol; and after scoring the quiz, pay particular attention to those areas in which you had misconceptions (T = True   F = False).

T   F   1.   Alcohol is correctly classified as a drug.

T   F   2.   After a drink, a person is pepped up because alcohol in small amounts is a stimulant.

T   F   3.   Excessive ingestion of alcohol can cause death by overstimulating the nerve cells to exhaustion.

T   F   4.   Alcohol is absorbed into the system and digested in the same way as food.

T   F   5.   Alcohol has no nutritional value.

T   F   6.   Alcohol has caloric value and can be used to produce energy.

T   F   7.   An alcohol hangover can be eliminated by eating high levels of carbohydrates before or during drinking.

T   F   8.   Drinking black coffee accelerates the sobering-up process.

T   F   9.   Between 50 and 75 percent of all alcoholics eventually develop cirrhosis of the liver.

T   F   10.   Alcohol cannot cross the placenta, thus even excessive drinking cannot significantly affect the fetus.

T   F   11.   For the average 150-pound individual, it would take the accumulation of five drinks to significantly affect driving skills.

T   F   12.   Social drinking is the primary cause of alcoholism.

T   F   13.   The development of alcoholism usually proceeds through predictable stages.

T   F   14.   Only individuals with seriously maladjusted personalities become alcoholics.

T   F   15.   Women become alcoholics primarily because they try to keep up with the drinking behavior of significant men in their lives.

T   F   16.   There is no effective treatment for alcoholism.

T   F   17.   Among teen-agers twelve to seventeen years old, alcohol is second only to marijuana as the most widely used drug.

Self-Test: ALCOHOL QUIZ (continued)

T   F   18.   Alcoholics Anonymous has been replaced by more modern treatments and is now used very seldom as a treatment modality.

T   F   19.   Because alcoholism is rare among employed individuals, few companies have developed employee alcohol programs.

T   F   20.   Accentuating guilt feelings is the most effective way to help a friend who is a problem drinker.

ANSWER KEY: 1. T   2. F   3. F   4. F   5. T   6. T   7. F   8. F   9. F   10. F   11. F   12. F   13. T   14. F   15. F   16. F   17. F   18. F   19. F   20. F

In reality, alcohol is the nation's number-one drug problem. Indications are that more than 10 million Americans are either alcoholics or problem drinkers whose drinking habits have adverse effects on themselves, family, employers, police, and society in general. On the average each of them affects the lives of four family members and more than sixteen friends and business associates in the community.

Slightly more than 7 percent of the nearly 150 million adults who are eighteen years of age or older have problems with alcohol. If we were talking about measles or the flu, that number would indicate an epidemic with historic significance, calling into action every health resource to deal with the problem. Of the adults who drink, one in three has a drinking problem. In addition to these adult problem drinkers, there are an estimated 3.3 million problem drinkers among youth between the ages of fourteen and seventeen. It is estimated that alcohol-related deaths may run as high as 205,000 per year in the United States. Alcohol contributes to slightly over 50 percent of our traffic accidents, and causes in excess of 28,000 fatalities, countless injuries, and immeasurable property damage each year. It is conservatively estimated that our national alcoholic problem costs us $50 billion annually.

ALCOHOL: THE FACTS

Chemically, an alcohol is an alkyl group with a hydroxyl (OH) group attached. The representative of this chemical group that has produced a good deal of social and medical concern and detailed study is ethanol, or ethyl alcohol, which is contained in all commonly ingested alcoholic beverages.

Ethanol has within its structure the chemical power to depress the action of the central nervous system; thus, it can definitely be classified as a mind-altering drug. With chronic use of ethanol, an individual's tolerance grows and he or she becomes physically and psychologically dependent on it.

The phenomenon of physiological tolerance to alcohol has long been recognized, though not understood. Tolerance is a condition in which it takes increasingly larger amounts of alcohol to produce the same effects previously felt at lower levels of alcohol intake. Many researchers believe that alcoholic tolerance is a process of adaptive metabolism whereby the cells of the body continuously develop the capability of metabolizing increased amounts of alcohol. Other investigators suggest that it is merely a process whereby the central nervous system adapts to the alcohol that is present; that is, much of tolerance is due to the learned ability to adjust to alcohol's physical effects on speech, vision, gait, etc. Observation of the day-by- day behavior of drinkers suggests that it is possible to diminish the outward signs of intoxication even though blood alcohol levels remain constant. It has been suggested that the reason for loss of tolerance in the first severe stages of alcoholism may be the permanent damage to or loss of cells that control these outward signs of tolerance.

When alcohol is ingested, it is immediately absorbed into the portal venous blood and taken directly to the heart, which sends a rich supply of blood (15 percent of the total blood pumped per minute) to the brain. Alcohol's first effects are manifested in the cerebral area and are due to depressant action on the central nervous system. As the tissues of the brain become exposed to the highly fat-soluble ethyl alcohol, the first cells to be depressed are those of the highest cortical areas, including the association areas of the cerebral cortex that house the centers of judgment, self-control, and other learned inhibitions. Thus, even small amounts of alcohol bring about some loss of inhibition. When learned inhibitions are removed from the government of behavior, antisocial behavior may occur, because inhibitions are a result of the socialization process. As children learn to live in their society, they must learn the social inhibitions that are impressed on them. Very early in life they learn to control their excretory processes, their tempers, and other reactions to social and physical stimuli. They learn that it is not wise to fight with older and bigger children—not acceptable, indeed, to fight at all. They are constantly being conditioned to the sexual and moral code of those around them and are expected to behave in a certain manner. As these social inhibitions are learned, they are apparently stored in the association areas of the brain as the guardians of logical, social behavior. It is obvious, then, that if these particular cells are removed, damaged, or chemically rendered inoperable by alcohol or other drugs, they will cease to guard social behavior, and the drinker will revert to more primitive behavior—the degree of reversion depending on the amount of alcohol ingested and on his or her temperament (Fig. 4.1).

It is, then, this release of inhibitions that may cause the drinker to feel stimulated when, in fact, the brain cells have been depressed. Alcohol is classified as a depressant, and it is this depressant action that brings about most of the commonly observed consequences of drinking. The first noticeable effects of alcohol result from depression of higher brain centers; as drinking continues, this depression spreads downward through deeper motor areas to the emotional centers buried beneath the cortex, and further down the brainstem to the most primitive areas of the brain. Thus, control over social inhibitions, motor coordination, speech and vision, and the waking state is progressively lost as greater amounts of alcohol are consumed. The final areas affected are those of respiration and heart rate control.

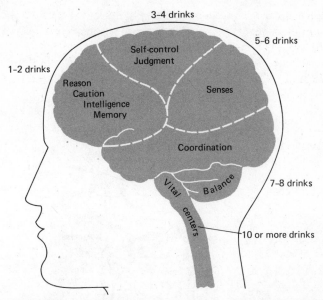

Fig. 4.1 Alcohol's effects on the brain. The effects of the number of drinks are dependent on factors such as the time period in which the drinks are consumed, weight of the drinker, and other individual considerations. This graphic shows the general depressive effects of alcohol on the brain.

Although most deaths attributed to alcohol are the result of chronic physical deterioration caused by many years of alcohol abuse, acute death from alcohol toxicity is caused by depression of the respiratory center located in the medulla. Whereas the lethal level of blood alcohol in most humans is between 0.40 and 0.60 percent, animals that are given artificial respiration can maintain life up to a blood alcohol level of 1.20 to 1.30 percent before cardiac failure causes death.

There is still much to discover regarding the way in which alcohol causes depression of central nervous system cells, but it appears to researchers that alcohol interferes with the sodium-potassium pump that is responsible for setting up the postsynaptic membrane potential. If the membrane cannot hold or reestablish its integrity, an impulse cannot pass through it, hence, the depressant action on the cell and/or system.

Ingestion and Absorption

Since alcohol is already in liquid form, it is ready for absorption into the blood immediately after ingestion. It is not changed chemically in the stomach or the intestine as is food during the digestive process. Some absorption of alcohol occurs in the stomach, but most of it takes place in the first foot of the small intestine just beyond the pylorus. In contrast, most food has to pass far into the latter two-thirds of the small intestine, the jejunum and ilium, before absorption can take place (Fig. 4.2).

Absorption of alcohol is very rapid because it has a low molecular weight,

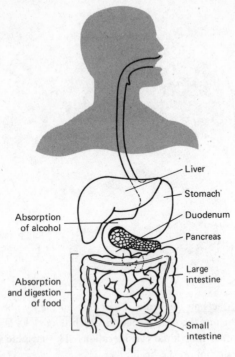

Fig. 4.2   Absorption of food and alcohol.

because it is highly fat- and water-soluble, and because the bloodstream in most instances has a lesser concentration of alcohol than the stomach or intestines so it simply flows down the diffusion gradient. This rapid absorption gives the blood of the portal circulation a much higher initial concentration of alcohol than that in the remaining vascular system; however, tissues with a rich blood supply, such as the brain, liver, and kidney, quickly reach a storage equilibrium with the blood. After a period of time other tissues of the body, such as the muscles, will reach this equilibrium also.

In addition to its effects on the central nervous system, alcohol has a local effect on the tissues with which it comes in contact. As alcohol is taken into the body through the digestive tract, that system is subjected to irritation and degeneration. Alcohol can damage the esophagus by direct irritation of the cellular lining, and by interference with normal muscular functioning, thereby causing an upward movement of stomach acid. The major complication is hemorrhage and difficulty in swallowing. Alcohol has been associated with a variety of inflammatory and bleeding lesions in the stomach. The degree of damage in the lining of the stomach appears to be related to the concentration of alcohol, with damage to the cells occurring rapidly after ingestion of especially highly concentrated drinks. In the intestines, alcohol can change the rate of peristaltic and propulsive waves. Diarrhea is frequently a problem to chronic drinkers. Intestinal malabsorption contributes to nutritional deficiencies as calcium, iron, and vitamin uptake is impaired. Problems associated with the pancreas and liver will be discussed later.

If nutritional elements are defined as those substances necessary for the growth, repair, and proper functioning of the body and not merely energy producers, then ethyl alcohol would not be on the list of nutritive substances. Alcohol is a highly caloric substance, but contains only trace amounts of vitamins, minerals, and proteins. Often the substance that is mixed with alcohol (for example, hops and grain in beer; grapes in wine) contains some protein and vitamins, but these amounts are too small to be of appreciable value to the human organism.

The main problem in the case of chronic alcoholics is that alcohol is not merely added to the diet, but is substituted for carbohydrates, fats, and proteins. Humans usually eat in accordance with their appetites, which are normally geared in part to their caloric needs. When the appetite has been satisfied (calorically), the individual stops eating even though vitamins, minerals, and proteins may still be inadequate. In chronic alcoholics, the result is often extreme vitamin deficiency that brings on polyneuritis from thiamine deficiency, fatty liver from protein deficiency, or a multitude of similar nutrition-related maladies.

In individuals who are excessive drinkers but who eat enough to meet their daily nutritional requirements, the problem is usually merely one of maintaining proper body weight because of the high caloric value of alcohol.

Calories

Chronic alcoholics have little difficulty maintaining energy levels even though they might consume little actual food. The calories expended for energy come from the alcohol, which for most alcoholics exceeds a fifth of a gallon per day. Alcohol is considered a high-calorie food, and the alcoholic who consumes more than a fifth of whiskey per day will absorb more than 2,200 calories from the alcohol alone. This may amount to as much as 75 percent of his or her normal daily intake of calories.

Alcohol yields seven calories per gram, which makes it more caloric than carbohydrates (four calories per gram) but less caloric than fats (nine calories per gram). A one-ounce shot glass of whiskey (50 percent alcohol) yields approximately 84 calories. A twelve-ounce can of beer (4.5 percent alcohol) runs a little higher at 150 calories, and a four-ounce glass of dry table wine has about 100 calories. For a more detailed listing of the caloric value of alcoholic beverages, see Table 4.1.

Like foods, alcohol must be metabolized into a chemical substance that the cells

Table 4.1 Alcohol Content and Caloric Value of Various Alcoholic Beverages

Beverage	Alcohol Content	Approximate Calories
Beer (4.5%), 12-oz can	0.54 oz	150
Highball, 1 oz whiskey, 4 oz ginger ale	0.50 oz	140
Manhattan, 1½ oz whiskey, ¾ oz sweet vermouth	0.75 oz	145
Martini, 1½ oz gin, ½ oz 12% vermouth	0.75 oz	150
Tom Collins, 1½ oz gin, lemon, sugar, mix	0.75 oz	154
100 proof scotch, gin, etc., 1 oz	0.50 oz	100
80 proof scotch, gin, etc., 1 oz	0.40 oz	80
Dinner wine (12%), 4 oz	0.50 oz	100
Dessert wine (22%), 4 oz	0.80 oz	160

can utilize. This biochemical process begins when the enzyme alcohol dehydrogenase changes ethanol into acetaldehyde. This is the first step in alcohol metabolism and occurs mainly in the liver, although very high levels of intake stimulate at least one alternative metabolic pathway which can increase the rate of alcohol clearance. Substances that stimulate this alternative pathway can be extremely dangerous and are still to be tried in human subjects.

The first breakdown of alcohol in the liver proceeds at a rate that varies somewhat from one individual to another, but the range of variation is quite small. The average amount of ethanol that is changed into acetaldehyde is one-quarter to one-half ounce per hour. This is the approximate alcoholic content of one twelve-ounce bottle of beer or one mixed drink. Within each person this phase of alcohol metabolism is quite uniform and little can be done to speed up the process. There are some individual differences in the amount of alcohol that can be stored in the body, but sooner or later this stored alcohol must be metabolized. Until that time, alcohol will continue to affect the central nervous system. Since the first phase occurs in the liver at a constant rate, the process of "sobering up" is dependent on the liver. This concept is extremely important for individuals who must drive or perform other activities after drinking.

The second phase of alcohol metabolism, that of oxidation of acetaldehyde into acetic acid, takes place not only in the liver but also in many cells of the body, including the cells of the brain and nervous system. The rate of this oxidation is very important because the accumulation of large amounts of acetaldehyde in the cell can have adverse effects on normal cell function.

Acetaldehyde serves as a substrate for several enzymes. Under normal circumstances, it is metabolized rapidly and does not interfere with cell function. However, the large amounts of acetaldehyde that accumulate after ingestion of large quantities of ethanol are significant in the development of headaches, gastritis, nausea, dizziness, and other symptoms, which, when they occur together, are commonly known as a hangover (Khanna & Israel, 1980).

The problem of the accumulation of acetaldehyde is compounded by the effects of alcohol on cellular metabolism. Ethanol is a general depressant of several endocrinological processes and associated metabolic events. This decrease in general metabolism also slows down the rate at which acetaldehyde is utilized (Davis & Welsh, 1970).

The third phase of alcohol metabolism is the energy phase, where acetic acid, the metabolic product of acetaldehyde, enters into the normal chemistry of energy production. It is chemically changed into acetyl coenzyme-A and is used in the Krebs cycle to produce energy, just as other foodstuffs are (Fig. 4.3). When alcohol is in the system it is used preferentially for fuel, leaving the foodstuffs to be stored as fat. With this a twofold problem occurs, one of gained weight and the other of an accumulation of fats that are not removed from the liver. The latter is instrumental in the liver disease that is seen in chronic drinkers.

The Hangover

The nausea, headache, gastritis, dizziness, and vomiting that often accompany excessive consumption of alcohol appear to be caused not only by high alcohol

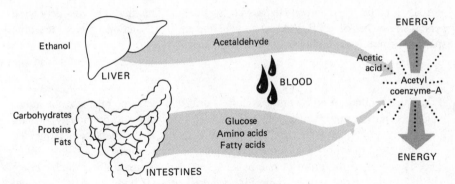

Fig. 4.3 Energy production from food and alcohol.

concentration in the blood but also by the increased amounts of acetaldehyde in the tissues. Accumulation of excess amounts of alcohol and acetaldehyde further depresses metabolic activity, thus increasing the amount of lactic acid and acetic acid in the body. Large amounts of lactic acid diminish alkali reserves and the alkali-binding power of the blood. Thus, impaired respiratory exchange, which decreases normal elimination of lactic acid and carbon dioxide, combines with increased acid accumulation due to decreased alkali-binding power to accentuate the symptoms of the hangover.

There remains some controversy as to the value of food substances in speeding up the oxidation of alcohol and the elimination of acetaldehyde and lactic acid buildup. Proteins have been shown to speed up metabolism of alcohol in individuals whose rate of metabolism is not at a maximum. A diet low in protein will tend to diminish the metabolic rate through depletion of the enzymes necessary for alcohol metabolism. Diets high in either fat or carbohydrates have not been shown to have any significant effect on the rate of metabolism of alcohol. Investigators have found some increases when glucose or insulin was given, but these increases occurred only in individuals who exhibited a lower-than-maximum alcohol metabolism. It can be concluded that individuals with normal alcohol metabolism cannot increase this metabolism by prior consumption of any dietary substance (Pirola, 1978).

The practice of drinking black coffee to aid in the sobering-up process has been followed for many years. However, sobering up or regaining control of the cells depressed by alcohol is entirely dependent on the breakdown of alcohol by the liver.

The caffeine contained in coffee is a stimulant and slightly increases the activity of cells in the central nervous system. While caffeine may or may not alleviate the intoxication symptoms, it does not speed up the metabolism of alcohol. It is generally assumed that alcohol metabolism is independent of overall metabolism and is not sensitive to the overall metabolic demands of the body. Conditions such as hyperthyroidism, physical activity, or exposure to low temperatures (all of which are capable of doubling overall metabolism) have little if any effect on the metabolism of alcohol and on the sobering-up process (Kendis, 1967).

Even though drinking coffee does not actually speed the sobering-up process, it still remains a sound practice so long as its effects are not overrated. The caffeine in the coffee is a central nervous system stimulant and may temporarily act as a partial stimulant to some cells depressed by alcohol. This may give the depressed person somewhat of a lift. And since sobering up is a function of time, the time spent in drinking the coffee may be of even more value!

Proof

If the same amount of equal-proof liquors is drunk in the same manner, one liquor is no less intoxicating than the other (Fig. 4.4). As was noted previously, we are speaking of one basic substance, ethanol. Whether it is distilled from fermented molasses, as rum is, or from fermented grains, as bourbon is, makes little difference. However, if the proof of one beverage is higher than another, the beverage with the higher proof will be more highly intoxicating if both are drunk in equal quantities: two ounces of whiskey are more intoxicating than two ounces of beer.

In the same vein, there is a common belief that mixing certain alcoholic beverages in certain ways will make one ill—"beer on whiskey, mighty risky"—whereas a different drinking pattern of the same drinks will not cause illness—"whiskey on beer, nothing to fear." Switching drinks throughout an evening may cause nausea, but probably more because of the amount drunk than because of the kinds consumed or the order of consumption.

The proof of a distilled beverage is its alcohol content and is roughly twice the given alcohol percentage (100 proof equals about 50 percent alcohol). A 100-proof spirit is an alcoholic beverage in which the alcohol has a specific gravity of 0.93426 at 60°F. This is the weight of the substance per volume compared to the weight of the same volume of water. It is said that in the early testing of alcoholic beverages the distiller mixed the whiskey with gunpowder, and if the alcohol content was too low the mixture would not light. If the whiskey was too strong, the gunpowder flamed up wildly. But if the alcohol content was near that desired, it would burn with an even, bright blue flame. This kind of flame was "proof" of good whiskey.

The proof, or percent alcohol, of a drink should be of concern to everyone who drinks or serves alcoholic beverages, so that one can intelligently judge the spacing

Fig. 4.4   Equal alcohol content.

of drinks and the proper waiting period before driving or taking on some other responsibility. As was pointed out earlier, the alcohol contained in one cocktail or a twelve-ounce bottle of beer is oxidized in approximately one hour.

Food, especially milk, fats, and meat, slows the absorption of alcohol. This allows more time for alcohol metabolism to proceed. Obviously, the rate of alcohol consumption is important, for if large amounts are consumed in a very short time, the concentration of alcohol in the stomach and intestine would cause rapid absorption. However, concentrations of alcohol above 50 percent (that is, beverages that are more than 100 proof—unusually strong) often exert a depressant effect on absorption. This may be due to a depression of stomach movement that delays the emptying of stomach contents into the intestine; or it may be that the high concentration of alcohol irritates the mucosal lining of the stomach and intestine, causing an increase in the secretion of mucus, and thus delaying absorption.

On the other hand, alcohol diluted to 10 percent or less, as in highballs, is absorbed slowly. The most rapid absorption usually occurs with wines and stronger mixed drinks such as martinis and manhattans, in which the percentage of alcohol is somewhere between 10 and 40 percent. Under most conditions, the drink with 40 percent alcohol would be absorbed more rapidly than the one with 10 percent because of the concentration being higher in the stomach than in the blood.

After alcohol is absorbed from the stomach or intestine, it passes into the portal system and is distributed throughout the body. When the blood alcohol level exceeds that of the tissues, alcohol is absorbed into the tissues and exerts its depressant effect there. Even though muscle tissue absorbs alcohol, the resulting depression of muscular activity is minor; the muscle tissue, in effect, stores the alcohol. Alcohol is not absorbed in fat tissue to the same degree as in muscles, probably because of the low water and protein content of fat.

ALCOHOL-RELATED DISORDERS

The following discussion presents extracts from the literature on alcoholism and its excesses.

Cirrhosis of the Liver

Laennic's cirrhosis is a chronic disease in which there is a progressive spread of connective tissue between portal spaces where there was once functional tissue. It is believed to develop by a process of fat accumulation followed by dysfunction and finally by fibrosis of the liver. It is also theorized that hepatitis may be a step in this disease process.

About 75 percent of all alcoholics show impaired liver function and approximately 8 percent of all alcoholics eventually develop cirrhosis, a rate of incidence that is about six times that of the nonalcoholic population. Cirrhosis has become the fourth leading cause of death for persons between the ages of twenty-five and forty-five in large urban areas.

Alcoholics have a greater chance of developing cirrhosis of the liver because (1) alcoholics tend toward malnutrition and this lack of nutritive elements allows the cirrhotic process to occur, and (2) alcohol itself (in the presence of adequate nutrition) causes cirrhosis.

The basis of the malnutrition theory of cirrhosis causation is that dietary deficiencies, especially a deficiency of proteins, result in a low level of lipotropic substances (such as choline, folic acid, and cynanocobalamin or vitamin B_{12}), which are necessary for normal removal of fat from the liver. In experimental animals, when these lipotropic substances are withheld from their diet, fatty liver results, and in most species cirrhosis follows. High-protein diets, especially those that include choline, may aid in the arrest of the cirrhotic process (Lieber, 1977).

Fatty liver is a logical forerunner of a fibrotic condition because:

1. Excess fat interferes with normal metabolism in hepatic cells, thus causing death of the cells.
2. Fat-filled cells next to each other tend to merge, thus creating a larger, nonworking complex that ruptures.
3. Excess fat causes a diminution of reproductive activity in hepatic cells, and as a result, worn-out cells are not replaced as quickly as they would be normally.
4. Fat obstructs normal blood flow in the liver cells, resulting in anoxia (oxygen deficiency) and death of the cells. Once liver cells die, the fibrotic process begins and will continue as more cells die. This is not a reversible process.

It has also been shown that high alcohol consumption has a direct deleterious effect on the liver. When the liver is forced to metabolize very large amounts of alcohol, there is an excess buildup of metabolites there that inhibits the production of energy from dietary fats. That is, the liver preferentially produces energy from alcohol rather than from other foods. This leads to deposition of fat in hepatic cells and holds much the same potential for liver damage as does fat deposition caused by dietary deficiency. Lieber and DeCarli (1974) have produced cirrhosis in baboons even when there was no dietary deficiency. It is important to note that these animals developed cirrhosis even though their diets were more than adequate.

Wernicke-Korsakoff Syndrome

The Wernicke-Korsakoff syndrome is a neurological syndrome that can occur in chronic alcoholics. The syndrome has two distinct phases. The acute phase is characterized by mental confusion, optical problems, and temporary nerve dysfunction, including some paralysis. The chronic or long-term effect is primarily memory loss. Research over the last ten years has shown that this condition develops over years of alcohol abuse and is due to both the direct effect of the alcohol and the interaction of the toxic effects of alcohol and malnutrition. (Malnutrition is often seen in alcoholics) (Butters & Cermak, 1980).

Cardiovascular Disorders

Alcohol plays a number of roles in the etiology of cardiovascular disorders. Most cardiologists now recognize the existence of a condition known as alcoholic heart disease which is caused by the direct toxic effects of alcohol on the heart muscle tissue. A cofactor in this condition seems to be malnutrition, especially thiamine deficiency. Hypertension is another cardiovascular disorder with varied etiology that has also been linked to excessive alcohol consumption (three or more drinks per day). The mechanism for this relationship has not been established. Some studies have shown that moderate drinkers are less at risk than nondrinkers for major coronary problems. A possible mechanism is that moderate amounts of alcohol increase high-density lipoprotein (HDL) which has been found to be inversely related to coronary atherosclerotic disease (NIAAA, 1982).

Endocrine Disorders

A review of recent literature has clearly shown that alcohol depresses testosterone levels both acutely and chronically. In addition, this depression may be somehow related to the metabolic tolerance a person develops with chronic alcohol use. Alcohol has been found by most investigators to increase the output of adrenal hormones but it is not clear at this time whether this is a direct result of the alcohol or of stress. Several other endocrine hormones have been found to be altered with chronic alcohol use and this is thought to be one of the primary mechanisms involved with both tolerance and physical dependence (NIAAA, 1982).

Cognitive Impairment

Alcoholics in treatment centers have been found to exhibit both brain abnormalities and cognitive impairment. CAT scan studies show that the brains of alcoholics have shrunk. The evidence on cognitive impairment suggests that the effects of drinking alcohol varies with consumption. There is very little impairment in a light drinker compared to sometimes severe impairment in alcoholics. In some respects, alcoholics manifest characteristics of premature aging while others do not (NIAAA, 1982).

Fetal Alcohol Syndrome

Fetal Alcohol Syndrome (FAS) is an abnormal pattern of growth and development that occurs in some children born to chronically alcoholic women. Children with FAS show a wide range of disabilities. Typically, FAS children are very small, have a similar facial appearance, and suffer major mental and motor retardation. The exact number of children affected by maternal alcoholism is unknown. Estimates are that one in every 750 to 1,000 live births may be FAS. Alcohol is suspected as the primary cause of the prenatal damage, although other factors such as heredity, nutrition, other drugs, and individual differences in susceptibility to alcohol may be involved (Sokol et al., 1980).

Recent studies of moderate and heavy drinking women, compared with abstainers and light drinking women, indicate alcohol may negatively affect the developing fetus—even when the mother is not alcoholic. These effects include reduced physical growth, increased spontaneous abortions and stillbirths, and damage to the central nervous system, as reflected in the infant's behavior and postnatal development. There are many scientific limitations in investigations of human pregnancies. This means that precise cause-and-effect relationships seldom can be demonstrated and that the amount of alcohol that is ''safe'' to consume during pregnancy cannot be established. The need for long-term assessment of children whose mothers drink different amounts of alcohol, in different patterns (such as daily drinking versus binge episodes), is essential to better understand the association between drinking during pregnancy and children's wellbeing.

Prevention efforts and public information programs have started and offer promise as one means of preventing damage to the developing child. Objective evaluation of these efforts is critical, as well as encouraging innovative strategies to reduce alcoholism and alcohol abuse among women in the childbearing years (Landesman-Dwyer et al., 1981; NIAAA, 1982).

Any drug that enters the bloodstream of a pregnant woman soon reaches the placenta, often in highly undiluted form. Many soluble materials are capable of crossing the placenta, entering the fetal bloodstream, and chemically acting on fetal structures. Alcohol is one of these substances.

The pregnant mother, by virtue of her adult status, has the ability to detoxify her body by breaking down foreign substances, but the unborn fetus has a number of handicaps that leave it much more vulnerable to a toxic drug.

1. The fetus has the anatomical disadvantage of an enormous surface area of placenta villi, which permits easy transfer of a substance such as alcohol from the mother's blood to the blood of the fetus.
2. Its gastrointestinal mucous membrane has a high degree of permeability.
3. The fetus is deficient in functional kidney structures (glomeruli) that help excrete unwanted substances from the body.
4. Fetus enzyme systems are insufficiently developed to effectively break down or metabolize foreign substances.

Thus, until the fetus leaves its uterine environment, its ability to metabolize or detoxify toxic substances is hampered.

A mother who is intoxicated during delivery will give birth to a child who is, to a degree, also intoxicated (depending on the amount of alcohol that the mother has consumed). Indeed, a child born to an alcoholic mother may have to be gradually withdrawn from alcohol just as a child born to an opiate addict must be withdrawn from that drug (Warner & Rossett, 1975).

DRINKING AND DRIVING

Consider these facts about drinking and driving:

- Alcohol is involved in about one-half of all highway deaths. About 22,000 people a year (400 a week) die because some people choose to drive while intoxicated.
- About one-half of those killed each year are *not* the ones who have been drinking.
- Sixty percent of the young-adult (16–24 years old) highway deaths are related to alcohol use; in other words, if it were not for drinking drivers, six out of ten young adults killed in automobile accidents would still be alive.
- The accidents tend to be one-car crashes. As many as 60 percent of all alcohol-related accidents are single-vehicle crashes. These accidents usually involve running off the road or running into something. The problem seems to involve judgment, vision, and car control.
- The accidents tend to involve speeding. About one-fourth of all accidents involving young adults are caused by speeding, usually over 40 miles per hour. The problem here is often emotional control and/or judgment.
- The accidents tend to occur at night and on the weekends, usually after 10:00 P.M. As many as 70 percent of all alcohol-caused crashes involving young adults occur on weekends.

As regards driving, the necessary skills are: (1) good judgment, (2) good emotional control, (3) ability to see well, and (4) skill and coordination.

Alcohol impairs a driver's judgment, making the necesary complex decisions even more difficult. For example, a driver needs to gauge his or her own speed and that of other cars. He or she must assess carefully whether there is time to pass, whether there is room to merge, stop, or turn, and whether to slow down when other cars seem to be slowing down.

Alcohol has been called "optimism in a bottle," causing drunk drivers to overestimate their ability to handle a car. They fail to critically evaluate their own performance. They truly do not realize that their driving performance has deteriorated. The ability of intoxicated drivers to see as well as sober drivers is an often overlooked hazard of drunk driving. Eye muscles, relaxed by alcohol, do not focus as well or as quickly. Visual acuity diminishes, and things start to look fuzzy. Night vision is a major problem for intoxicated drivers. Both glare vision and glare recovery are impaired by alcohol. Finally, peripheral vision and depth and distance perception are also impaired.

The most common driving errors are: driving too fast, changing from fast to slow without reason, running over curbs, driving on the wrong side of the road or in the wrong lane, weaving, straddling lanes, starting in a quick or jerky manner, running stop signs, not signaling turns, or giving the wrong signal. Obviously, anyone who drives in this manner should allow someone else to do the driving, but that usually does not happen because the affected driver is unable to see his or her own mistakes.

Although individuals differ in their reactions to ingested alcohol, one cocktail is usually not likely to interfere with one's driving skill. For instance, a small person drinking a cocktail on an empty stomach may be adversely affected by the drink, but for most people the approximate blood alcohol content (0.02 to 0.03 percent) resulting from one cocktail is not high enough to make a difference in driving ability.

Blood alcohol levels are given in milligrams of alcohol per 100 milliliters of blood: If a person had 50 mg of alcohol per 100 ml of blood, he or she would have a blood alcohol content of 0.05 percent. Roughly speaking, four to five ounces of whiskey in an average-weight individual (154 pounds) ingested over a period of one hour would give a blood concentration of about 0.10 percent in two hours.

It is generally found that at a blood alcohol level of 0.02 percent there is no discernible intoxication. Between the levels of 0.05 and 0.09 percent there are various signs of intoxication, but these levels would not be legal proof of drunken driving in most states. Most individuals are, however, unmistakably drunk at a level of 0.15 percent, and at a level of 0.3 percent *any* drinker would be intoxicated. At 0.45 percent, intoxication is severe and further ingestion of alcohol could well result in death; indeed, levels as low as 0.35 to 0.45 percent have been known to cause death. Levels above 0.55 percent are usually fatal in untreated patients. For a thorough summary of the effect of various levels of blood alcohol concentration, see Table 4.2.

There are numerous ways of regarding what exactly constitutes the so-called drug problem in the United States, and one need not look very far to find a lively

Table 4.2   Psychological and Physical Effects of Various Blood Alcohol Concentration Levels*

Number of Drinks[†]	Blood Alcohol Concentration	Psychological and Physical Effects
1	0.02–0.03%	No overt effects, slight feeling of muscle relaxation, slight mood elevation.
2	0.05–0.06%	No intoxication, but feeling of relaxation, warmth. Slight increase in reaction time, slight decrease in fine muscle coordination.
3	0.08–0.09%	Balance, speech, vision, and hearing slightly impaired. Feelings of euphoria. Increased loss of motor co-ordination.
4	0.11–0.12%	Coordination and balance becoming difficult. Distinct impairment of mental facilities, judgment, etc.
5	0.14–0.15%	Major impairment of mental and physical control. Slurred speech, blurred vision, lack of motor skill. Legal intoxication in all states (0.15%).
7	0.20%	Loss of motor control—must have assistance in moving about. Mental confusion.
10	0.30%	Severe intoxication. Minimum conscious control of mind and body.
14	0.40%	Unconsciousness, threshold of coma.
17	0.50%	Deep coma.
20	0.60%	Death from respiratory failure.

*For each one-hour time lapse, 0.015% blood alcohol concentration, or approximately one drink.
† The typical drink—three-fourths ounce of alcohol—is provided by:
   a shot of spirits (1½ oz of 50-percent alcohol—100-proof whiskey or vodka)
   a glass of fortified wine (3½ oz of 20-percent alcohol)
   a larger glass of table wine (5 oz of 14-percent alcohol)
   a pint of beer (16 oz of 4½-percent alcohol).

debate on the subject. However, one topic on which the vast majority of people agree is the problem of drinking and driving. Those who do not agree are the drinking drivers who constitute the problem. Safety experts use the term "problem drinker" to describe about two-thirds of the drinking drivers who cause fatalities on the highways, not only because their consumption of alcohol is far beyond normal levels but also because they have experienced problems with alcohol in the past. Studies of drivers responsible for alcohol-related fatal accidents show that as many as two-thirds of these drivers have had a problem with alcohol before, as indicated by previous arrest, hospitalization, or a social agency contact in which excessive drinking played a role.

Experts disagree on their estimates of the number of problem drinkers who drive, but most agree that fewer than 10 percent of registered drivers have a drinking problem. In numbers, this still leaves about eight million problem drinkers on the road responsible for alcohol-related deaths and serious injuries. That is about one out of every fifteen drivers, yet they are involved in two-thirds of all alcohol-related traffic deaths. Approximately 30,000 people lose their lives each year because society cannot deal with those individuals who have a known problem with alcohol.

This is one drug-related topic where the statistics speak loud and clear, leaving no room for misinterpretation. Studies have firmly established a significant relationship between blood alcohol concentration (BAC) and relative risk of accident. Below 0.05 percent BAC risk, on the average, remains at essentially the same level as for drivers who have not been drinking. Between 0.05 percent and 0.10 percent BAC, the curve rises to about seven times that of nondrinking drivers. Above this BAC level, risk rises very rapidly from 20 to 50 times that of drivers who have not been drinking.

Table 4.2 summarizes the psychological and physical effects of various blood alcohol concentration levels. This information is important enough to be put another way and displayed again. Figure 4.5, prepared by the National Highway and Traffic Safety Administration (NHTSA), can serve as a usable, ready reference for your own weight and drinking situation. Find your weight and memorize how many drinks you can safely handle before you drive. It could save your life and the lives of others.

ALCOHOLISM

Alcoholism is a general term describing a whole set of physical, psychological, and sociological conditions, yet is specific enough to be used as a name for a "drinking disease." Alcoholism in the following discussion will be regarded mainly as a medical and psychological problem, in other words, drinking that has become pathological, chronic, and progressive, with true addictive aspects. It is well known that alcoholism does not start on one specific day in a long number of drinking days, but rather at some point when the chronic drinker can no longer control his or her appetite for alcohol.

Approximately 75 percent of American adults of drinking age and approximately 80 percent of high school students have consumed alcohol. Surveys indicate that one-half of the teenagers who drink do so at least once a month, but no accurate breakdown into specific frequency categories has been made for this age group. In

| | Drinks Two-Hour Period | | | | | | | | | | |
Weight	1½ oz 86° Liquor or 12 oz Beer										
100	1	2	3	4	5	6	7	8	9	10	11	12
120	1	2	3	4	5	6	7	8	9	10	11	12
140	1	2	3	4	5	6	7	8	9	10	11	12
160	1	2	3	4	5	6	7	8	9	10	11	12
180	1	2	3	4	5	6	7	8	9	10	11	12
200	1	2	3	4	5	6	7	8	9	10	11	12
220	1	2	3	4	5	6	7	8	9	10	11	12
240	1	2	3	4	5	6	7	8	9	10	11	12

Be careful	Driving	Do not drive
BAC to .05%	impaired	.10% & Up
	.05–.09%	

Fig. 4.5 Effect of number of drinks on responsible driving. The unshaded area shows the number of drinks that may not affect responsible driving depending on one's weight. Beyond that, the probability of being seriously affected becomes much greater.

the adult drinking groups, approximately 9 percent are classified as heavy drinkers, 18 percent as moderate, 31 percent as light, and 42 percent as either abstainers or infrequent drinkers. As has been discovered about other drugs, consumption of alcohol is slightly higher on the east and west coasts and lowest in the southern states.

A good definition for alcoholism is any drinking behavior that is associated with dysfunction in a person's life. This goes beyond the concept of alcoholism as a disease and encompasses both the temporary and ongoing behavior which compromises a person's physical and emotional well-being as well as the ability to function optimally at work and in interpersonal relationships. The disease model of alcoholism does help explain and describe much of the behavior of alcoholics; however, it should not be our only conceptualization. Using a disease orientation, E. M. Jellinek (1952) conducted a classic study that developed into the dominant philosophy of treating alcoholics in the last two decades. While that concept is now under fire because it is not all-encompassing of alcoholism in its broadest context, it describes the behavior of a large percentage of alcoholics and is therefore valuable. Jellinek interviewed over 2,000 alcoholics and found a characteristic pattern that constituted the "road to alcoholism." With a knowledge of this characteristic pattern, problem drinkers may recognize their problem earlier and control their drinking habits before the habit controls their lives.

The phases that most alcoholics follow appear to go from controlled social drinking to complete alcohol addiction. These phases can be summed up as follows (Fig. 4.6).

Prealcoholic Phase

1. *Controlled social, cultural drinking.* The first phase is that of controlled social or cultural drinking. It is said that some drinkers become alcoholics with their first drink, but complete loss of control to alcohol usually progresses over a period of ten to twenty years or longer.

2. *Occasional escape from tensions.* Just as social drinkers do not become alcoholics overnight, they also have no warning that their drinking has gone beyond that of social or cultural drinking and has progressed to a purposeful drinking—to escape from tensions. About 20 percent of the nation's drinkers fall into this category.

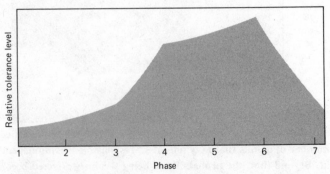

Fig. 4.6   Tolerance to alcohol during characteristic phases of alcoholism. (Modified from Jellinek, 1952, p. 67.)

3. *Frequent escape drinking.* The third phase is entered as innocuously as was the second. As drinkers find that they can temporarily escape the tensions and frustrations of their everyday lives through the use of alcohol, they begin to turn to this escape from real life more often.

During these first three stages, the drinker's tolerance to alcohol steadily increases, but in Phase 3 alcohol tolerance takes a sharp upswing and he or she must drink more liquor to achieve the same nirvana that was previously experienced (see Fig. 4.6).

Early Alcoholic Phase

4. A progression of drinking takes the escape drinker into the fourth phase, which appears to begin with the occurrence of the first blackout. The blackout is not merely passing out from drinking too much, but is more like temporary amnesia. One may carry on a conversation, move about, even drive a car—but will remember none of these actions later. It has been hypothesized that this phenomenon is due to the drinker's willpower—he or she wishes to remain in control of his or her body to prove the ability to handle the liquor, but the drug effect still overtakes part of the brain so that memory patterns are not established.

Tolerance continues to develop slowly during this phase and will continue through Phase 5, where it reaches its peak.

The actions of problem drinkers during this phase may be characterized as a progressive preoccupation with alcohol. When social functions are announced, they are more interested in whether drinks are to be served than in who will be attending the function. Before attending social functions, they fortify themselves with alcohol, and at parties they are in continual pursuit of an alcohol supply. These drinkers are far past the social drinking stage. They may begin to drink alone, gulping down the first few drinks to obtain an immediate effect, and their behavior may begin to be embarrassing to others, especially their spouses. Also, during this phase, problem drinkers may develop conscious or unconscious guilt feelings about their drinking and offer "good excuses" for taking a drink. No longer do they brag about their alcohol consumption, but rather they tend to underestimate the number of drinks they have consumed. They begin to avoid conversation concerning alcohol altogether (Bacon, 1973).

At this time, changed drinking patterns (drinking at a different time of day, switching to a new alcoholic beverage, using a different mix, etc.) may be used as a means of controlling one's drinking habits, and there may even be periods of total abstinence to prove that alcohol is still on a "take-it-or-leave-it" basis.

True Alcoholic Phase

5. Again, let it be emphasized that these phases are not definite periods of time made obvious by calendar dates or road signs. Over a period of time, chronic drinkers move from the early alcoholic stage to the true alcoholic phase, in which everything in their being revolves around alcohol. Appearance, home relations, job, and possessions are neglected and begin to deteriorate. Family members change their habits to avoid confrontations with the alcoholic, and as a result of this, deep resentment and self-pity are manifested in the alcoholic. He or she may go through extended periods of constant drinking for consolation.

It is during this phase that the drinker can no longer stop after one drink. It has been suggested that perhaps by this time the alcoholic's first drink of the day or evening affects those cortical cells that control drinking judgment, and thus he or she cannot stop after one drink.

6. The sixth phase is ushered in by regular morning drinking, drinking that usually continues throughout the day. The alcoholic is now in danger of withdrawal symptoms if alcohol is not kept in his or her system at all times.

This phase is often represented by the comic figure who hides bottles all over the house and office. But at this point the alcoholic is really a tragic figure, who neglects proper nutrition and whose family life deteriorates to the point of complete disruption. Alcohol is the alcoholic's purpose for living; he or she has become totally addicted to the drug.

7. The last phase of alcoholism is one in which social, medical, and psychological help must be given to the alcoholic or death will occur. By this time, he or she may have severe liver damage and possible brain tissue damage.

In this or the previous stage the alcoholic is most likely to experience the DT's, or delirium tremens. This reaction is characterized by delirium, muscle tremor, confusion, and hallucinations or delusions (mainly visual, such as moving animals, but tactile hallucinations may occur, a feeling that small animals or bugs are crawling on the skin). DT's do not generally occur until the alcoholic has been in the last two phases of alcoholism for several years, and at the onset of DT's the alcoholic may hallucinate only occasionally, but the symptoms gradually increase in duration and intensity. The psychotic episode lasts from two days to two weeks, frequently terminating in a long, deep sleep. In about 10 percent of the cases death occurs, mainly due to pneumonia, complete renal shutdown, or cardiac arrest (Lieber, 1977).

During any one of these phases, alcoholics may change their drinking pattern to one of partial or complete abstinence. It is believed that once chronic drinkers can no longer control their drinking, that is, they can no longer stop at one or two drinks, they cannot return to a social drinking status, but must become totally abstinent. Alcoholics Anonymous calls for this complete abstinence and it has been the most effective agency in the nation in helping alcoholics to recover.

The Causes of Alcoholism

Many authorities on alcoholism and its treatment feel that, in general, only individuals with serious personality maladjustments become chronic alcoholics. Various studies on alcoholism have shown that alcoholics tend to be insecure, anxious, oversensitive, and dissatisfied with themselves and their lives. Without alcohol they feel inferior to others and find it difficult to socialize or feel at ease in most social situations (Dudley et al., 1974).

Alcoholics have been compared to psychiatric patients in personality profile, which has led many researchers to conclude that alcoholism is but a symptom of deeper, more profound psychiatric disturbances. Many alcoholics have been found to exhibit such personality characteristics as dependence, low self-esteem, compulsivity, confusion of sex roles, immaturity, and low frustration tolerance, which can be identified as "addiction-promoting" traits (Blane & Barry, 1973). Other variations of the psychological model of alcoholism lean more toward learned behaviors. That is, drinking alcohol is a learned coping device that aids the drinker in dealing with excess stress. The more severe and frequent the stress, the more alcohol is used to solve the problem, thus completing the reinforcement loop. Of course, the more personality deficiencies one has, the more chance there is of interpreting life as being stressful (Russell & Mehrabian, 1975).

Although personality maladjustment may be a basic characteristic of the alcoholic, it is not the only hypothesized "cause" of alcoholism. A second proposal or theory is that alcoholism is the result of a biochemical defect, a lack of certain body chemicals, perhaps enzymes or hormones (Hoff, 1968). This theory contends that due to a genetic deficiency, certain enzyme systems are not produced in the body. This creates a biological state or balance that can be maintained only by the intake of alcohol. Animal studies have been conducted showing that rats with a vitamin B_1 deficiency prefer a mixture of water and alcohol to water alone (Lieber, 1977).

Studies among family members, between twins, and between adoptees and their adoptive and biological parents have provided persuasive data linking hereditary factors with alcohol-related behaviors. This evidence in no way diminishes the importance of environmental influences, it only serves to illustrate the impact of both nature (biology) and nurture (environment). It is impossible to study the genetic influence of some physiological factors on human subjects. However, studies with rats and mice have demonstrated a genetic influence on ethanol consumption, central nervous sensitivity, acquired tolerance, and withdrawal symptoms. The evidence suggests that alcohol consumption, as well as some of the physiological actions of alcohol, may be influenced by differences in heredity, metabolism, and some brain amines (Belkaup, 1980).

Another perhaps genetically related physical theory of causation is the formation of the tetrahydroisoquinolines (TIQ) in the body. TIQ might act as a false transmitter amine; it is theorized as being able to mediate some of the chronic effects of ethanol. TIQs have been found to produce an increased preference for alcohol in rats that continued after TIQs were discontinued (Duncan & Deitrich, 1980). While little is yet known about the action of the TIQs, several researchers believe that they may hold the answer to the physical causation theory of alcoholism (Goldstein, 1983; Hamilton et al., 1980).

A third basic causative factor that has been proposed is that of cultural readiness, which depends on the following conditions:

1. The degree to which the society brings about a need for escape—how much the society causes inner tensions in its members. In search of society-set goals, individuals may become so pressured that they must find an escape, and alcohol provides that escape (Crosby, 1975).

2. The kind of attitudes toward drinking that the society engenders in its members. Because drinking has become a sign of being grown-up and is often regarded as the socially acceptable behavior, typical American youth may actually be pressured into drinking alcohol. Adult drinkers set the trend for the younger members of society. When alcohol is used in the home without fanfare or is used for religious purposes, it is less likely that members of those homes will use alcohol unwisely (Jessor & Jessor, 1975).

3. The number of suitable substitute means of satisfaction that the society provides. When a society offers a variety of desirable outlets for its members to occupy their thoughts and release tensions, self-destructive habits such as chronic drinking or drugs will be less prevalent than in societies offering no socially acceptable escapes. For instance, some societies may offer religion as a form of escape. Also, a habit as simple as eating food may become a substitute escape mechanism.

A fourth basic theory is moral in substance. Even though this theory has strong historical and religious roots, it seems to be losing support in all but the most fundamental moralist circles. To the moralists, alcohol is an evil substance that has the power to accentuate the moral human weaknesses. If one knows the power of alcohol, then drunkenness and alcoholism must therefore be willful. The alcoholic is regarded as a sinner who freely chooses to drink, and drinking is considered a sign of moral weakness. As extreme as this position may sound, do not be too quick to dismiss its influence in the list of causes of alcoholism. If the drinker's family and friends judge the alcoholic as weak, or even as a sinner, that judgment can lead to feelings of guilt, self-hate, and alienation in the drinker, which further intensify the problem. The vicious circle is well known: increasingly bitter family quarrels, mounting debt, job difficulties, punishing remorse, self-condemnation, hate of others, and even worse, self-hate.

The moral issue is more often associated with the discussion of female alcoholics. The force of public condemnation is more pronounced in the case of a woman because of the remnants of the double standard, which brands alcohol abuse in a wife and mother as more shocking and "unnatural" than in a husband and father. The increased shame and guilt are only one special problem faced by women drinkers. The others create a constellation of causes and consequences special enough to examine in a separate section.

The Woman Alcoholic

Heretofore, the drinking problems of women have been largely ignored. Alcoholism has long been considered a man's illness. But we now know better. Some authorities believe that women never had fewer drinking problems than men, but women have been more hesitant to seek help because of society's harsher judgment of the woman alcoholic. Trapped by society's mythical image of the alcoholic female as a "fallen woman," a woman suffered doubly by being considered not only sick, but immoral as well. It is no wonder women alcoholics and their families labored to conceal, disguise, and deny the problem.

Recent evidence suggests that sex differences play an important role in both the etiology and the biomedical consequences of alcohol abuse. Evidence is reviewed which suggests that the associated morbidity and mortality (completed suicide, accidental death, and death resulting from cirrhosis of the liver) due to alcoholism and alcohol-related problems is greater among women than men. For example, studies completed in a number of countries now demonstrate that the alcoholic woman is more susceptible to developing cirrhosis of the liver in association with a lower level of daily alcohol consumption and following a shorter history of heavy drinking than her male counterpart. Further work is needed to determine the exact nature of the mechanisms involved (autoimmunity, endocrine, or other) in this increased risk in order that successful intervention can be implemented. Because of the previously meager efforts to study women alcoholics, further research is also needed to determine whether women may be at greater risk for developing cancers, cardiovascular disorders, brain damage, and other complications as a result of their excessive drinking.

Also, because of the comparatively minor efforts to study women in the past, evidence is currently lacking regarding etiological factors. For example, while it has been demonstrated through use of adoption studies that genetic factors play an important role in the development of alcoholism in men, the evidence is now inconclusive regarding alcoholism in women (Wilsnack, 1980).

Studies comparing male and female alcoholics in treatment indicate that, once far enough advanced, the alcoholic syndrome is much the same for both sexes, but that important differences exist in the kinds of life experiences and social problems encountered. Data from general population surveys show that among drinkers men have a higher prevalence of problems than women, but when frequency of intoxication is held constant (which is almost never done) most of these differences disappear.

Prevalence of depressive disorder is higher among female alcoholics, while prevalence of sociopathy is higher among males. This sex differential is also found in the general population. It may be that there exists a genetic predisposition and that it manifests itself in these different ways because of the influence of cultural training for gender roles. Marriages of alcoholic women show a much higher frequency of disturbance than those of men, and the prevalence of alcoholic husbands in these marriages is especially striking and deserves exploration. Many studies have addressed the question of sex role conflict in women as an influence on drunkenness and alcoholism.

Most authors agree that no "typical female alcoholic" exists and that women alcoholics are a highly heterogeneous group. Attempts have been made to identify discrete subtypes using such classifying variables as type of psychopathology, personality type, and demographic variables. There is a consensus that most female alcoholics suffer from common problems of low self-esteem and poor self-concept, although it remains unclear as to whether such traits are the cause or result of problem drinking (NIAAA, 1982).

As a group, women suffer a great deal of stress, and some of the stresses are very different from those faced by men. Since the traditional roles that society has defined for women and men produce quite different behavior, goals, self-images, and life experiences, women face certain problems in common that are not relevant to men.

From childhood, females have been taught that as the "second sex" they can expect to derive their sense of self-worth primarily through their relationships with men, rather than through their own achievements and activities. Until recently, women were rarely encouraged to develop as independent persons with strong, secure identities. This is not to say that women's drinking problems stem entirely from their role in society, but regardless of what women do with their lives, they cannot escape judgment that, on some very basic level, they are inadequate because they are women.

Studies repeatedly show that women drink primarily to relieve loneliness, inferiority feelings, and conflicts about their sex roles, regardless of their life style.

The Woman at Home.   Many women derive great satisfaction from a full-time career as a mother and homemaker. Yet it drives other women to drink. Not every woman is interested in being a housewife, but many women abandon outside career goals for a home-centered life because of pressure to fulfill their role. It is not an easy compromise to make. Feeling trapped in a life style at odds with their real interests and goals, many women become increasingly overwhelmed with frustration and anger as the years go by. At the same time, they may fight enormous guilt feelings for wanting a life beyond the home. Caught in a paralyzing conflict, and finding that a couple of drinks have a way of dissolving feelings of anxiety, they begin to depend more and more on alcohol to shield them from their feelings. Before they realize it, they are relying on regular doses of liquor simply to get through the day. Without knowing it, they become alcoholics.

Another often-described situation dealing with the housewife is the absent-nest syndrome. The children grow up and leave home, a serious illness strikes in the family, an unexpected divorce occurs. For many women, the center of their lives, the home, is suddenly gone. They have few resources, no job, few close friends, no real outside interests. Anxiety and aloneness set in. For these women, drinking often relieves the pain.

The Working Woman.   Even when a woman decides to work outside the home, she often finds that she is labeled as inferior and must constantly work twice as hard just to prove that she is as competent as her male counterparts. The pressure not to fail can become overwhelming and, like the situation described for the housewife, she may find that alcohol seems to reduce the pain and anxiety, that the three-martini lunches and five o'clock pick-me-ups are the best part of the day. As the pain and pressure increase, so do the visits to the bar and the amount drunk during each visit.

A special case with regard to the working woman is when she is also head of the household. Over nine million American women are faced with this situation. While most seem to make it, many find this unbearable and seek relief from the harsh reality through alcohol. The stresses involved in these circumstances are obvious. Working, keeping a house, and caring for children is usually accomplished by two adults. The financial difficulties are such that few of these women are in jobs that pay well enough to allow for household help. Although busy with work and household chores, the woman in this situation is often alone, since there is little time for socializing. Again, it is easy to see how, when a few drinks temporarily reduce the pain, anxiety, and pressure, the motivation to take another drink to prolong the high is almost irresistible (Beckman, 1975).

Looking at the problem encountered by the woman alcoholic drives home the point that there is no one cause for alcoholism, but probably a combination of various factors. At the present stage of our knowledge we can only say that this disorder is due to some complex combination of an individual's biological and psychological makeup, reacting to another complex combination of external factors that precipitate the dependency on alcohol (see Fig. 4.7).

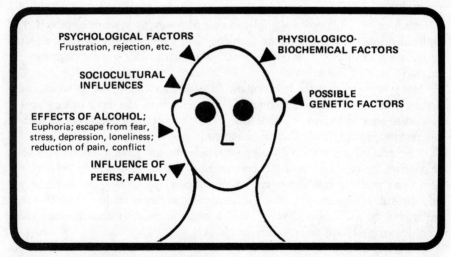

Fig. 4.7   **Causative factors in alcoholism.**

Adolescent Alcoholics

Studies show that alcohol is the most commonly used drug of adolescents between the ages of twelve and seventeen. These studies also reveal that problem drinking increases sharply with age, and that adolescent problem drinkers are more likely to use other illicit drugs than are nondrinkers. Adolescent drinking problems are related to other delinquent and social problems, and as expected, to poor performance in school as well.

The factors associated with prevalence of alcohol use are varied and include both parental and peer influence. Attitudes about drinking as well as the actual drinking behavior influence the adolescent. Other factors are academic achievement and religious affiliation and commitment. It is clear from the research that adolescent drinkers share a variety of personality and psychosocial characteristics. It is important to remember that programs designed to prevent adolescent drinking problems must also vary in their approach and techniques (Mayer & Filstead, 1980).

Treatment

In recent years, there has been a cultural shift in attitudes toward alcoholism. This has led to more people acknowledging their problem with alcohol and seeking treatment. It has also allowed alcoholics to reduce their denial of their problem and to refer themselves to treatment. The increase in number of self-referrals and the number of individuals seeking treatment in the early stages of alcoholism improve the success rate. The situation has brought to light the problem of the possible inappropriateness of treatment techniques that were primarily designed for more advanced stages of problem drinking. While controlled studies have not been done, it is assumed that treatment in the earlier phases of alcoholism would be both different and more effective than the more usual forced treatment of severe alcoholism.

Much emphasis is now being placed on early warning systems of detection of problem drinkers. These systems are dependent on the ability to recognize the periodic steplike increase in one's consumption pattern that usually culminates in excessive alcohol intake.

Many barriers to early intervention remain. Likewise, there is no clear-cut evidence on which treatment technique is most effective. The mode of treatment is dependent on a definition of alcoholism and a philosophy of causation, so finding and researching the most effective treatment is elusive.

It is generally agreed that once a person falls into the "true addiction" phase of alcoholism, he or she is thereafter considered an alcoholic. Many recovered alcoholics may prefer to call themselves "nonpracticing" alcoholics, but do admit that they are still alcoholics. Alcoholics Anonymous members readily admit that they are alcoholics, and appear proud to say it because to them it means that they know their disease and have done something about it.

Although there is no known "cure" for alcoholism, treatment is available to alcoholics at any stage in their drinking career. However, most alcoholics make their appearance in the hospital wards and rehabilitation groups only after their drinking has reached a critical point. Upon presentation for medical service, the alcoholic is given vitamin (especially vitamin B) shots, is put on a special diet, and goes through a "drying out" period during which he or she is watched very closely for symptoms of withdrawal and for which he or she is given medication (usually tranquilizers). After this initial medical phase has removed the alcoholic from imminent physical danger, social and psychological rehabilitation must follow in order to keep the patient from lapsing back into alcohol use.

There are as many reasons for drinking as there are drinkers and, accordingly, there are nearly as many different kinds of alcoholic treatment programs as there are alcoholics. Careful scrutiny of the literally thousands of programs will show that each is an adaptation of the few basic techniques that are discussed below.

Psychotherapy forms the basis for many programs operating on the assumption that excessive drinking is (1) a psychoneurotic behavior that offers escape from grief, pain, anger, and guilt; (2) a release from anxiety, hostility, or feelings of inferiority; or (3) a means of dealing with unresolved feelings of sexual inadequacy, social weakness, or general rejection.

In addition to the use of psychotherapy, treatment modalities may involve the use of behavior modification. Aversion therapy is an example of how behavior modification is used in the treatment of alcoholism (Elkins, 1975). It involves teaching deeply relaxed patients to visualize themselves drinking, becoming sick, and eventually vomiting, or to first visualize distasteful scenes, then think of drinking. Later, they are taught to visualize feelings of well-being and associate these with being sober. Hypnosis may be used, especially with subjects who find drinking euphoric and pleasurable. In some cases, effective use has been made of posthypnotic suggestions such as, "I will never drink another drop in any form, for alcohol is meaningless and I am indifferent to it and to people who use it." Electrotherapy is also used as a conditioning device in aversion therapy. Techniques vary, but one common practice is to attach electrodes to the subject's fingers or ear. Then, in a barroom setting, the patient is allowed to drink at will, but receives shocks when he or she does so; the shocks continue until the drink is rejected.

A more popular reeducation program involving aversion therapy is conducted with the help of the drug Antabuse (disulfiram). This drug interferes with the metabolism of alcohol; after the alcohol is converted to acetaldehyde, further breakdown is blocked. The toxic acetaldehyde causes flushed face, headache, increased heart rate, heart palpitations, nausea, vomiting, and breathing difficulty. When this drug is used in treatment, the alcoholic knows that ingesting alcohol will make him or her physically ill. It is in a sense a chemical conscience for the alcoholic.

Another drug occasionally used in the treatment of alcoholism (not in aversion therapy) is LSD. The therapeutic actions are in the form of breaking down defenses and allowing the alcoholic to relive traumatic experiences so that the anxiety associated with them might be reduced. In addition, a transcendental occurrence can provide a powerful emotional experience that may give the patient the feeling of change through the gaining of new insights into feelings and behavior.

The idea of gaining power and control over one's self is an ego-building experience that helps reinforce self-control. Biofeedback instrumentation has been used in this manner as patients are taught to control brain waves (alpha, beta, theta states) at will, reduce muscle tension, or voluntarily change the temperature of a particular body site. This not only aids in reducing anxiety and tension but also gives the feeling of self-control over behavior that has been found to carry over into those situations that previously led to drinking.

Exercise programs have also been successful in the treatment of alcoholism. The alcoholic individual develops poor health habits, is out of touch with his or her body, and forgets what it is like to feel good physically. Exercise increases fitness, develops self-confidence, and reduces tension and anxiety. The importance of reducing tension and anxiety cannot be overemphasized—it is the reason why most programs use tranquilizing drugs in some part of their treatment regimen.

All psychological treatment is not on an individual basis: Group therapy is also a widely accepted treatment modality. It is usually less expensive and gives the patient a chance to develop abilities by which to deal effectively with social situations. Psychodrama, role playing, and sensitivity group interaction break down defense mechanisms and allow patients to see themselves in a more positive light and to analyze their relationship to the rest of society, especially to their family. Family sessions helping to reestablish communication and to analyze problems that caused frustration are worked out with the help of a therapist.

Trends in Treatment. One major trend in alcoholism treatment programs is the development of specialized programs to meet the needs of special populations. Individuals tend to do better in programs when they are placed in a group with peers who have a similar cultural background and/or social status.

Family therapy is being used increasingly in alcoholic rehabilitation programs. Also included in these programs is treatment for the children of alcoholics. At least twelve million American schoolchildren have alcoholic parents. Children of alcoholics also appear to be at greater risk for developing a variety of dysfunctional conditions. Children in these programs are treated for their own problems to help them and not the alcoholic. However, the therapy does provide a model for positive change in the family.

The value of continuing to support hospital detoxification and primary treatment has still not been determined. The trend seems to be moving away from the hospital setting. The controversy between the medical and social models of treatment still exists. The social model seems to be gaining in popularity and a number of programs have been developed.

A larger group approach, Alcoholics Anonymous, is perhaps the most successful of all group treatment modalities. This organization's basic aim is to help alcoholics stop drinking. Through group discussions with others who have similar problems, the alcoholic can come to realize that his or her problem is not unique and that other individuals have met the challenge of alcoholism successfully. Alcoholics Anonymous offers group identity, status, and prestige, qualities sorely lacking in the life of the alcoholic. With self-identity restored (or gained for the first time), the nonpracticing alcoholic is able to work toward regaining a normal life.

Since AA was founded in 1935 it has provided help for hundreds of thousands of people. The first step, that of admitting powerlessness over alcohol, is a difficult one and may be taken only after other forms of individual treatment have been exhausted. But once this is achieved, the alcoholic usually is able to refrain from taking the first drink, while each day of sobriety adds to his or her self-confidence. AA does not demand any long-term "I will never drink again" pledges. Forty years of accumulated wisdom has shown the folly in such gestures. Instead, AA follows what it calls the 24-hour plan. It encourages the alcoholic to concentrate on not drinking for 24 hours and then take each day, 24 hours at a time. This is but one example of the realism, honesty, and simplicity that spell success for this most unique treatment. Unique is an understatement, for in this day of government subsidies, political activism, and programs that change with each new research report, AA stands as a model. There is only one requirement for membership—a desire to stop drinking. There are no dues or fees for AA programs. AA is not allied with any sect or religious denomination, although many of its doctrines rely on a Power greater than the drinker alone. As a group, AA is not allied with any political party, organization, or institution; it does not support or engage in research or medical or psychiatric treatment, nor does it endorse any causes or engage in any controversy. Its single purpose is to help members remain sober. Its methods, support, and fellowship from others with similar problems sound too simple to be effective until you take a closer look at the basic underlying causes of alcoholism. The now famous Twelve Steps of AA further describe their approach:

Twelve Suggested Steps of Alcoholics Anonymous

We admitted we were powerless over alcohol—that our lives had become unmanageable.

Came to believe that a Power greater than ourselves could restore us to sanity.

Made a decision to turn our will and our lives over to the care of God *as we understood Him.*

Made a searching and fearless moral inventory of ourselves.

Admitted to God, to ourselves and to another human being the exact nature of our wrongs.

Were entirely ready to have God remove all these defects of character.

Humbly asked Him to remove our shortcomings.

Made a list of all persons we had harmed, and became willing to make amends to them all.

Made direct amends to such people wherever possible, except when to do so would injure them or others.

Continued to take personal inventory and when we were wrong promptly admitted it.

Sought through prayer and meditation to improve our conscious contact with God, *as we understood Him,* praying only for knowledge of His will for us and the power to carry that out.

Having had a spiritual awakening as the result of these steps, we tried to carry this message to alcoholics, and to practice these principles in all our affairs.

AA is a way of life for the nonpracticing alcoholic; a club or fraternitylike atmosphere develops and most social activities of AA members revolve around that group. Members become dedicated to helping others remain sober, which becomes a form of egotistic altruism. By helping others they help themselves.

In addition to the help given the alcoholic, AA offers aid in understanding the alcoholic mate or parent through its Al-Anon and Ala-Teen groups. Here, nonalcoholic family members may learn about the disease of alcoholism and, more important, that the nonalcoholic is not responsible for the actions of the alcoholic. Guilt is an emotion common to family members of alcoholics, since they are apt to feel that they are the cause of the situations that drive the alcoholic to drink (Bean, 1975).

At the beginning of this chapter, we mentioned the staggering cost of alcoholism to society. Millions are spent on rehabilitation, but this amount is minuscule when compared to what absenteeism, turnover, and accidents cost business and industry. For that reason, a constantly increasing number of industries in the United States are now providing facilities for the early detection and treatment of alcoholism in their employees. Recent court decisions and shifts in public attitudes emphasizing the concept of alcoholism as a disease, together with changing insurance company policy, have been largely responsible for this movement. While some segments of society have not responded, thus denying treatment-cost benefits provided for by health care programs, many insurance companies have recognized alcoholism under their mental health benefits. A major stumbling block is the standard insurance company provision that treatment be undertaken in a strictly medical setting in an accredited hospital (which usually offers very limited, expensive, and inefficient programs for the alcoholic). However, with the increasing development of data on treatment effectiveness, cost, licensing, and certification of facilities, insurance companies are expected to expand their coverage (Kurtz et al., 1984).

Drug abuse occurs throughout the work force in all types of companies and may involve as many as six million workers. A 1981 report by the General Accounting Office estimates that more than 5 percent of the work force suffers from alcoholism. Many industries have developed employee assistance programs to help workers with alcohol and drug abuse problems. Such programs are designed to identify troubled employees through observation of impaired job performance, and to encourage and assist them in obtaining help. Now, 57 percent of Fortune 500 companies have such programs. These programs are the product of labor-management cooperation and recognition of the extraordinary costs of alcohol-related problems through absenteeism, accidents, sick pay, and lost productivity at every level of corporate activity. Employers report that after employee assistance programs are established, they experienced significant reductions in lost work hours, disability payments, and accidents. The strategy encourages the use of employee assistance programs to reduce the health and economic costs of alcohol- and drug-related problems.

The major goals of occupational alcohol programs which have developed can be summarized as:

- Reaching employed problem drinkers in order to reduce the costs of poor performance and absenteeism associated with drinking.
- Minimizing grievances and arbitrations associated with employee alcohol problems.
- Recovering the health and on-job efficiency of valued employees.
- Providing assistance to families of employed problem drinkers and/or to the family members with drinking problems.
- Intervening early enough to obtain substantial rehabilitation.

The scope of activities in an occupational program can range from the development and dissemination of the company's written policies, procedures, and response to the problem of employee alcohol abuse, to the implementation of an in-house treatment program.

A variety of terms have been used to designate the range of programmatic options in work-place intervention and treatment of health problems, such as employee assistance or troubled employee. Both physical and mental conditions may be included, as well as employees at every level, and sometimes even their families. The problems addressed may be either personal or work-related, but are all costly to the individual and to the company. Alcoholism services paved the way programmatically, but today a "broad brush" or general assistance concept is prevalent, intervening and referring for treatment any employee whose work impairment appears related to health or emotional problems. Recognition of the value of the experienced, trained employee, as well as increased social responsiveness, have stimulated new corporate services and increased program options. Unions have also taken a leading role in urging expanded treatment modalities. Poor work performance has been the most important variable in motivating employee participation, and current data suggest that program costs ultimately are recovered in savings in sickness and accident benefits, grievances, training, absenteeism, etc. (Mojer & Gaylord, 1984).

SOMEONE CLOSE DRINKS TOO MUCH

A recent opinion survey indicated that almost two-thirds of the adults in the United States know someone who "drinks too much." In one-third of those instances, the individual was a family member or close friend who has had a drinking problem for more than ten years. With between 9 and 10 million problem drinkers and alcoholics in this country, each affecting at least four other persons, that makes approximately 36 to 40 million people who share alcohol problems. However, to look at it another way, there are 40 million potential helpers who have a personal reason to help problem drinkers find the way to health and well-being.

If you find you are one of these potential helpers, the National Institute on

Alcohol Abuse and Alcoholism has published an informative booklet on how to help a problem drinker who is affecting your life. If you are one of these people, there are some things that you may want to know. First of all, three-quarters of the problem drinkers who go through treatment recover or at least show marked improvement. Many health professionals therefore consider alcoholism to be the most untreated treatable illness in America. The most difficult step is getting the drinker to accept help. The goal is to guide the troubled drinker to treatment (U.S. Department of Health, Education and Welfare, NIAAA, 1976).

That is not as easy as it sounds, for even though the moral stigma of alcoholism has begun to fade, it is still something most drinkers will not admit to, and therefore, will not seek treatment. Pressure and preaching are very seldom effective in guiding the problem drinker to help. Instead, a nudge or push at the right time might just be the start on the road back. Push may come to shove when the drinker's troubled life spills over into yours, and you must decide to save your own "sanity." Often, the choice between losing family or job and going to treatment is the push that helps get a drinker to accept help. While preaching usually increases guilt and worsens the drinking problem, do not be afraid to talk about the person's drinking problem honestly and openly. It is easy to be polite, or to just sweep it under the rug. While it does not help to nag, it does help to let the drinker know that you are aware of his or her drinking problem, that you still care about him or her nevertheless, and that you are willing to talk about it.

As you talk with the problem drinker (there is more than a semantical difference between "talk with" and "talk to"), try to remain calm, unemotional, and factually honest. By now, you should have done your homework and informed yourself about alcohol and its effects. Let the problem drinker know that you have researched groups like AA and are attending Al-Anon or Ala-Teen. Show them you still care about them and would like to see them change their behavior. Try to live life as normally as possible and include them in your activities as much as possible. However, do not tolerate their drunkenness. Do not cover up or make excuses for them. The problem drinker must take responsibility for his or her actions. There is a difference between action that produces guilt and action that fosters self-responsibility. Likewise, do not try to shelter the problem drinker from alcohol by hiding bottles, or by not going to affairs where alcohol is served. They must want to not drink. Above all, never try to show support by drinking along with problem drinkers, never argue with them when they are drunk, never drive with them when they are drunk, and above all, *do not accept guilt for their behavior*.

If it is not already, it will soon become apparent that dealing with a problem drinker is very difficult, so do not try to go it alone. If you discreetly ask around, you will easily find someone else who has gone through it. He or she will be a good source of information. Seek the help of professionals. The best source is a university counseling service. Many large universities employ full-time counselors who specialize in alcohol-related problems. Other sources of help are community mental health units, local chapters of Alcoholics Anonymous and their support groups, Al-Anon and Ala-Teen. If you look around, you will be surprised at the amount of help that is available. Alcoholism is a big problem and you are not the only one who must cope with it.

Symptoms of Excessive Drinking:

1. Frequent blackouts
2. Chronic hangovers
3. Changes in study or work habits caused by drinking
4. Change in drinking habits that signal more drinking

HEALTHY DRINKING BEHAVIOR*

Having a good-tasting, thirst-quenching, slightly intoxicating beverage that goes along with pleasurable activities is the proper use of alcohol. It is called Drinking and Fun, not Drinking for Fun—that is, drinking in moderation to add to the pleasure of whatever else is going on. Heavy drinking—drinking to get high or to get drunk—signals the beginning of an alcohol problem. Few people will readily admit that being intoxicated is pleasurable, even after they hear about all the crazy things they did while drunk. There is little pleasure in being hardly able to walk, unable to converse coherently with friends, having one's senses dulled, being blacked out, or being unable to perform sexually.

Actually, most people do not start out to get drunk. They just wind up that way when they get into certain situations. To avoid slipping from a pleasurable high into intoxication, Kingsley Amis, in his book *On Drink* (1973), suggests:

- The atmosphere should be relaxing, and whatever can be done to make everyone mix should be done. One reason people drink too much at social gatherings is that they cannot seem to get conversations going.
- The volume of music should be low enough to allow people to socialize—again, when you cannot talk, you drink more.
- Food should be served. It not only slows down the absorption of alcohol, it satisfies some nervous oral needs in addition to the continual sipping of drinks. Good food also takes some of the spotlight off alcohol. Foods that have some protein content are best—for example, cheese and crackers, Swedish meatballs, hard-boiled or deviled eggs, cheese fondue, pizza, and bite-sized cold cuts.
- There should be activities going on, and some effort should be made to get everyone involved. Dancing, games, sports, or good conversation quickly become the focus of a mixer and drinks can then just add to the enjoyment.

Wine Classes. Many colleges and universities conduct wine-tasting courses in which students are taught not only to appreciate good wines but also to accentuate the positive and responsible uses of alcohol. Good wine is an enhancer, it is never the main focus. Once one is knowledgeable about wine, a moderate wine and cheese party becomes a very pleasurable social event.

Beer Busts. If you or your organization are the host, take some responsibility to see that your guests have a good time and get home safely. While you will get some points with some people for serving a record number of kegs of beer, most people

---

*The following section is extracted from D. A. Girdano, G. Everly, Jr., and D. E. Dusek, *Experiencing Health* (Englewood Cliffs, N.J.: Prentice-Hall, 1985).

will be satisfied with having enough to drink and a lot of "fun" activities. Consider the needs of nondrinkers and provide some good nonalcoholic drinks. The acme of thoughtfulness would be to have a taxi squad or bus to take the overintoxicated home. Word will soon get around campus that not only do you throw a good party but you also care about your guests (U.S. DHEW, 1977).

REFERENCES

Amis, Kingsley. *On Drink*. Orlando, Fla.: Harcourt Brace Jovanovich, 1973.

Bacon, S. D. "The process of addiction to alcohol: social aspects." *Quarterly Journal of Studies on Alcohol* 34(1):1–27, 1973.

Bean, M. "Alcoholics Anonymous I." *Psychiatric Annals* 5(2): 7–61, 1975.

Beckman, L. J. "Women alcoholics: a review of social and psychological studies." *Journal of Studies on Alcohol* 36(7):696–824, 1975.

Belkaup, J. K. "Genetic factors in the effects of alcohol," in H. Riger and J. C. Crabbe, eds. *Alcohol Tolerance and Dependence*. North Holland: Elsevier, 1980, pp. 157–180.

Blane, H. T., and H. Barry III. "Birth order and alcoholism: a review." *Quarterly Journal of Studies on Alcohol* 34(3):837–852, 1973.

Butters, N., and L. S. Cermak. *Alcoholic Korsakoff's Syndrome: An Information Processing Approach to Amnesia*. Orlando, Fla.: Academic Press, 1980.

Crosby, W. H. "Those two martinis before dinner every night." *Journal of the American Medical Association* 231(5):509, 1975.

Davis, V. E., and M. J. Welsh. "Alcohol, amines, and alkaloids: a possible biochemical basis for alcohol addiction." *Science* 167:1005, 1970.

Dudley, D. L., et al. "Heroin vs. alcohol addiction—quantifiable psychosocial similarities and differences." *Journal of Psychosomatic Research* 18(5):327–335, 1974.

Duncan, C., and R. A. Deitrich. "A critical evaluation of tetrahydroisoquinoline induced ethanol preference in rats." *Pharmacology, Biochemistry and Behavior* 13:265–281, 1980.

Elkins, R. L. "Aversion therapy for alcoholism." *International Journal of the Addictions* 10(2): 157–210, 1975.

Girdano, D. A., G. Everly, Jr., and D. E. Dusek. *Experiencing Health*. Englewood Cliffs, N.J.: Prentice-Hall, 1985.

Goldstein, Dora B. *Pharmacology of Alcohol*. New York: Oxford University Press, 1983.

Hamilton, M. G., K. Blum, and M. Hirst. "In vivo formation of isoquinoline alkaloids: effect of time and route of administration of ethanol." *Advances in Experimental Medical Biology* 126:13–86, 1980.

Hoff, C. E. "Pharmacologic and metabolic adjuncts," in R. J. Catanzaro, ed. *Alcoholism*. Springfield, Ill.: Charles C Thomas, 1968, pp. 175–185.

Jellinek, E. M. "Phases of alcohol addiction." *Quarterly Journal of Studies on Alcohol* 13: 672, 1952.

Jessor, R., and S. L. Jessor. "Adolescent development and the onset of drinking: a longitudinal study." *Journal of Studies on Alcohol* 36(1):27–51, 1975.

Kendis, J. B. "The human body and alcohol," in D. J. Pittman, ed. *Alcoholism*. New York: Harper & Row, 1967, pp. 23–30.

Khanna, J. M., and Y. Israel. "Ethanol metabolism." *International Review of Physiology* 21:275–315, 1980.

Kurtz, N. R., et al. "Measuring the success of occupational alcoholism programs." *Journal of Studies on Alcohol* 45(1):32–45, 1984.

Landesman-Dwyer, S., A. S. Ragozin, and R. E. Little. "Behavioral correlates of prenatal alcohol exposure: a four-year follow-up study." *Neurobehavioral Toxicology and Teratology* 3(2):135–145, 1981.

Lieber, C. S. *Metabolic Aspects of Alcoholism.* Baltimore, Md.: University Park Press, 1977.

Lieber, C. S., and L. M. DeCarli. "An experimental model of alcohol feeding and liver injury in the baboon." *Journal of Medical Primatology* 3:153–163, 1974.

Mayer, J. E., and W. J. Filstead, eds. *Adolescence and Alcohol.* Cambridge, Mass.: Ballinger, 1980.

Mojer, G., and M. Gaylord. "Successful referral of resistant employees within a corporate EAP." *EAP Digest* May/June, 20–24, 1984.

National Institute of Alcohol Abuse and Alcoholism (NIAAA). *Alcohol and Health Monograph Nos. 1, 2, 3, 4.* Washington, D.C.: Department of Health and Human Services, 1982.

Pirola, R. C. *Drug Metabolism and Alcohol.* Baltimore, Md.: University Park Press, 1978.

Randell, C. L., and E. P. Noble. "Alcohol abuse and fetal growth and development," in N. K. Mello and J. H. Mendelson, eds. *Advances in Substance Abuse.* Greenwich, Conn.: JAI Press, 1980.

Russell, J. A., and A. Mehrabian. "The mediating role of emotions in alcohol use." *Journal of Studies on Alcohol* 36(11):1508–1536, 1975.

Sokol, R. J., S. I. Miller, and G. Reed. "Alcohol abuse during pregnancy: an epidemiological model." *Alcohol Clinical and Experimental Research* 4(2):135–145, 1980.

U.S. Department of Health, Education, and Welfare, National Institute on Alcohol Abuse and Alcoholism. *Someone Close Drinks Too Much.* Washington, D.C.: GPO, 1976.

_____ *The Whole College Catalog About Drinking.* Washington, D.C.: GPO, 1977.

Warner, R. H., and H. L. Rosett. "Effects of drinking on offspring: an historical survey of the American and British literature." *Journal of Studies on Alcohol* 36(11):1395–1420, 1975.

Wilsnack, S. C. "Prevention of alcohol problems in women: current status and research needs," in *Alcoholism and Alcohol Abuse Among Women: Research Issues.* NIAAA Research Monograph No. 1. Rockville, MD.: NIAAA, 1980, pp. 163–186.

SUGGESTED READINGS

Carmody, A. P. *Alcoholism and Problem Drinking.* Washington, D.C.: Veterans Administration, 1977.

Duryea, Elias J. "An application of inoculation theory to preventive alcohol education." *Health Education* Jan./Feb., 4–7, 1984.

Estes, Nada J. *Alcoholism: Development, Consequences, and Interventions.* St. Louis, Mo.: C. V. Mosby, 1977.

Ewing, J. A., and B. A. Rouse. *Drinking: Alcohol in American Society.* Chicago: Nelson-Hall, 1978.

Greenblatt, M., and M. A. Schuckit. *Alcoholism Problems in Women and Children.* New York: Grune and Stratton, 1976.

Hewitt, K. *The Whole College Catalog About Drinking.* Washington, D.C.: NIAAA, 1976.

Heyman, M. M. *Alcoholism Programs in Industry: The Patients' View.* New Brunswick, N.J.: Rutgers Center of Alcohol Studies, 1978.

Landstreet, B. F. *The Drinking Driver.* Springfield, Ill.: Charles C Thomas, 1977.

Milt, H. *Alcoholism, Its Causes and Cure: A Handbook.* New York: Scribners, 1976.

National Institute on Alcoholism and Alcohol Abuse. *The Community Health Nurse and Alcohol Related Problems.* Washington, D.C.: U.S. Government Printing Office, 1978.

National Institute on Alcoholism and Alcohol Abuse. *Planning a Prevention Program.* Washington, D.C.: U.S. Government Printing Office, 1977.

Novak, D. G., and R. L. Jones. *Alcoholism: General Issues and Perspectives.* Austin, Tex.: Texas Commission on Alcoholism, 1976.

Paolino, T. J. *The Alcoholic Marriage.* New York: Grune and Stratton, 1977.

Savage, Tom V. "Investigating the social aspects of alcohol use." *Health Education* Jan./Feb., 49–50, 1984.

Stewart, D. *The Adventure of Sobriety.* East Lansing: Michigan State University Press, 1976.

Tarter, R. E., and A. A. Sugerman. *Alcoholism.* Reading, Mass.: Addison-Wesley, 1976.

W., Bill. *Alcoholics Anonymous.* New York: Alcoholics Anonymous World Services, 1976.

Warner, H. S. *An Evolution in Understanding of the Problem of Alcohol: A History of College Idealism.* Boston: Christopher, 1966.

Zylman, R. "Fatal crashes among Michigan youth following reduction of legal drinking age." *Quarterly Journal of Studies on Alcohol* 35:283–286, 1974.

CHAPTER 5

MARIJUANA

HISTORY

Alcohol became a symbol in a social class struggle in the nineteenth and early twentieth centuries; with the increase in popularity of marijuana in the 1960s, many similarities between its prohibition and the prohibition of alcohol were drawn. However, marijuana represented a symbol of differences not between the working-class immigrant and the aristocracy, but between the generations, in their life styles, values, and social and political philosophies.

During the 1930s, headlines told of crimes committed by normally law-abiding citizens who were under the influence of the killer weed, marijuana. One-sided congressional hearings were quickly convened and the result was the Marijuana Tax Act. Compared to that of alcohol, the prohibition of marijuana was relatively quiet and unopposed. This was the atmosphere in which early attitudes toward marijuana developed, and little else was heard on the subject until the easy-going, pleasure-seeking "hippie" life style engendered fear of social disorder in the greater population, lack of responsibility, and moral decay in a country run by a "straight" majority. Marijuana soon became the symbol of a disagreement between social and moral stability and individual freedom. Law enforcement agencies were caught in the middle, as legal enforcement of the prohibition of marijuana was found to be virtually impossible. The costs were staggering, not only in monies for police, lawyers, and judges, but in the misery of those jailed for possession and use of what many regarded as a harmless drug.

In 1970, a Presidential Commission, the President's Commission on Marijuana and Drug Abuse, was established to separate fiction from fact and to recommend a uniform policy that would not only reflect the attitudes of the majority but also to provide legally and morally for the freedoms of the individual (National Commission on Marijuana and Drug Abuse, 1972). The Commission's survey showed that dominant opinion still opposed marijuana use, so it could not recommend legalization of marijuana or even a position of neutrality toward it. Instead, the Commission recommended a social policy of discouragement, asking for increased efforts by schools, churches, and families to implement this policy. Such implementation would decrease the need for legal regulation.

The Commission also recommended that the possession of marijuana for personal use no longer be a criminal offense, while marijuana possessed in public would remain contraband, subject to seizure. It further recommended that states adopt a uniform statutory scheme similar to the proposed federal laws, whereby private possession would not be considered a criminal offense, possession of small amounts in public would be punishable by a fine, and sale would remain a serious offense with stringent penalties.

To help educate society and to make sure that lawmakers and politicians were kept abreast of the latest scientific information, the pot lobby (the National Organization for the Reform of Marijuana Laws, or NORML) was formed in 1970. NORML used a middle-class, pragmatic, time-honored lobbying style to get legislators to accept the recommendation of the President's Commission, that of decriminalization of marijuana users (not legalization of marijuana). They continually emphasized that while the scientists debate the question of the dangers of marijuana, thousands are being punished for using what might be found later to be a relatively harmless drug.

These historical events have led us to our current laws that have generally decriminalized possession of small amounts (usually one ounce) of marijuana, while keeping strict enforcement regarding import and sales of the drug. Each state legislates its own marijuana laws.

The remainder of this chapter presents the facts about marijuana as they are known to date.

CANNABIS

Nearly any student of drugs knows that marijuana is derived from the flowers and the top leaves of the female Cannabis sativa plant, a weed of the hemp family that flourishes without the need for special cultivation. The resin, a sticky yellow substance, is produced by the plant as a protective shield against the elements; marijuana plants grown in hotter, sunnier climates produce more resin in order to protect themselves from the sun's heat. The resin contains the active drug ingredients of the plant. Marijuana contains 421 chemicals from 18 chemical classes, but the most important active ingredient is thought to be tetrahydrocannabinol—specifically, delta 9 tetrahydrocannabinol (THC)—with possible synergistic effects from other cannabidiols and cannabinols (Turner, 1981). It has been found that THC in its active form may be retained in the body for as long as forty-five days after its initiation into the body.

There are a number of strains of cannabis, the strength of each depending on the amount of active THC that it contains. In the United States, the weakest, and most widely used, preparation is derived from the tops of uncultivated flowering shoots and is simply called marijuana (or "pot," "grass," "weed," or other nicknames). Much of the marijuana used in the United States is grown here and is of a very weak variety; it is usually olive-green in color. The native Cannabis sativa is being hybridized with the potent Asian Cannabis indica and a rapid-growing Cannabis ruderalis from the Soviet Union to form a new "super strain" of marijuana (Macdonald, 1983). Cultivation techniques that include destruction of the male plant and removal of seeds from the female plant have produced the potent sinsemilla strains. Foreign (or imported) marijuana is generally stronger than domestic, and some are identified by color, such as Panama Red, Acapulco Gold, and the dark brown plants from Jamaica and Colombia.

Cannabis used in the preparation of *bhang* in India is of similar potency to American marijuana, and appears to be widely used there as a mild intoxicant with no great health or social hazard (Fort, 1968). For a cannabis product of greater potency than *bhang,* the small red leaves and resinous material are treated in such a manner that one solid mass is formed. This preparation is called *ganja* by the Indians. The most potent source of THC is the pure resin, which is carefully removed from the leaves of the plant. This gummy substance is called *charas* in

India, but Americans are more likely to know it as hashish. Its potency is five to ten times that of marijuana, depending on growing conditions and its use. The resin hardens into a brown lump, a darker color signifying increased potency. Reports vary, but hashish usually has between 10 and 20 percent THC. Liquid hashish, called hash oil, may have concentrations of 30–40 percent, with the highest recorded concentration in the United States being 43.8 (Turner, 1981).

Contraband marijuana seized by law authorities is regularly monitored for component chemicals and THC content at the NIDA laboratory at the University of Mississippi. Reports from this laboratory make it apparent that THC concentration in the marijuana available in the United States has been increasing since 1965 (Macdonald, 1983). Table 5.1 shows that the percentage of THC concentration of "street" marijuana in 1965 was from 0.1 to 0.2 percent, while in 1983 it was from between 2 and 4 percent. Table 5.1 shows THC concentrations in the United States from 1965 to 1983 (Macdonald, 1983).

In the Western world, cannabis is usually smoked, and in this form it is considered more potent than when taken orally in drinks or food preparations, as is the practice in Eastern countries. Smoking allows more control over the use of cannabis, because the effects can be felt much more rapidly and intake can be altered accordingly. The effects of ingestion last longer, but nausea and vomiting may occur as an aftermath. As with most other drugs, the effects of marijuana are dose-dependent.

Since marijuana is the lowest potency among cannabis preparations, in its lower concentrations it must be considered a sedative-hypnotic, much like alcohol. Stronger THC preparations such as high concentration marijuana, hashish, and hash oil may be considered psychedelic or hallucinatory.

Until 1977, Mexico supplied the largest amount of marijuana for the United States, but Mexican officials at that time launched an effective campaign against marijuana growing and smuggling. During this crackdown, marijuana fields were sprayed with paraquat, an herbicidal solution that was found to be associated with lung damage in smokers of marijuana coming from sprayed fields. As the trade in Mexican marijuana slowed down, Colombian marijuana began to fill the gap. In 1980, Colombia not only provided about two-thirds of the marijuana smoked in the United States, but it was also considered the largest supplier of marijuana in the world. The Colombian marijuana crop provided more revenue to the local economy than did coffee or other field crops, with the approximately 250,000 acres of marijuana potentially yielding six billion pounds of marijuana per year. Each pound was worth $600 on the streets of the United States. Although the Colombian farmer saw only about 1 percent of that $600, at $6 per pound he still had a more profitable crop than corn or cotton (Willis, 1984).

Table 5.1 THC Concentrations: 1965–1983

1965	0.1–0.2%		
1970	1.0%		
1983	2–4% (average)	5–6% (high grade)	13.56% (highest)

Although United States officials confiscate millions of pounds of marijuana yearly, Drug Enforcement Agency officials estimate that they intercept only a small percentage of the marijuana entering the country. The remainder plays a major role in the multibillion dollar per year business that supplies American smokers, who consume more than 130,000 pounds per day. Through the use of independent and government surveys concerning patterns of marijuana use, we can tell something about who these users are, their patterns of use, and the trends that are occurring in our country.

MARIJUANA DEMOGRAPHY

Two surveys conducted nationally on the use of marijuana appear to have enough validity to allow the use of their results with a measure of confidence. The first of these, the National Household Survey, was conducted in 1971, 1972, 1974, 1976, 1977, 1979, and 1982. The second survey, an annual sampling of high school seniors, has been done yearly since 1975 (National Institute of Drug Abuse, 1984). Although these surveys (as with all surveys) have loopholes and may miss some segments of the population, the positive input of the gathered information overshadows the limitations of the survey.

The results of these surveys are summarized here to illustrate the trend of marijuana use in America in the last decade (Miller et al., 1983).

Marijuana use in America remains a strongly age-graded phenomenon that peaks during the young adult years. Experimental use is not usually the norm, as weekly or near-daily use is not uncommon. Fewer than one-third of the 12–17-year-olds who have ever used marijuana say that have used it on only one or two occasions. Data as early as 1976 indicated that marijuana is frequently used in combination with alcohol and other drugs, and that the abuser of marijuana generally abuses other drugs as well (Dusek & Girdano, 1976). About 25 percent of "ever-users" aged 18–25 report that they usually had an alcoholic drink when they used marijuana. Of the 18–25-year-olds, 21 percent report having used marijuana on a near-daily basis (i.e., twenty or more days out of a single month) at some point in their lives.

It appears that the percentage of today's youth (age 12–17) who report ever having tried marijuana is slightly lower than it was in 1979 (26.7 percent versus 30.9 percent, respectively). In the next age category (young adults, age 18–25), the 1982 survey showed that only 64.1 percent said that they had ever tried marijuana versus 68.2 percent in 1979. Trends in annual prevalence (marijuana use in the year prior to the survey) also showed 1979-to-1982 decreases in the young and young adult groups.

A downward trend also appears in both youth and young adult groups in current prevalence of marijuana use (i.e., use during the *month* prior to the survey). In the 1977 and 1979 surveys, nearly 17 percent of all 12–17-year-olds reported current use, but by 1982, the figure had dropped to 11.5 percent. The parallel drop in current use for young adults was 35.4 percent in 1979 to 27.4 percent in 1982.

In the older adult age group (26 and over), lifetime prevalence increased while current use did not increase. This pattern is explained by the changing composition of the older group; i.e., those moving into that age group carry past marijuana experience with them.

EFFECTS OF MARIJUANA

Research concerning the effects of marijuana has been controversial since the 1960s, as the desire to achieve certainty about the effects of the drug led many researchers to ignore what is generally known about drug effects in general, and the importance of frequency of use, dosage, and setting. One fact that holds back our ability to make a complete statement on the effects of this (or any other) drug is that it takes many years of use by millions of users for implications to become clear. The research on the effects of cigarette smoking is an example. It took from the outbreak of the smoking epidemic (World War I) until 1964 before a definitive statement linking smoking with its danger to the smoker's health was presented to the American public (U.S. Public Health Service, 1964). Widespread habitual use of cannabis has occurred for fewer than twenty years in America. In addition, early studies tried to compare casual users with habitual or heavy users.

Although many more "smoker-years" will be needed to confirm long-term effects of smoking marijuana, some of the effects of the drug are constant enough in the literature to merit comment. With a brief overview of the physical, psychological, and psychosocial effects that have been suggested to date, we offer a word of caution to those who study the research documents regarding marijuana. When perusing each document, determine the number of subjects used, the presence of control groups, the potency of the substance in terms of the THC content per kilogram of body weight, mode of administration, setting, and other aspects of valid experimental research. When comparing newer research with older research, remember that the THC content of marijuana is rising.

Although there are many biochemical aspects of marijuana that are yet to be uncovered, the stockpile of known physiological effects has grown remarkably in the last twenty years (Glantz, 1984).

Physiological Effects

Chronic administration of cannabis results in the development of tolerance to a wide variety of the acute drug effects in both humans and experimental animals. Though scientific opinion is more divided on the question of dependence on cannabis, there is now substantial evidence that at least mild degrees of dependence, both psychological and physical, can occur (Kaymakcalan, 1981; Ninth Report to the U.S. Congress, 1982).

Acute Effects

Heart rate and blood pressure. The most verified effect of marijuana on humans is a dose-related temporary increase in heart rate. Blood pressure tends to drop if the person is standing, but remains the same or even rises if the person is sitting or reclining. Health scientists at the National Academy of Sciences Institute of Medicine indicate that marijuana use may be a threat to those with hypertension, cerebrovascular disease, and coronary atherosclerosis (Institute of Medicine, 1982). It appears, however, that there are minimal changes in the electrocardiograms of healthy young adults after smoking marijuana (Aronow & Cassidy, 1975).

Conjunctival congestion. With the smoking or ingestion of marijuana, there is a reddening of the eyes due to vasodilation of blood vessels.

Psychomotor performance. Research confirms early findings that marijuana use decreases hand steadiness and increases body sway while standing erect. When experiments demand uncomplicated responses to a simple stimulus, marijuana has little effect on reaction time, but when the task is complex, performance is impeded. What appears to be involved is the inability of the marijuana user to display continuous attention or to digest complex information processing. Tracking is an example of a task that requires continuous attention, and has special importance to marijuana smoking because it is a task involved in driving, piloting a plane, and the operation of other machinery. In tracking tasks where overload to the point of inability to track is applied, it has been found that deficits in performance due to marijuana may last for as long as ten hours after initially becoming high (Moskowitz et al., 1981).

Subjects are also adversely affected by marijuana in experiments where they are asked to detect and respond to peripheral light cues in their visual field. These effects may also hinder driving and other machine-operating skills.

Driving skills. Simulator studies show that marijuana intoxication impairs driving skills. In situations that closely simulate actual driving conditions, there is a greater deficit in ability to perform them while high. It has been found in simulator study that the greatest impairment due to marijuana occurs in the area of perceptual demands rather than car control, but when more lifelike conditions were produced by a computer-controlled simulator, marijuana users were significantly less likely to be able to control car velocity and proper positioning in response to wind gusts and driving curves. Also affected are the ability to maintain proper distances and lane position as well as response to route signs. The responses seen in simulator study would have resulted in accidents in actual driving situations (Smiley et al., 1981). It has also been shown that glare recovery time (after driving into headlights at night, for example) is lengthened in marijuana intoxicated drivers.

Pilots have also been found to have impaired flying abilities following social doses of marijuana. They were found to be unable to maintain flight pattern and to remember where they were in their flight sequence (Janowsky, 1976).

Although attempts have been made to determine driving fatalities or accidents that involve marijuana, there is still a serious missing link for such research—measurement of blood cannabinoid levels. These levels drop within twenty minutes after smoking, and may decrease to such a low level within two hours that they cannot be readily detected. In addition, the relationship between cannabinoid level and decreased performance has not yet been established, either. There have, however, been several studies that have linked marijuana use with causality of automobile accidents and deaths (Warren et al., 1981; Hingson et al., 1982a). It was found by Hingson et al. (1982a) that teen-agers who drove more than six times per month after having smoked marijuana were nearly 2.5 times more likely to have been involved in traffic accidents than those who did not smoke and drive. Heavier users (fifteen or more times per month) were nearly three times more likely to have had an accident. Studies such as these do give indication that marijuana increases the danger of driving under its influence. It is suspected that the involvement of marijuana in traffic accidents and deaths is underestimated due to lack of proof by legal authorities and also due to underrating the effects of marijuana by users when estimating their abilities to drive while high.

Chronic Physiological Effects

Respiratory. Research suggests that marijuana smoke has many harmful effects on the respiratory system in much the same way as does cigarette smoke. A comparison of tar content, however, shows that a marijuana cigarette is more harmful to the lungs (one joint contains five milligrams of tar; one cigarette contains 1.2 milligrams of tar). Because delta 9 THC localizes in body fat, particularly in the liver, lung, and testes, and disappears slowly, these tissues may be more susceptible to damage (Aronow & Cassidy, 1975).

A recent study showed that marijuana smokers displayed decreased lung diffusion capacity, specific airway conductance, and forced expiratory flow after two months of smoking an average of about five marijuana cigarettes daily (Tashkin et al., 1980). Smokers of marijuana show greater lung impairment than comparable tobacco smokers, at least partially due to the fact that they inhale very deeply, retain the smoke in their lungs for a longer period of time, smoke the joint clear down, and the smoke is not filtered.

Studies of hash smokers have found that heavy use of that drug is related to occurrence of bronchitis, asthma, sinusitis, and there is evidence that marijuana smoke and smoke residuals contain carcinogenic substances that are related to malignant cellular changes of lung tissue and exposed skin in experimental animals (Glantz, 1984).

Reproduction. Although there has been no conclusive statement regarding a possible long-term effect on sperm count in males, studies have shown that delta 9 THC lowers the concentration in blood serum of pituitary hormones (gonadotropins) that control reproductive functions. Delta 9 THC appears to have a modest reversible suppressive effect on sperm production in men, but there is no proof that it has a deleterious effect on male fertility (Ninth Report to the U.S. Congress, 1982).

Although delta 9 THC is known to cross the placenta readily and to cause birth defects when administered in large doses to experimental animals, no adequate clinical studies have been carried out to determine if marijuana use can harm the human fetus. There is no conclusive evidence of birth defects in human offspring, but a slowly developing or low-level effect might be undetected by the studies done to date. The effects of marijuana on reproductive function and on the fetus are unclear, but there is a consensus that the use of marijuana during pregnancy is contraindicated. Hingson and colleagues found that pregnant women who used marijuana during pregnancy were five times more likely to deliver infants who showed features seen in the fetal alcohol syndrome (1982b). The relationship, however, does not prove cause and effect.

Scientific evidence to date suggests that there are no mutagenic or cytogenic effects that occur from marijuana use, but investigation should not be considered complete until we experience many more smoker-years of marijuana use.

Immunity. Some studies of the immune system demonstrate a mild, immunosuppressant effect on human beings, but other studies show no effect (Glantz, 1984). The jury is still out on this issue until more time can be given to its study. Long-range, large-scale studies in this area have yet to be done, and most smokers are relatively young, and still have a healthy degree of immunity.

Brain. Early studies suggest that marijuana use was related to atrophy of the brain, but these results could not be replicated. Current studies also fail to find persistent EEG changes related to marijuana use. Although there appears to be no permanent change in brain structure due to marijuana use, behavioral changes are apparent (Glantz, 1984).

Behavior. From the time of early popularization of marijuana, users have reported negative experiences that range from mild anxiety to acute panic, and an acute brain syndrome that included disorientation, confusion, and memory impairment was reported as early as 1969 (Talbott & Teague, 1969). These negative experiences usually occur in inexperienced users, those who encounter an unexpectedly high potency, or those who use higher doses than usual. In the United States, cannabis psychosis is not commonly reported, but a Swedish study reported a causal link between heavy hashish use and a schizophreniclike state that included aggressiveness, confusion, and affective lability (Palsson et al., 1982).

The phenomenon of "flashbacks" is well known in the literature on drug abuse, but it is usually associated with LSD or other hallucinogenic experiences. Some investigators have reported such occurrences, but others seriously doubt that flashbacks stem from marijuana use.

It appears likely that chronic marijuana use is related to amotivation in many young and older users alike. It is difficult to say which came first, the amotivation or the smoking of marijuana. In a recent NIDA report (1982), there was strong conviction that motivational effects are highly related to use and that normal motivation may return following cessation of use of the drug. It was also noted that more than half of the high school seniors who quit marijuana use said they did so because of "loss of energy or ambition," and about 40 percent of the daily users thought that it interfered with their ability to think and contributed to their loss of interest in other activities.

Of grave concern is the possible behavioral effects of marijuana on the social and psychological growth and development of child and adolescent users. Eight percent of American 12- and 13-year-olds have used marijuana on at least one occasion, and 24 percent of 14- and 15-year-olds have done so, too (Miller & Cisin, 1983). Clinicians who treat children and adolescents who are heavy users are convinced that such use seriously interferes with functioning and development (NIDA, 1982). This interference can be reasonably assumed, as the drug experience is a temporary pleasure device, totally unreal, and thus unrelated to ongoing life.

Such experiences tempt the user to go back for a better feeling. Overemphasis on the "feeling" world of subjective experiences may lead the user to withdraw in order to search for triggers of such experiences, resulting in self-absorption and selfishness, which diminish motivation to participate in the search for what Abraham Maslow, the great educational philosopher, terms "growth experiences." Growth experiences are those for which the individual feels responsible; they are active and creative and are used as stepping stones toward additional growth, and are activities that meet long-term, psychological needs such as self-respect, self-esteem, and self-love. Growth experiences are often directed outward to others, helping the individual to overcome feelings of separateness and fulfilling the need to belong. If drug use inhibits this process, especially in the adolescent years, social and psychological growth could be severely retarded.

Psychological and Psychosocial Effects

Several specific types of psychological performances are impaired by marijuana use. These include digit/symbol substitution, digit span, serial subtraction, reading comprehension, and overestimation of time. All of these effects are dose-related. The more complex, unfamiliar, and demanding the task, the greater the impairment is apt to be. Because of these findings, it is apparent that marijuana use has disruptive effects on classroom abilities.

Marijuana use also alters perception of sight, sound, and touch; it affects mood and social interaction. For some, it is these effects that are sought in the marijuana high.

The psychological tests currently available for use cannot detect significant differences between moderate users and nonusers of marijuana, but they show that chronic marijuana use seems to correlate with manifest psychopathology. A revealing study by Mirin et al. (1971) identified some of the personality differences between casual users (one to four times per month) and heavy users (twenty to thirty times per month). They found abusers of marijuana to be psychologically similar to abusers of other drugs. Heavy marijuana users were discovered to be multiple drug users who exhibited some degree of psychological dependence, manifested by anxiety when supply was uncertain, and a self-perceived inability to relate to the world in general when not high. Heavy users were judged to have a poorer work adjustment and a self-reported inability to master new problems. In addition, heavy users expressed a poor heterosexual adjustment and were found to be more depressed and hostile toward society, and to have more anxieties than casual users. The average casual user was not unlike the average nonuser in the above-mentioned categories.

More recent longitudinal and cross-sectional study has shown that heavy marijuana use is associated with poor academic performance and motivation, various kinds of delinquent behavior, problems with authority, and lack of self-esteem (Glantz, 1984). These aspects of psychosocial behavior have generally been found to precede the drug use, although individual case studies may show that the drug use precedes diminished motivation and performance.

It appears that predictors of future marijuana (and other drug) users may include:

Rejection of parental and school authority (rebellion)
A dislike for school
A sense of alienation
Truancy
Valuing independence more than achievement
Being more peer-oriented than parent-oriented
Having a more positive attitude toward drug use in general
Theft and vandalism
Lying
Interpersonal aggression

Predictors may also include lower self-esteem, and a greater degree of personal dissatisfaction and depression.

Generally, young people who are highly peer-oriented will be more likely to use drugs. Users are much more likely than nonusers to have friends who are users, also.

Another issue with marijuana use has continually arisen. This issue is the "stepping stone" theory, i.e., that the use of marijuana leads to the use of other illicit drugs. There is statistical certainty that marijuana use (especially heavy use) is associated with use of other drugs, including alcohol and tobacco. Because of the relationship between the use of marijuana and that of licit drugs, prevention strategies are being broadened to include the licit drugs.

MEDICINAL MARIJUANA

Reports found in ancient Chinese and Indian texts of the medicinal use of cannabis show that it was recommended for hundreds of problems, including insomnia, pain, anxiety, and tension, and used as such sporadically throughout history. By the early 1900s, however, Western medicine had nearly given it up, since the extract was of a varying potency and was considered to have a poor shelf life. Also, because of its poor water solubility, a physician had no way of knowing whether or not it was absorbed by the patient. The final death knell for the medicinal use of marijuana was sounded by the Marijuana Tax Act in 1937, when the drug was officially classified as a narcotic. Physicians found it easier and safer to prescribe other drugs.

Recent research regarding the medical effects of THC on certain maladies has been positive, and special approval for experimentation and/or prescription has aided individuals with glaucoma, asthma, those who suffer nausea and vomiting from cancer therapy, and those with epileptic seizures (Ninth Report to the U.S. Congress, 1982; Council on Scientific Affairs, AMA, 1981; Hollister, 1983).

Because of the side effects of smoking marijuana (e.g., bronchial irritation), because of the difficult chemical properties of cannabis, and because cannabis cannot be patented by pharmaceutical companies (Montgomery, 1978), the cannabis products that may be recognized in the United States will most likely be synthetic analogs of THC tailored to avoid some of the effects of the natural drug. The ideal agent would demonstrate stability and water solubility, and would selectively cause vasodilation, sedation, or whatever effect is sought, with as few side effects as possible. In all cases of its use, there is the possibility of undesirable psychological side effects, which makes it necessary for the physician to administer this drug selectively.

REFERENCES

Aronow, W. S., and J. Cassidy. "Effect of smoking marijuana and of a high-nicotine cigarette on angina pectoris." Clinical Pharmacology and Therapeutics 17(5):549–554, 1975.

Council on Scientific Affairs, American Medical Association. "Marijuana: its health hazards and therapeutic potentials." *JAMA* 246(16):1823–1827, 1981.

Dusek, Dorothy, and Daniel A. Girdano. "College drug use—a five-year survey." *Journal of the American College Health Association* 25(2):117–119, 1976.

Fort, J. "Has the world gone to pot?" *Journal of Psychedelic Drugs* 2(1):1–8, 1968.

Glantz, Meyer D., ed. *Correlates and Consequences of Marijuana Use.* Washington, D.C.: Department of Health and Human Services, 1984.

Hingson, R., et al. "Teenage driving after using marijuana or drinking and traffic accident involvement." *Journal of Safety Research* 13(1):33–38, 1982a.

Hingson, R., et al. "Effects of maternal drinking and marijuana use on fetal growth and development." *Pediatrics* 70(4):539–546, 1982b.

Hollister, L. "Cannabis: finally a therapeutic agent?" *Drug and Alcohol Dependence* 11:135–145, 1983.

Institute of Medicine, National Academy of Sciences. "Behavior and psychosocial effects of marijuana use," in *Marijuana and Health.* Washington, D.C.: National Academy Press, 1982.

Janowsky, D. S. "Marijuana effects on simulated flying ability." *American Journal of Psychiatry* 133(4):384–388, 1976.

Kaymakcalan, S. "The addictive potential of cannabis." *Bulletin on Narcotics* 33(2):21–31, 1981.

Macdonald, Donald. *Drugs, Drinking and Adolescents.* Chicago: Yearbook Medical Publishers, 1983.

Miller, J. D., and I. H. Cisin. *Highlights from the National Survey on Drug Abuse: 1982.* Rockville, Md.: NIDA, 1983.

Miller, J. D., et al. *National Survey on Drug Abuse: 1982.* Rockville, Md.: NIDA, 1983.

Mirin, S. M., et al., "Casual versus heavy use of marijuana: a redefinition of the marijuana problem." *American Journal of Psychiatry* 127(9):54–60, 1971.

Montgomery, B. J. "High interest in medical uses of marijuana and synthetic analogues." *JAMA* 240(14):1469–1470, 1978.

Moskowitz, H., et al. "Duration of skills performance impairment," in *Proceedings of the 25th Conference of the American Association of Automotive Medicine.* San Francisco: The Association, 1981.

National Commission on Marijuana and Drug Abuse. *Marijuana: A Signal of Misunderstanding.* Washington, D.C.: U.S. Government Printing Office, 1972.

National Institute of Drug Abuse (NIDA). *Marijuana and Youth—Clinical Observations on Motivation and Learning.* Washington, D.C.: U.S. Government Printing Office, 1982.

National Institute of Drug Abuse. *Student Drug Use in America 1982.* Washington, D.C.: U.S. Government Printing Office, 1984.

Ninth Report to the U.S. Congress. *Marijuana and Health.* Washington, D.C.: Department of Health and Human Services, 1982.

Palsson, A., S. O. Thulin, and K. Tunving. "Cannabis psychoses in south Sweden." *Acta Psychiatrica Scandinavica* 66:311–321, 1982.

Smiley, A. M., H. Moskowitz, and K. Ziedman. "Driving simulator studies of marijuana alone and in combination with alcohol," in *Proceedings of the 25th Conference of the American Association for Automotive Medicine.* San Francisco: The Association, 1981.

Talbott, J. A., and J. W. Teague. "Marijuana psychosis: acute toxic psychosis associated with the use of cannabis derivatives." *JAMA* 210:299–302, 1969.

Tashkin, D. P., et al., "Respiratory status of seventy-four habitual marijuana smokes." *Chest* 78:699–706, 1980.

Turner, C. E. *The Marijuana Controversy.* Rockville, Md.: American Council for Drug Education, 1981.

U.S. Public Health Service. *Smoking and Health.* Washington, D.C.: U.S. Government Printing Office, 1964.

Warren, R., et al. "Drugs detected in fatally injured drivers in the Province of Ontario," in Goldberg, L., ed. *Alcohol, Drugs, and Traffic Safety.* Stockholm: Almqvist and Wiksell, 1981.

Willis, D. K. "Global war on drugs." *Denver Post,* Feb. 19–23, 1984.

SUGGESTED READINGS

AMA Drug Evaluations, 4th ed. Littleton, Mass.: Publishing Sciences Group, Inc., 1980.

Chapple, Steve. *Outlaws in Babylon.* New York: Long Shadow Books, 1984.

Cohen, Sidney. "Marijuana and the public health: an analysis of four major reports." *Drug Abuse and Alcoholism Newsletter,* 1984, XI:10.

Council on Scientific Affairs of the American Medical Association. "Marijuana: its health hazards and therapeutic potentials." *JAMA* 246(16):1823–1826, 1982.

Dackis, C., et al. "Persistence of urinary marijuana levels after supervised abstinence." *American Journal of Psychiatry,* 139(9):1196–1198, 1982.

Frytak, S., and C. G. Moertel. "Management of nausea and vomiting in the cancer patient." *JAMA,* 245:393–396, 1981.

"Grass was never greener." *Time,* August 9, 1982.

Grinspoon, L. *Marijuana Reconsidered.* Cambridge, Mass.: Harvard University Press, 1971.

Kaplan, John. *Marijuana: The New Prohibition.* New York: World Press, 1970.

Mann, Peggy. *Marijuana Alert.* New York: McGraw-Hill, 1985.

National Academy of Sciences Institute of Medicine. *Marijuana and Health: Chemistry and Pharmacology of Marijuana.* Washington, D.C.: National Academy Press, 1982.

Roffman, R. "A therapeutic approach to problematic marijuana use: promoting abstinence or moderation," presented at Marijuana and Health Symposium, Oakland, Calif., June 20, 1982.

Smith, D. "Acute and chronic marijuana toxicity," presented at Marijuana and Health Symposium, Oakland, Calif., June 20, 1982.

Smith, D. *The New Social Drug.* Englewood Cliffs, N.J.: Prentice-Hall, 1970.

Soueif, M. I. "Chronic cannabis consumption: suggestions for future research." *Drug and Alcohol Dependence* 11:57–61, 1983.

Syzmanski, H. V. "Prolonged depersonalization after marijuana use." *American Journal of Psychiatry* 138:231–233, 1981.

CHAPTER 6

HALLUCINOGENS

Few of the drugs that are classified as "hallucinogens" truly cause hallucinations as they are generally used. Hallucinations are entirely made up in the mind. Most of the drugs in this classification more often cause illusions, sights and sounds occurring during the drug experience that are based upon physical objects and real sounds. Perhaps a more encompassing description for most of these drugs, especially LSD and the other synthetic analogs, is "psychedelic." This term connotes other-than-normal sights, colors, sounds, movement, and so on. It is also important here to note that too much of any substance or condition (such as sensory deprivation) may cause illusions or hallucinations. Some of the drugs described in this chapter are combinations of psychedelic substance and amphetamine, or some other substance. Regardless of their chemical basis, these drugs are discussed here because of their street use, danger, or abuse.

The neurochemical action of LSD, the prototype of psychedelic drugs, and the action of other psychedelics (see Table 6.1) occur mainly in the midbrain. All of the drugs listed in Table 6.1 contain an indole nucleus, a chemical configuration that is also basic to the neurotransmitter serotonin. The mechanism of action of these hallucinogens is believed to be related to their interference with the neurons that use serotonin as their transmitter substance. The serotonin-mediated neurons of note here are found in the reticular area of the brainstem, the hypothalamus, and the limbic system (refer to Chapter 3). LSD apparently stimulates the same cells that are stimulated by amphetamines in the reticular formation, and also alters the function of fiber tracts that use serotonin. The stimulant effects of LSD increase sensory information delivery to the cortex, while serotonin pathway interruption results in a decreased ability to selectively damp out sensory input (Holbrook, 1983).

Since LSD is the prototype of the psychedelic drugs, its actions and the drug taker's reaction to it are detailed fully in this chapter. Some of the LSD drug experience can be carried over into that of other psychedelic drugs. In addition, the background material from the 1960s helps explain current use of some of the other psychedelic drugs, especially the recent use of MDMA.

LSD, THE PROTOTYPE

A century of research into the chemistry of ergot alkaloids preceded the first written account of the synthesis of LSD by Stoll and Hofmann in 1943. Ergot is derived from the fungus *Claviceps purpurea,* which parasitizes rye and wheat kernels, and

Table 6.1 Hallucinogens Containing an Indole Nucleus

Indole amines or substituted indole alkylamines:
    Lysergic acid diethylamide (LSD)
    Psilocin
    Psilocybin
    Dimethyltryptamine (DMT)
    Diethyltryptamine (DET)

from some varieties of morning glory plants containing lysergic acid, the precursor of LSD.

Four years after Stoll and Hofmann's report, Stoll reported the accidental and experimental psychedelic experiences of Hofmann (1947). Since that time we have witnessed the ebb and subsequent flow of the hippie culture: the classification of LSD and other psychedelic drugs as illegal, the diminution of interest in LSD as a front-page story, the overall decrease in use of the hallucinogens but with sporadic surges of popularity of new drugs such as MDMA—the "ecstasy drug" in 1985.

Pharmacology

Ingredients used in the synthesis of LSD are lysergic acid, diethylamine, and trifluoroacetic acid. Lysergic acid is controlled by the Federal Drug Administration, but illicit manufacturers produce it in clandestine labs using *Claviceps purpurea* and mannitol. About one kilogram of lysergic acid will make one-half kilo of LSD. When legal authorities look for signs of illicit LSD manufacture, they look for these basic ingredients in the laboratory and for an ice-cream freezer, because the temperature of the mixture must be lowered to approximately twenty degrees Fahrenheit in order to complete synthesis.

The latency period (time elapsed between taking the drug and feeling its effects) depends on the amount taken and the mode of administration. Oral ingestion offers the longest latency, while intrathecal injection (under the membranes covering the spinal cord) causes an almost immediate onset of effects. Although sniffing or injecting LSD produces more rapid results, the oral route is the more common one. Cohen (1968) reported an average latency period of 45 minutes for an oral dose of two micrograms per kilogram of body weight (that is, 140 micrograms in the 70-kilogram male).

LSD is absorbed into the blood very rapidly, and upon absorption from the gastrointestinal mucosa (through oral administration), it is quickly distributed throughout the body, with the highest concentrations appearing in the liver, kidney, and adrenals. A high proportion of the ingested LSD is found in the bile, since this is the preferred route of excretion.

Although LSD apparently crosses the blood-brain barrier with ease, as little as 1 percent of the ingested dose has been found to actually concentrate in the brain. Upon examining levels of LSD in various parts of the monkey brain, Snyder and Reivich (1966) found the highest concentrations in the pituitary gland and pineal gland, but high levels were also found in the hypothalamus, the limbic system, and the auditory and visual reflex areas. Surprisingly low concentrations were found in the cortex, the cerebellum, and the brainstem. This information helps to explain the electrical storms found (via depth electrodes) in areas within the limbic system in LSD subjects, while electroencephalogram records of other brain areas show no change.

Physiological Effects, Tolerance, and Dose

If LSD is ingested, a number of physiological effects will become increasingly apparent as the latency period comes to an end. Among these are a tingling in the hands and feet, a feeling of numbness, nausea (and sometimes vomiting), anorexia (lack of appetite), a flushed appearance, sensations of chilliness, and dilation of the pupils (mydriasis). Mydriasis, along with increased heart rate, body temperature, blood pressure, and blood sugar level, persists throughout the experience, but the other physiological effects subside after their initial occurrence. LSD does impair intellectual processes; the user cannot or will not perform given tasks, has difficulty concentrating, and shows an overall air of confusion.

Tolerance to LSD develops quite rapidly. Abramson et al. (1956) found that there was a quite noticeable decrease in subjective symptoms when the same moderate dose was given daily for several days; hence, those who use LSD for "kicks" must either space their use or take ever-increasing doses if they use it daily.

A standard dose of pure LSD for the average person is considered to be 30–50 micrograms, while an average dose of "street acid" may be around 100 micrograms. Dosages as high as 1500 micrograms have been reported in supervised medical treatment, and occasionally a chronic user will report taking dosages as high as 10,000 micrograms. In addition to dosage, effects depend also on the frame of mind of the user and his or her personality and environment. To date, no deaths have been reported from overdoses of LSD in humans, but some connection was made in the 1960s between the taking of LSD and suicide.

The LSD Experience

In a supportive setting, the LSD user usually first shows signs of being affected by the drug by becoming extremely emotional. A minor remark or incident may set off an intense laughing or crying episode. Of all the senses, tactile sensitivity is most universally affected, and the most dramatic effects are those of hallucinations, although they are unusual.

As the drug begins to take hold on the user, one of the first visual effects is that of ever-changing colors and shapes of objects in the room, and the appearance of rainbowlike halos around lights. The senses are further affected, and synesthesia, a crossing of sense responses (hearing colors and seeing sounds), may occur. All this time may be spent in awe of the deepness of colors, the beauty of one object, the pureness of sound; but while LSD enhances visual and auditory perception, it also works on other central nervous system centers. Time and space perception are quite lost, and because of its stimulatory nature, LSD permits many extra stimuli to enter thought processes. Sounds and sights may flash on and off, tripping thought processes that have been long forgotten.

If a large enough dose is taken, the drug taker will begin to lose touch with the outside "concrete" world and begin to feel part of some greater living cosmos in which ego boundaries have been erased. The ineffable nature of this feeling seems to parallel Maslow's "peak experience"—that of being one with all things, an ecstasy of spirit (Maslow, 1968). Especially in a supportive setting, LSD takers report seeing divine figures, enchanting places, and other images of religiosity.

LSD and Spiritual Search

The increase in use of psychedelics had roots deep into the American culture of the 1940s and 1950s. At that time, the country had emerged from a depression and entered a postwar boom. Parents strove to obtain the possessions they lacked in the days of the depression, and vowed that their children would have the best of everything and be without worry of hunger and want. The "war babies" (children of soldiers coming back from World War II) knew a greater security than many of their parents had known; they experienced a new kind of freedom. Perhaps out of this very freedom and security grew their disdain for material wealth and the superficial life that often accompanied it. Established practices were challenged in increasing numbers with increasing vigor, and a new movement was under way with an ethic of love, individual freedom, and personal honesty. McGlothlin (1968) likened the young people of this movement to the early Christians: both groups preached a doctrine of love, rejection of earthly possessions, avoidance of pride and other aspects of vanity, and support from communal living. Also like the early Christians, the individuals involved in this movement (who became known as *hippies*) were rejected by the established society. McGlothlin did not point out some of the obvious differences between the two groups, such as attitudes toward drug use, sexual behavior, and so forth. It is interesting to note that the hippie movement waned after ten years, while Christianity has continued to live for nearly two centuries.

During this time, Timothy Leary, a Harvard professor, was discovering the religious wonders of psychedelic drugs and began making a case for their inclusion in religious ceremony. He wanted everyone to have religious experiences whereby they might learn the answers to four basic spiritual questions (Leary, 1970):

1. The Ultimate-Power Question (What is the power that moves the universe?)
2. The Life Question (What is life?)
3. The Human-Destiny Question (What is man's role?)
4. The Ego Question (What is my role?)

These questions were being asked by the youthful revolutionaries who were turning away from organized religion to a religion of their own. LSD and marijuana became the drugs of choice as both were linked to a passive, introspective life style.

In 1967, a group of San Francisco Bay Area physicians who were concerned with the effects of psychedelic drugs sponsored a symposium entitled, "The Religious Significance of Psychedelic Drugs," in which legal, social, and cultural aspects of the psychedelic religious movement were discussed (Symposium, 1968). At this meeting, one of the panelists, Reverend Laird Sutton, focused on cultural and spiritual vacuums that he felt were contributing factors in the hippie movement. He felt that the replacement of the love ethic by a duty ethic in the larger society was a cultural vacuum that the hippies were trying to fill. Sutton's religious vacuum was many-faceted, but highly insightful into the 1960s culture. He pointed out that in the United States at that time, there were but a few acceptable forms of worship, and that society felt a profound distrust of mysticism and perpetuated a secrecy toward human spirituality. He also stated that the education of most young people lacked specific periods of time that were set aside specifically for individual religious development, and that there were few opportunities in our society for one to engage in philosophical or religious search for the meaning of life and existence. In addition, he pointed to a paucity of religious literature dealing with the psychedelic or spiritual experience. For many in the hippie movement, these served as motivations for examining a new way of life and a more profound type of spiritual experience than was then available in the name of Protestantism, Catholicism, or Judaism.

At this symposium, an air of optimism was apparent—there was a general feeling that this new love ethic could spread and give our society new life.

Such optimism was not seen by Huston Smith, an MIT professor, who in 1966, even before the great hippie upsurge, predicted that the whole movement would not have a religious impact because it did not have an established, stable community or church; it had no guidelines for behavior; it failed to formulate an integrated social philosophy demonstrating how the psychedelic experience influenced ongoing life; and it failed to convince the established society that what it was experiencing was meaningful (1970). Smith did prophesy the demise of the large hippie communities, such as the Haight-Ashbury community of 1967–1968, but we see vestiges of this original movement in communes throughout the world; in general, an age of greater awareness was stimulated by the movement.

The death of the Hippie-Haight lay at the hands of the very people involved there, for the Haight (and other hippie communities, such as Greenwich Village in New York) was a mixture of all people. Yablonski (1973), described it as a mixture of "High Priests" (the philosophers of the scene), novitiates or the army of aspirants, and finally the "plastic hippies" who were subdivided into groups of hippie drug addicts, teenyboppers, severely emotionally disturbed people, and a miscellany of "others." Yablonski, in his continental visit into the hippie community during its peak, saw the movement as composed of a few philosophers (10–15 percent), a larger group of true seekers (35 percent), and then a group of fringe people who were part-time dropouts, teenage runaways, or drug addicts who used the movement as a shield of immunity from established society. Also from his experiences with and in the movement, Yablonski estimated that 20 percent of the total number involved were seriously emotionally disturbed young people who were using the movement as a place to hide or a method of dealing with their psychoses.

This breakdown of the characters involved in the movement facilitates the understanding of why large communities died out. There were large numbers of individuals who were not committed to a deep philosophy and were rather like leeches drawing their lifeblood from the community. The underlying philosophy of the movement was to "do your own thing." As Noyes, the founder of Oneida, one of the longest-lived communes in the United States in the 1800s, discovered, without rules a community is faced with three major disruptive forces: lethargy, antiorganization or anarchy, and sexual irresponsibility. This absence of rules and organization also appeared in the many communes that grew out of the counterculture movement of the 1960s, and it caused their early demise. Groups of individuals who sought to remove themselves from the rules of the "Establishment" failed in their efforts when they rejected organization.

And so the strong, concentrated movement of the 1960s became a low-key, more personal search for human interaction based on honesty, love, and individual freedom, and the psychedelic drug scene subsided in a similar manner. No longer do the media romanticize the "trip" or its users; the psychedelic clichés have been replaced by new jargon; and the fear of chromosome damage is overshadowed by marijuana and other more popular drugs. But the psychedelics are still being used, with about 20 percent of adults 18–34 years old having tried them (Miller et al., 1983).

Current vestiges of the early psychedelic movement are the parapsychology search and research being conducted all over the world, and the resurgence of the Eastern philosophies of Taoism and Zen with their inherent holistic life styles. On the West Coast in particular, the holistic health movement is tied with these philosophies so that individuals are relating their health to all aspects of their lives and taking responsibility for the healthful integration of body, mind, and spirit.

With parapsychology and the Eastern philosophies, as with the psychedelic experience, come the belief in reincarnation, which expands the Western view of death and dying; astral projection, which defies our "normal" concept of time and space; and other aspects of consciousness yet unexplored by the Western world. Such areas as ESP and Kirlean photography (which captures energy emanating from living forms) are becoming more commonplace in popular newsprint, and it appears that more scientists, physicists, and physicians are accepting the possibilities of the paranormal aspects of consciousness. Although the concepts of parapsychology seem new and different to most of the Western world, they are, in fact, older than Christianity.

Deceit and Dangers

Surveys show that many street users who think they are purchasing mescaline, peyote, psilocybin, or other organics are actually buying acid, PCP, or some other more easily manufactured hallucinogens. This deceit could be a hazard to those who expect one kind of drug reaction, but find themselves in an entirely different experience. Since the intensity and length of the trip depend at least in part upon the drug and the dosage, the street buyer must exercise caution.

Although there has been an atmosphere of adventure surrounding the psychedelics, they are not without drawbacks. Two dangers involved in psychedelic use that were given a great deal of coverage in the early days of the hippie movement were bad "trips" and flashbacks. These phenomena are related in that both probably involve the memory process and other intricacies of the central nervous system. Cohen (1968) estimated that about 0.1 percent of normal individuals who take LSD under favorable laboratory conditions suffer serious reactions. However, most of the psychedelic drug use in America today is not done under laboratory supervision.

The bad drug experience, or "freakout" as it once was called, can be triggered by various stimuli. The panic that might result from loss of time-space perception, the acute physiological reactions of heart palpitation, chilliness, and nausea, or mere confusion from the experience could initiate a bad experience. Users might get so involved in their pseudohallucinations (true hallucinations occur only with high dosages and/or a very supportive setting) that they can no longer extricate themselves from their environment. If they panic, lose self-control and judgment, and perhaps become incoherent or violent, they and those around them are in a potentially dangerous situation. Since LSD wears off gradually over a period of ten to sixteen hours, the user cannot come out immediately except with the use of an anti-LSD drug such as chlorpromazine. However, the use of such a drug should be weighed against the possible harmful effects of subsequent psychological problems and a higher probability of flashbacks. In many, if not most, cases, a person having a bad experience can be talked back into a calm state; violence and restraint should be used only as a last measure. One should never tell users in this condition that they have lost their mind or damaged it permanently, because they are already in a frightened, irrational state and unable to think calmly or to use logical reasoning.

The bad experience can occur from an unexpected upsurge of memories that are normally repressed. It is not wise for a person with an unstable personality to take LSD, because the problems he or she has during an undrugged state may be amplified by LSD. It is not known exactly how LSD works, but it appears that normal selective damping of incoming stimuli no longer takes place and electrical storms occur in various parts of the brain.

A danger to many initial users is an intense expectation that doors will open, truth will be seen, and the soul will truly be enlightened. Expectation may be so great that anything short of an extremely moving experience may induce depression and a bad trip may ensue.

Another acute psychological danger is that ego boundaries may disappear; for example, the floor may seem to become part of the body, and to step on the floor may evoke bodily pain. Ego may be inflated to heights beyond compare—to pure omnipotence—or to extreme lows, where suicide may seem to be the only way out.

Thinking loses its logic. There is a danger that users will begin to be fanatically set on illogical "truths" that occur to them during an LSD experience. They may believe they can read minds, can transmit ESP messages, can will themselves to do anything, or can even make themselves believe beyond a doubt that others are trying to kill them or are fiendishly plotting against them. Because of this inability to separate idea from reality during the drugged state, a striking number of LSD users strongly believe in magic.

It appears that mental stability, a supportive environment, and a good frame of mind upon going into an LSD experience are essential. Taking LSD in an angry or apprehensive mood has been shown to increase the likelihood of a bad experience; hence, one should never be given LSD when he or she is unwilling to take the drug. Above all, LSD should never be given to individuals who are unaware that they are taking it, for they will not be prepared for the effects, which sometimes even chronic users cannot handle.

Flashbacks

A well-publicized chronic reaction to LSD is the *flashback*, and although this phenomenon does not occur to everyone who takes LSD, it is impossible to predict who will experience it. It seems to occur most often in cases where the user has had a bad experience. Feelings of paranoia, unreality, and estrangement are often experienced in the flashback along with distorted visual perceptions and anesthesias or paresthesias (prickly or tingling sensations) creeping over the body. It has been shown that the body rids itself of LSD quite completely in about 48 hours; it is not known how the body will react in an LSD-induced manner after that time has lapsed. Fischer (1971) attributed the flashback experience to a "stateboundness" which is initiated by a stimulus identical to one previously experienced. An example of this is the sudden reflection or reliving of an experience of a departed parent upon smelling her perfume or his pipe tobacco. Experienced drug users can sometimes cause a flashback by setting the environment that surrounded them in a previous experience; this is called a "free trip," for it occurs without the use of a drug. Those who do not use drugs experience the same free trip when they have a moving memory of a happy experience.

Flashbacks have been known to last from a few minutes to several hours, to occur once a month or several times a day, up to eighteen months after LSD use, and to happen in many different settings. It has been found that other drugs may trigger a flashback, and flashbacks frequently occur while one is driving or going to sleep; thus it would seem that they occur during a time when the reticular formation is not forwarding a large number of stimuli into the cortex. This may permit random thoughts or an overriding influence of any one thought or stimulus to trigger a state-bound experience. Flashbacks can be set off by stressful situations, but may occur at nonstressful times as well.

There appear to be three kinds of flashbacks: perceptual (seeing colors, hearing sounds of the original experience), somatic (experiencing tingling sensations, heart palpitations, etc.), and emotional (reliving of depressive, anxious, or otherwise emotional thoughts that may have been triggered by the initial trip). The first two usually elicit reactions of panic, fear, and hysteria in those who do not understand the nature of them, but the third type may be the most dangerous: the persistent feeling of fear, remorse, loneliness, or other emotions that occur may lead to extreme depression or suicide.

Chronic Psychosis

Another psychological danger is that of prolonged psychosis or neurosis resulting from LSD use. This is not a flashback, but is a continuing problem after the LSD experience. Paranoiac and schizophreniform psychoses have been seen to occur as a result of LSD, and the conditions have continued after the intoxication has worn off (Ungerleider & DeAngelis, 1981). Severe depression accompanying these psychoses has been thought to be the cause of homicidal and suicidal actions that followed.

The Chromosome Issue

Numerous studies from the 1960s to the present report LSD's potential for causing chromosomal breaks, and although the significance of such breaks has not been definitely established, they have been found to occur in animal and human white blood cells (Dipaolo et al., 1968), and in fetuses exposed to LSD after conception (Alexander & Miles, 1967). Researchers have found meiotic chromosome change in mice directly exposed to high doses of LSD, and have indicated that LSD may have serious effects on size of litters, congenital malformations, and frequency of leukemia and other neoplastic diseases (that is, diseases involving the growth of nonfunctional tissue). On the other hand, there are numerous studies that report no cytogenic effects (harmful effects on the cells) and no teratogenic effects (harmful effects on the fetus) in rodents, rabbits, and humans (Hecht, 1968).

The complexity of the chromosome issue and the sophistication of the research tends to be somewhat confusing to the lay reader. Caution should be exercised in reading, analyzing, and comparing studies. Pitfalls such as method of analyzing breaks, subject selection (possibility of other drug contamination), type of experimental animal, weight of animal, purity of LSD used (pure chemical, dry LSD mixed with saline, street mixtures), time of examination after exposure to LSD, and probably most important, amount of LSD per kilogram of body weight must be considered. Further consideration must be given to the type of teratogenic or cytogenic effect being studied. Chromosome breakage is of doubtful importance unless the germ cells are affected. Dishotsky et al. (1971) pointed out, however, that many reports of chromosome damage come from studies in which subjects have ingested illicit (not pure) LSD, and therefore, the harmful effects observed may have stemmed from adulterating substances rather than from the LSD. Most researchers, who have no control over interpretations of their work by news reporters and the public, caution their readers against extending their findings to situations not covered by physical and/or statistical controls. The research papers on the potential dangers of LSD are too numerous and too well-executed to ignore, however, and women who are contemplating pregnancy or are in early pregnancy are warned against taking any unprescribed drug, especially in the first trimester.

LSD Use in Psychotherapy

LSD has been used with limited success in psychotherapy. It must be understood that, where found successful, the drug has been only a tool, just as a scalpel is a tool. In the hands of a competent surgeon, the scalpel can be used to benefit the patient, but in the hands of others it can be a dangerous object. Therapeutic use of LSD has not increased greatly over the years because of its limited success, legal implications, difficulty in procuring the drug, adverse reactions to the drug (even in a controlled environment, bad trips can and do occur), and the problem of rapid tolerance buildup in the patient.

LSD therapy has been tried by psychotherapists to help resolve various problems of their patients. It has had limited use in cases of alcoholism, autism, paranoia, and schizophrenia, and various other mental and emotional disorders (Grof, 1967). Results of these uses have ranged from "no improvement" to "complete cure," but the largest percentage lies in the "slightly improved" category (Ditman & Moss, 1968). LSD does not work for every therapist or every patient. When the drug does contribute to the improvement of a patient, it is the combination of patient, therapist, and drug, all working together, that effects a cure.

When the beneficial effects of therapy are presented as a rationale for using the drug in a nonmedical setting, one must realize that (1) the argument is based on therapy with limited use and limited success, and (2) the question is one of *psychedelic therapy* as opposed to *psycholytic therapy*. Psycholytic therapy, the use of LSD in a medical setting, calls for a low dosage (50–70 micrograms) administered repeatedly over a long period of time. This low dosage appears to facilitate recall, catharsis, abreaction, and other patient reactions that may aid in psychoanalysis. As one can see, this is *not* the nontherapeutic LSD experience, where a larger dose is taken and stronger reactions occur. Therefore, in rationalizing the nontherapeutic use of LSD, one cannot cite the beneficial effects of psycholytic therapy, because this use is quite different from street use in dosage and in effects.

Psychedelic therapy, which is used on occasion, is a specialized form of intensive therapy on a "one-shot" basis. A dose of 200 micrograms or more is used to create a typical LSD experience, in which it is hoped that the patient will "find himself." This type of therapy is used with patients who have a basic loss of self-respect, self-esteem, and self-image, in the hope that the drug experience will allow them to accept themselves once again. This experience must be preceded by extensive therapeutic preparation for several weeks prior to the therapy session. The setting must be extremely supportive—special music, lighting, pictures, etc., are used—and most important, a trained therapist must be with the patient constantly during the 10- to 12-hour trip, shaping, directing, and guiding the trip. The therapist provides reassurance, averts anxiety, and is responsible for the success of the experience. The session is followed up with supportive therapy to help redirect the patient.

Not all sessions of psychedelic therapy produce effective results, and bad trips are known to occur in therapy as well as in street use. In the last several years, the drug MDMA (see page 114) has been used by therapists to help clients break down communication barriers, trust themselves and others, deal with jealousy in a positive manner, and to solve other personal growth issues. Adler et al. (1985) reported that Lester Grinspoon and Norman Zinberg (both of Harvard Medical School and both long-standing experts in drug study) found MDMA to be a helpful therapeutic tool.

Creativity

Because creativity stems from mood, perception, thought, and other workings of the mind, it is not easily judged; it is therefore difficult to determine whether LSD might enhance creativity.

LSD subjects have expressed the feeling of being more creative during the LSD experience, but the activities of drawing and painting during a trip are hindered by the motor effects of LSD and the products of creative effort under the influence of LSD largely prove to be inferior to those produced prior to the drug experience. Paintings done in LSD-creativity studies have been reminiscent of schizophrenic art.

Harman et al. (1966) found that a very light dose of mescaline (a derivative of the peyote cactus) equivalent to 50 micrograms of LSD proved helpful to a select group of engineers, scientists, and administrators who had specific problems that they could not solve before the drug experience. A majority of these subjects developed solutions to their problems after the drug experience. Whether or not they could have arrived at a similar solution in a brainstorming session or some other nondrug experience is impossible to say. However, these were highly select, competent subjects who apparently possessed a certain degree of creativity before the drug experience.

McGlothlin et al. (1970) tested twenty-four college students and found, through the use of creativity, attitude, and anxiety tests, that three LSD sessions (200-microgram doses) had no objective effect of enhanced creativity six months later. However, many of the subjects said that they *felt* they were more creative. This paradox is noted in many areas of LSD study—subjects feel that they have more insights, are more creative, and have more answers to life's questions, but they do not demonstrate these feelings objectively. Their overt behavior is not modified and these new insights are shortlived unless they are reinforced by modified behavior.

In general, it has been found that LSD subjects report a greater interest in art and music after an LSD experience, and this greater awareness of the arts may give rise to some of the subjective feelings of creativity that have been reported.

The literature reveals that outstanding drug researchers, such as Hoffer and Osmond (1967) and Cohen (1968) felt that LSD did not enhance creativity in a noncreative mind. The drug may alter electrical patterns so that sensations are different and thus evoke a new idea from existing knowledge. A person who does not know music will not become a pianist by taking LSD; however, he or she may become more interested in music.

OTHER HALLUCINOGENS

All hallucinogens produce similar reactions in the human body, but the intensity of the reaction varies among the different drugs. The preceding discussion of the psychotherapeutic use of LSD gives an idea of the difference between the less intense reactions produced by a 50-microgram dose and the typical LSD experience caused by a dose of 200 micrograms or more. The difference in intensity of other hallucinogens parallels this type of continuum. It is found that an oral dose of 0.1 milligram (100 micrograms) of LSD produces psychedelic effects comparable to those produced by 5 milligrams of psilocybin or PCP, 30 milligrams of inhaled DMT, or 300 to 500 milligrams of mescaline (Holbrook, 1983; Senay, 1983).

Other drugs in this classification that have seen high abuse, other than LSD, are mescaline, psilocybin, DMT and DET, STP, and PCP. The recent appearance of MDMA as a street drug also warrants attention. There are so many hallucinogens of minor popularity, such as nutmeg, certain morning glory seeds, jimson weed, ibogaine (obtained from a plant grown in equatorial Africa), and countless others that time and space will not allow a complete description of each. However, the effects of these are very similar to those described for LSD, if they are taken in large enough doses.

There is the ever-present danger to users of the more popular hallucinogens that street supplies of these drugs are regularly mislabeled and misrepresented. It appears that PCP is involved in most of the street drug misrepresentation.

LSD has been described in detail in this chapter; the remainder of the chapter is devoted to other drugs that are commonly placed in this classification, even though they may also have amphetaminelike or anesthetic qualities. Also in this chapter is a review of the Comprehensive Drug Abuse Prevention and Control Act and its amendments that govern not only the psychedelic drugs, but the other drugs of abuse as well. It is presented here because it is the main legal tool to control the drugs of abuse described in the following chapters.

Mescaline and Peyote

Mescaline is one of the principal alkaloids found in the peyote cactus (Fig. 6.1) (*Lophophora williamsii*) and is apparently responsible for the visual hallucinations that occur when one eats peyote.

Peyote intoxication differs somewhat from mescaline intoxication because peyote also contains alkaloids other than mescaline. A dose of 300 to 600 milligrams of mescaline can produce hallucinations and other psychedelic effects, whereas more than 50 times that amount of peyote must be ingested in order to produce similar reactions. Duration of effects for mescaline is five to twelve hours, but longer periods have been reported (Smith, 1969).

Mescaline may be marketed as a powder, as a gelatin capsule, or in liquid form, thus making it possible to sniff, ingest, or mainline the substance. However, it is reported that most mescaline is taken orally. Peyote is taken orally in the form of mescal buttons, the brown, dried crowns of the cactus. These buttons are either chewed or sucked to extract the hallucinogenic substances within.

Peyote is the only drug of its kind that is legal in the United States. The reason is that it is part of the ritual ceremony performed by the Indians of the Native American Church of North America, a religious group of nearly a quarter million members, which preaches brotherly love, high morality, and abstention from alcohol. However, the drug must be used strictly for religious ceremony, and peyotists must deal with legal suppliers for their drug.

The peyote ceremony usually consists of an all-night gathering inside the ceremonial meeting place, where the worshippers sit in a circle around a fire. Peyote is taken and works its effects as the worshippers are led in prayer, chanting, and

Fig. 6.1   The peyote cactus.

meditation by a "road-man." The meeting ends in the morning with a communal meal (Widener, 1985).

Peyote intoxication first brings on a feeling of contentment and hypersensitivity, then one of nervous calm during which visual hallucinations are apt to occur. Brilliant flashes of color, defying description, are seen prior to the visual hallucinations. It appears that visual hallucinations occurring from peyote ingestion follow a pattern. First, geometric figures appear, then familiar scenes and faces, followed by unfamiliar scenes and objects. It is this visual phenomenon that makes peyote revered by peyotists—this is their way of communicating with their spirits.

If this drug and its derivative, mescaline, were used only as religious objects, they would be of little concern. However, the use of these hallucinogens has entered the pleasure-seeking world, and if they are taken in sufficient dosage, their use and the problems they cause become similar to those described for LSD. Like LSD, no physical dependence on these drugs has been observed, but the need for further psychological gratification may provide the impetus for repeated use. Tolerance to mescaline develops, as does cross-tolerance between mescaline, LSD, and psilocybin.

Psilocybin

In 1958, A. Hofmann (who discovered the hallucinogenic effects of LSD) isolated psilocybin, the hallucinogenic agent in *Psilocybe mexicana,* a small mushroom that grows in marshy places (Fig. 6.2). This mushroom has been used for centuries in religious ceremonies. The Aztecs used it as a sacrament and to produce visions and hallucinations.

This drug (along with another *Psilocybe mexicana* derivative, psilocin) also has fallen into street use as a psychedelic. It is available in powder or liquid form, and a dose of 4 to 8 milligrams will produce effects similar to those of mescaline, including initial nausea, coldness of the extremities, and mydriasis, followed by abrupt mood changes and visual hallucinations. The intoxication, lasting about eight hours, is followed by mental and physical depression, lassitude, and distortion of one's sense of time and space.

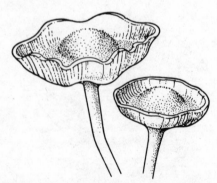

Fig. 6.2 The mushroom *Psilocybe mexicana,* from which psilocybin is produced.

Psilocybin use has been shown to cause development of tolerance. No physical dependence has been observed, but psychological dependence is a danger.

DMT and DET

DMT (dimethyltryptamine) was labeled the "businessman's trip" because a 70-milligram injected dose will cause an onset of hallucinatory effects within two to five minutes, with the condition subsiding within half an hour to an hour. Both of these drugs are not orally active and therefore must be smoked or injected.

DMT was originally obtained from seeds of *Piptadenia peregrina* and *Piptadenia macrocarpa,* legumes that are found in the Caribbean islands and in South America. The natives of these areas pulverized the seeds and then inhaled the substance as snuff through a tube.

DMT sold on the street is a semisynthetic that is easily produced from common materials, and is thus inexpensive to buy. It is very similar in chemical structure to psilocin, the substance into which psilocybin is converted in the body and which subsequently causes the psychedelic experience to occur. It is usually smoked in a mixture of parsley, marijuana, tobacco, or tea.

DMT (and its close chemical variant DET, diethylatryptamine) has not been found to cause physical dependence, but tolerance does develop, as may an intense desire to continually repeat the experience. In addition, no cross-tolerance develops between DMT and LSD, mescaline, or psilocybin (Jaffe, 1980).

STP (DOM)

Psychotomimetic amphetamines are a group of amphetamines that produce hallucinogenic effects along with the typical amphetamine reactions to be discussed in Chapter 7. This group of psychoactive drugs is exemplified by DOM (dimethoxymethylamphetamine), more popularly known as STP. The nickname STP seems to have been derived from the popular motor oil additive "scientifically treated petroleum" or from the words *serenity, tranquility, and peace.*

As has been mentioned, STP is capable of producing typical LSD-type reactions or amphetamine action, or both. As with most other drugs, the reaction depends on the dose. In clinical studies, reactions have been observed with doses varying from 2–14 milligrams, while street doses appear to be around 10 milligrams.

Ingested doses of fewer than 3 milligrams produce heart rate increases, pupillary dilation, increase in systolic blood pressure, and increase in oral temperature. The experience at this dosage has been described as a mild euphoria. The duration of reaction at low doses is from eight to twelve hours, with peak reactions occurring between the third and fifth hours (Snyder et al., 1968).

With higher doses reactions may last from sixteen to twenty-four hours. This duration may be responsible for the high incidence of acute panic reactions associated with this drug. In the extreme hyperactive condition, the even larger increases in heart rate, blood pressure, and body temperature, along with pupillary dilation, an extremely dry mouth, nausea, and profuse sweating, all seem to be endless. These effects are accompanied by LSD-type alterations in perception (such as enhancement of details), visual and auditory hallucinations (including blurred multiple images, distorted shapes, and vibration of objects), and a slowed passage of time. The mind becomes flooded with a variety of irrelevant and incoherent thoughts, then becomes absolutely blank, exacerbating the feeling that one is going crazy (Snyder et al., 1968). Also, as is the case with LSD, flashbacks or recurrent reactions have been reported to occur, but no mechanism for this phenomenon has been substantiated (Holbrook, 1983).

The significance of these hallucinogenic breaks with reality is that they allow for gross misinterpretation of the amphetaminelike somatic effects over an extended period of time. This combination of hallucinogenic and amphetaminelike effects appears to be the primary danger of psychotomimetic amphetamine compounds like STP. The pharmacological effects have not been widely investigated, but the limbic system, the thalamus, and the hypothalamus seem to be affected. These are the hypothesized sites of action because they are the sites of the greatest accumulation of STP in the brains of experimental animals.

MDMA

In the last several years MDMA (methylenedioxymethamphetamine) has become popular on campuses and on the street because it appears to relax inhibitions and enhance communication. Used since the 1970s as a tool in psychotherapy because of its ability to make people feel good about themselves, MDMA is now undergoing legal classification as a Schedule I drug (drugs with abuse potential, but no medical use). Thereapists are seeking to continue its legal use, however.

This drug has been touted as being "all that LSD was supposed to be, but was not." However, it is not a true hallucinogen, and unlike LSD, it does not diminish the drug taker's ability to distinguish between fantasy and reality (Adler et al., 1985). The drug is related to amphetamines, mescaline, and MDA (a potent stimulant).

Adler et al. (1985) report that the Haight-Ashbury Free Medical Clinic in San Francisco has seen patients in their detoxification unit who have taken ten to fifteen 100-milligram doses of MDMA in one day. It is still too early to map future trends with this drug, but its nickname, "Ecstasy" may help predict an upswing in its trial use.

PCP

Phencyclidine piperidine HCl (PCP) is a popular street drug that has been used by more than seven million people in the United States. It has stimulant, depressant, hallucinogenic, and analgesic properties, thus making the drug difficult to classify, but it has been proposed that it be put in the class "dissociative anesthetic." We include its discussion here because of its frequent misrepresentation of other psychedelic drugs. The drug is used legally as an animal-immobilizing agent, but was originally developed as a human anesthetic. In 1965 its manufacturers, Parke, Davis

& Company, requested that the use of PCP with human subjects be discontinued because of frequent postoperative side effects ranging from mild disorientation to delirium.

PCP first appeared on the street in 1965 on the West Coast; because of the dangerous side effects of the drug, it quickly gained a poor reputation and its use diminished. In 1977 this drug was associated with at least 100 deaths and more than 4,000 emergency room visits—signs that PCP use was increasing. It seems that the ease with which PCP can be synthesized and the change in mode of use from oral ingestion to smoking or snorting, which enables the user to control its effects better, have caused an increase in its abuse. For instance, in one year (1976–1977), the number who had used PCP nearly doubled for the 12–17-year age group.

PCP is generally sprinkled on marijuana or parsley and smoked, with the amount in a joint varying from 1 to 100 milligrams. If swallowed, the effects last longer and are less controlled than if inhaled. The effects of 2–10 milligrams of orally ingested PCP last up to twelve hours and then a prolonged comedown period follows.

If sold in granular powder form, PCP is usually 50 to 100 percent pure, but may run only 5 to 30 percent pure if sold in other forms, especially when sprinkled on leaves. When misrepresented in street sales, PCP is most commonly sold as THC, but is also sold as cannabinol, LSD, mescaline, psylocybin, or even amphetamine or cocaine. PCP has been used in combination with heroin, cocaine, methaqualone, LSD, barbiturates, procaine, and other drugs. Because of the many nicknames for PCP, the street misrepresentation of the drug, and its use in combination with other drugs, it is difficult to get an accurate picture of the use of PCP in the United States.

The acute effects of PCP are so unpleasant for most users that one wonders how the drug could survive on the street market. The most frequently reported effect at moderate doses is one of depersonalization, where the user senses distance and estrangement from the surroundings. Sensory impulses in distorted form do reach the neocortex, but body movement diminishes, time appears to slow down, impulses are dulled, coordination fails, speech becomes senseless, and numbness sets in. Somatic effects include an increase in heart rate and blood pressure. At higher doses auditory hallucinations may occur, as may convulsions. Feelings of impending doom or death are common, and bizarre behavior, such as nudity in public, has also been reported. Users of PCP may also feel a sense of invulnerability and power that may lead to acts of violence.

Chronic users report memory problems and speech difficulty persistent over time; after chronic daily use these effects may last for as long as a year. Mood disorders such as depression and anxiety occur, especially after a two- to three-day run. With long-term chronic abuse, the PCP user may become paranoid and violent. (Violence appears to be a recurrent side effect of this drug.)

The continuing popularity of PCP is puzzling when one considers that even users acknowledge the persistent negative aspects of the drug. But some aspects such as heightened sensitivity, stimulation, mood elevation, and relaxation or tranquilization are positive motives given by users on at least some occasions. Continued use of PCP may also represent a desire for a prolonged altered state of consciousness, the risk taking that is inherent in this drug, or the fact that it helps in attaining new perspectives not found with other drugs such as marijuana or LSD.

A patient suffering from PCP overdose (doses of 0.5 gram or more in adults can be life-threatening) would exhibit some of the following symptoms: coma or stupor, vomiting, pupils in midposition and reactive, repetitive motor movements, shivering, muscle rigidity on stimulation, fever, flushing, and/or decreased peripheral sensations. These symptoms can be expected to occur with doses of 5 to 10 milligrams. At still higher levels (more than 10 milligrams) the symptoms may be prolonged coma (from twelve hours to many days), hypertension, convulsions, decreased or absent gag and corneal reflexes, hypersalivation, and decerebrate positioning.

In life-threatening situations, intensive medical management is called for initially, followed by isolation to reduce sensory stimulation. Often patients are so violent and unmanageable that restraints are necessary during this period. Constant vigilance is also required to monitor vital signs.

Some patients experience a psychotic phase, which lasts from several days to several weeks. The initial phase is one of violent psychotic behavior, followed by a more controlled restlessness and lessening of delusional activity, and then a final stage of rapid improvement of thought disorders and paranoia (Luisada & Brown, 1976). Often, during this phase, PCP abuse is misdiagnosed, since the symptoms so closely resemble an acute schizophrenic episode.

Low dosages (7 milligrams orally) of PCP have effects that are similar to those of barbiturate intoxication, whereas larger amounts (12 to 15 milligrams) produce the psychedelic reactions generally seen with high doses of LSD. At the high dose end of the scale (15 milligrams and up) hallucinations and paranoid psychosis occur, and there are reports of self-destructive behavior during intoxication at these amounts.

Diazepam can be used medically to counteract severe psychoneurotic reactions or when there is risk of convulsions. Death from PCP overdose occurs due to convulsions and/or depression of the respiratory centers.

AFTERWORD

Even though the psychedelic drugs were more of a 1960s phenomenon than a present one, it appears that their effects will be sought by drug takers and therapists in the future. Their ability to induce a state of consciousness that many link to loss of ego boundaries and to spirituality will most likely keep them in the licit and illicit pharmacopeia. As Adler et al. (1985) recently quoted the famous contemporary drug expert, Dr. Lester Grinspoon of Harvard Medical School, "One of the things that strikes me about the psychedelic story is that it is unfinished."

LEGAL RESTRICTIONS

The Federal Food, Drug and Cosmetic Act was passed in 1938 to control prescription as well as over-the-counter drugs. The Durham-Humphrey Amendments of 1951 provided even stronger control of prescribed barbiturates and amphetamines, and further amendments classified synthetic hallucinogens, such as LSD, as dangerous drugs. Penalties for the illegal possession of dangerous drugs varied from state to state.

The drugs that were classified as "dangerous drugs" are now controlled by the Comprehensive Drug Abuse Prevention and Control Act of 1970 and its subsequent amendments. In this act, the hallucinogens were placed in Schedule I (see below). A review of this act is given here because of its legal control of not only the hallucinogens but also the amphetamines, cocaine, sedative-hypnotics, opiates, and other drugs of abuse covered in this book. This law, as amended, accomplished the following:

1. Enforcement authority was taken out of the hands of the Treasury Department and given to the Bureau of Narcotics and Dangerous Drugs (BNDD). This direct control of drugs replaced the confusing attempts at control through excise taxes. Subsequently the new Drug Enforcement Administration (DEA) was created to uniformly enforce drug laws.

2. It simplified the classification problem by creating five categories (schedules) based not on chemical nature but on the potential for abuse and the need for medical use of the substance.

Schedule I contains those substances that have no recognized medical use and have a high potential for abuse. Some popular examples are heroin, marijuana, peyote, mescaline, LSD, DET, DMT, and THC. Prescription provisions do not apply to these drugs because their only legal use is for research, not for the practice of medicine.

Schedule II is made up of those drugs formerly known as "class A narcotics" plus the amphetamines. These drugs have some medical use, but possess a high potential for abuse. Some examples are codeine, opium, morphine, Dilaudid, Dolophine (Methadone), Demerol, Benzedrine, Dexedrine, Dexamyl, Bamadex, Ambar, Methedrine, Desoxyn, and cocaine. More recently included in this group as drugs of high abuse potential are amobarbital, pentobarbital, secobarbital, methaqualone, and Tuinal. In order to obtain these drugs, a written prescription is required, and this prescription cannot be refilled, as can prescriptions for Schedule III, IV, or V drugs.

Schedule III is made up of drugs formerly known as "class B narcotics," as well as some nonnarcotic depressants and some nonamphetamine stimulants. These drugs have a moderate to high potential for abuse and are used medically. Some popular examples are paregoric, Empirin with codeine, ASA with codeine, Doriden, Preludin, and Ritalin. A prescription is needed and may be refilled up to five times in six months.

Schedule IV contains drugs that have low potential for abuse and are used in medicine. Some examples are phenobarbital, chloral hydrate, paraldehyde, Equanil, and Miltown. A prescription is needed and may be refilled up to five times in six months.

Schedule V contains drugs formerly known as "exempt narcotics" such as cough syrups containing codeine. Prescription requirements are the same as those for Schedules III and IV.

3. It established more stringent penalties for pushers, dealers, and those involved in organized crime, and placed lesser penalties on the user.

	Fine		Imprisonment
Possession			
First offense	up to $ 5,000	and	1 year*
Second offense	up to $ 5,000	and	2 years
Sale			
First offense	up to $25,000	and	15 years
Second offense	up to $50,000	and	30 years

*Probation or suspension allowed.

4. It provided for liberal appropriations of funds for research and education.

5. It provided for appropriations for several hundred more agents to aid in enforcement of the act.

6. It established a commission to study marijuana.

It remains difficult to list specific laws and penalties for each state because of the variations that exist. Many states are in the process of making long overdue changes in their statutes. The present system permits too much inequality by allowing too great a difference between states and too wide a range of penalties. The federal statutes serve as guidelines for the states. The reader is urged to research state and local statutes, for it is the local laws that will apply to the offender.

HALLUCINOGENS AND RELIGIOUS FREEDOM

Several cases concerning the use of psychedelics have been tested on the grounds of religious freedom. The cases of *California* vs. *Woody* in 1969, *United States* vs. *Leary* in 1967, and *United States* vs. *Kuch* in 1968 are a few examples. In the first of these, the Supreme Court of California held that the use of peyote was a cornerstone of the religion in question and that its use was protected by the Constitution. However, in most states, members of the Native American Church (the religion in question in this case) must be of one-quarter Indian blood and be registered by the state, and all peyote used must be secured from legal sources and registered.

In both the Leary and Kuch cases, the courts rejected the argument that the Constitution protected the use of hallucinogenic substances. They concluded that the use of hallucinogens constituted a threat to society and that overt acts prompted by religious belief are not totally free from legislative restrictions. Although the Native American Church has been able to prove that peyote is essential to its religious practice, neither the Neo-American (in the Leary case) nor the Hindu religion (in the Kuch case) has been able to establish this foundation (BNDD, 1969).

REFERENCES

Abramson, H. A., et al. "LSD: XVII. Tolerance and its relationship to a theory of psychosis." *Journal of Psychology* 41:81, 1956.

Adler, J., et al. "Getting High on 'Ecstasy'," *Newsweek,* April 15, 1985, p. 96.

Alexander, G. I., and B. E. Miles. "LSD: injection early in pregnancy produces abnormalties in offspring of rats." *Science* 157:459–460, 1967.

Bureau of Narcotics and Dangerous Drugs (BNDD). *Handbook of Federal Narcotics and Dangerous Drug Laws.* Washington, D.C.: U.S. Government Printing Office, 1969, pp. 72–73.

Cohen, Sidney. "A quarter century of research with LSD," in J. T. Ungerleider, ed. *The Problems and Prospects of LSD.* Springfield, Ill.: Charles C. Thomas, 1968.

Dipaolo, J. A., et al. "Evaluation of teratogenicity of LSD." *Nature* 220:290–491, 1968.

Dishotsky, N., et al. "LSD and genetic damage." Science 172:431–440, 1971.

Ditman, K. S., and T. Moss. "The value of LSD in psychotherapy," in J. T. Ungerleider, ed. *The Problems and Prospects of LSD.* Springfield, Ill.: Charles C. Thomas, 1968.

Fischer, R. "The flashback: arousal-statebound recall of experience." *Journal of Psychedelic Drugs* 3(2):31–39, 1971.

Grof, S. "Use of LSD 25 in personality diagnostics and therapy of psychogenic disorders," in H. A. Abramson, ed. *The Use of LSD in Psychotherapy and Alcoholism.* Indianapolis, Ind.: Bobbs-Merrill, 1967.

Harman, W. W., et al. "Psychedelic agents in creative problem solving: a pilot study." *Psychological Review* 19:211, 1966.

Hecht, F., et al. "LSD and cannabis as possible teratogens in man." *Lancet* 2:1087, 1968.

Hoffer, A., and H. Osmond. *The Hallucinogens.* Orlando, Fla.: Academic Press, 1967.

Holbrook, J. M. "Hallucinogens," in G. Bennett et al., eds. *Substance Abuse: Pharmacologic, Developmental, and Clinical Perspectives.* New York: Wiley, 1983, pp. 86–101.

Jaffe, J. H. "Drug addiction and drug abuse," in A. Gilman et al., eds. *The Pharmacological Bases of Therapeutics.* New York: Macmillan, 1980.

Leary, Tim. "The religious experience: its production and interpretation." *Journal of Psychedelic Drugs* 3:76–86, 1970.

Luisada, P., and B. Brown. "Clinical management of phencyclidine psychosis." *Clinical Toxicology* (4):539–545, 1976.

Maslow, A. H. *Toward a Psychology of Being.* New York: Van Nostrand Reinhold, 1968.

McGlothlin, W. H. "Hippies and early Christianity." *Journal of Psychedelic Drugs* 1:24–37, 1968.

McGlothlin, W. H., et al. "Long lasting effects of LSD on normals." *Journal of Psychedelic Drugs* 3(1): 20–36, 1970.

Miller, J. D., et al. *National Survey on Drug Abuse 1982.* Rockville, Md.: NIDA, 1983.

Senay, E. C. *Substance Abuse Disorders.* Boston: John Wright, 1983.

Smith, D. E., ed. *Drug Abuse Papers.* Berkeley: University of California Press, 1969.

Smith, H. "Psychedelic theophanies and the religious life." *Journal of Psychedelic Drugs* 3(1): 87–91, 1970.

Snyder, S. H. and M. Reivich. "Regional location of lysergic acid diethylamide in monkey brain." *Nature* 209:1093, 1966.

Snyder, S. H., et al. "DOM (STP): a new hallucinogenic drug." *American Journal of Psychiatry* 125:113–120, 1968.

Stoll, A. "Lysergsaure-diathy-amid, ein phantasticum aus der mutterkorngruppe." *Schweizer Archiv fur Neurologie und Psychiatrie* 60:279, 1947.

Symposium, "Psychedelic drugs and religion." *Journal of Psychedelic Drugs* 1:45–71, 1968.

Ungerleider, J. T., and G. G. DeAngelis. "Hallucinogens," in J. H. Lowinson and P. Ruiz, eds. *Substance Abuse: Clinical Problems and Perspectives.* Baltimore, Md.: Williams and Wilkins, 1981.

Widener, Sandra. "The peyote path to God." *The Denver Post Magazine,* June 16, 1985, pp. 14–23.

Yablonski, L. *The Hippie Trip.* Baltimore, Md.: Penguin Books, 1973.

SUGGESTED READINGS

deRios, M. S. *Hallucinogens.* Albuquerque: University of New Mexico Press, 1984.

Hofmann, Albert. *LSD My Problem Child.* Los Angeles, Calif.: Tarcher, 1983.

O'Brien, R., and Sidney Cohen. *The Encyclopedia of Drug Abuse.* New York: Facts on File, Inc., 1984.

Stoll, A., and A. Hofmann. "Partialsynthese von Alkaloiden von Typus des Ergobasins." *Helvetica Chimica Acta* 26:944, 1943.

Tennant, F. S., Jr. "Treatment of dependency on stimulants and hallucinogens." *Drug and Alcohol Dependency* 11:111–114, 1983.

Wagner, G. C. et al. "Tolerance following the repeated administration of high doses of phencyclidine." *Drug and Alcohol Dependency* 13:225–234, 1984.

Weil, Andrew, and W. Rosen. *Chocolate to Morphine.* Boston: Houghton-Mifflin, 1983.

Zinberg, Norman. *Drug, Set, and Setting.* New Haven, Conn.: Yale University Press, 1984.

STIMULANTS:
COCAINE,
AMPHETAMINES,
AND CAFFEINE

INTRODUCTION

For centuries, drugs that stimulate the central nervous system have been in use. Natives of the high Andes chewed on coca leaves to help them contend with a harsh high-altitude existence, and coffee beans and tobacco have long been used for their stimulatory qualities. Suspecting that synthetic substances could produce an adrenalin-type of effect, researchers discovered the amphetamines in the 1920s. Because of the response of the sympathetic nervous system elicited by the various stimulants, these drugs have come to be abused. Hammer and Hazleton (1984) suspect that whenever there is a release of norepinephrine or dopamine in certain parts of the brain, a reward response is experienced that makes the repetition of the behavior that caused the neurotransmitter release to be highly unlikely.

The central nervous system stimulants include cocaine, caffeine, nicotine, amphetamines, and amphetamine-related psychostimulants (see Table 7.1).

The mechanism of the stimulants appears to be that of mimicking the action of, increasing the release of, or decreasing the reuptake of, one or both of the neurotransmitters, dopamine and norepinephrine, in specific brain areas such as the cortex and reticular activating system (Holbrook, 1983). A false transmitter called P-hydroxynorephedrine has been found in the spinal fluid after amphetamine administration, but at this time its significance is unclear (Cohen, 1981).

Analysis of both the physiological and behavioral effects suggests that the site of amphetamine action is in the brainstem, closely related to the reticular activating system, which accounts for the effect of alertness, and in the hypothalamus, which explains behavioral reactions such as the elevation of mood and loss of hunger. The site of cocaine action is thought to be in the forebrain (Hammer & Hazleton, 1984).

Table 7.1 Amphetamines and Amphetamine-Related Psychostimulants*

Principal Amphetamine Compounds		Amphetamine-Related Psychostimulants	
Generic Name	*Trade Name*	*Generic Name*	*Trade Name*
Racemic amphetamine sulfate	Benzedrine	Benzphetamine	Didrex
Dextroamphetamine sulfate	Dexedrine, Ferndex	Chlorphentermine	Pre-Sate
		Chlortermine	Voranil
Dextroamphetamine HCl	Daro	Diethylpropion	Tenuate
Dextroamphetamine tannate	Obotan	Fenfluramine	Pondimin
Methamphetamine HCl	Dexoxyn, Methampex	Methylphenidate	Ritalin
		Phendimetrazine	Plegine
Amphetamine complex	Bephetamine	Phenmetrazine	Preludin
Amphetamine combined	Obetrol, Delcobese	Phentermine	Ionamin
d-amphetamine + amobarbital	Dexamyl		
d-amphetamine + prochlorperazine	Eskatrol		

*Morgan, 1981.

The pharmacological effects of the amphetamines and other CNS stimulants mentioned in this chapter are typically those of an activated sympathetic nervous system. These combined reactions of alertness, wakefulness, and attentiveness are characteristics of the stress reaction, or the "fight-or-flight" syndrome. The following physiological reactions occur:

1. Constriction of blood vessels
2. Increased heart rate and strength of myocardial contractions
3. Rise in blood pressure
4. Dilation of the bronchi
5. Relaxation of intestinal muscle
6. Mydriasis (dilation of the pupil)
7. Increased blood sugar levels
8. Shorter blood coagulation time
9. Increased muscle tension
10. Stimulation of the adrenal glands

At one time, the amphetamines were the most highly abused stimulant, but legal regulation combined with increasing supplies of cocaine and other possible socioeconomic conditions have shifted the spotlight to cocaine as the main target for abuse prevention and education in the United States in the 1980s.

This chapter presents background information and current developments in the use of cocaine, amphetamines, and caffeine, three of the most highly abused stimulants in America. Nicotine, also a strong, highly abused stimulant, will be discussed in detail in Chapter 8, *Smoking and Health*.

COCAINE

Cocaine is a powerful, central nervous system stimulant derived from the leaves of the shrub *Erythroxylon coca* native to South America, especially in Peru and Bolivia, where it thrives in the warm valleys around 5,000 feet above sea level. In favorable conditions the plant yields crops four or five times a year for about forty years.

Cocaine is one of the oldest drugs known, with recorded use dating back hundreds of years. Coca's oldest use was in religious ceremonies as an inducer of meditative trance and as an aid for communicating with nature. The Incas reserved coca use for the nobility and priests, and those who were granted permission to use it were in extreme imperial favor. The leaves were offered in sacrifice to the gods, chewed during worship, and placed into the mouths of the dead to ensure a favorable welcome in the next life. For a while after the Spanish conquest of Peru, coca use was forbidden, until the Spanish discovered that the Indians could perform more work on less food while using the drug. A daily ration was then provided for the laborers. That practice became a habit that has never been relinquished. Even today Indians carry on their long, arduous journeys with a bag of coca leaves and a bag of plant ash. The leaves dipped in a small amount of ash are made into quid in the mouth and chewed for hours. When physical exertion is to be increased, so too is the amount of leaves to be chewed.

The coca plant from which cocaine is derived was introduced to Europe in the sixteenth century, but went practically unnoticed until the late nineteenth century when scientific investigation into its potential was begun. In 1884 one of its most ardent supporters, Sigmund Freud, began a series of experiments and published numerous reports on its beneficial effects. Freud was an enthusiastic user of cocaine, which he called the "magical drug." He proclaimed that it possessed almost un-believable curative power and could relieve a number of disorders, including mor-phine addiction, depression, and chronic fatigue. Although Freud never publicly retracted his broad endorsement of cocaine, he eventually acknowledged its dangers and conceded that it had failed as a cure for morphine addiction.

In America, during that same era, cocaine was enjoying considerable popularity as a remedy for numerous ills and became a common ingredient in many medicinal tonics. The most famous of these was the original Coca-Cola, which included flavoring from imported coca leaves. The government soon became alarmed at the number of Americans with the "cocaine habit" and moved to ban its consumption. In 1906 the Pure Food and Drug Act was enacted in part to control cocaine use. Later, in 1914, the Harrison Narcotic Tax Act legally classified cocaine as a nar-cotic, imposing the same penalties for illegal possession of cocaine as for heroin, opium, and morphine. This gave rise to the lingering misconception that cocaine is a narcotic, which, of course, it is not. The inclusion of cocaine in this Act did not go unopposed since cocaine enjoyed wide popularity. It was argued that cocaine was the greatest of all drugs, curing melancholy and restoring vigor to men. Cocaine was said to bring on liveliness, creativity, energy, glamor, and even lust. And when consumed by people aware of its potential dangers, it would cause no harm. The one argument that proved an accurate prognostication was that prohibition would result in underground traffic and enormous profits for the dealers, who would seek out and entice new customers.

For the next forty years, cocaine use seemed to reach an all-time low. But confiscation at border checkpoints and medical reports in the late 1970s signaled an increase in cocaine traffic and use; during the first half of the 1970s, cocaine became one of the most popular street drugs. The reasons for the sudden increase in pop-ularity are still not known. Some experts hypothesized that publicity created a snowball effect in a culture increasingly enamored with drug consumption in gen-eral.

Incidence of Use

In 1983, Miller et al. reported that nearly 7 percent of youth aged 12 to 17 reported having tried cocaine, but lifetime experience with this drug was concentrated in the 18-to-25 (young adult) years and in the 26-to-34 age group. Twenty-eight percent of 18-to-25-year-olds and 22 percent of 26-to-34-year-olds said that they have tried cocaine on at least one occasion. In contrast, about 4 percent of persons aged 35 and older report having used cocaine. Among young adults it appears that cocaine use is leveling off after the rather dramatic increases in lifetime prevalence reported in earlier surveys conducted during the 1970s.

Of all youth who have ever tried cocaine, the majority say that they have used it on just one or two occasions, but for older persons, experimental use is not the norm. About 12 percent of the entire 18-to-25 age group say that they have used cocaine on more than ten occasions. About 10 percent of all young adults say that on the occasions when they take cocaine they usually use marijuana also. In fact, in every age group, the majority of those who have ever used cocaine say that they have used marijuana on the same occasion that they took cocaine.

In the "high-risk" 18-to-25 age group, cocaine use is more likely among males than females, and more likely among whites than among persons of other races. Cocaine use also appears to be concentrated among young adults in large metropolitan areas in the Northeast and West, and in higher-education groups (Miller et al., 1983).

Cocaine Supply

Today, cocaine is sold to street-drug buyers at a high price, but certainly lower than during the sixties and seventies. Because cocaine was scarce and expensive, it became the "champagne of drugs," known in the drug subculture as the "rich man's drug." Its scarcity, its processing, and its elaborate distribution network all contributed to its high price. With the increasing amount of cocaine coming into the country, its use now appears regularly in the middle class, young and old alike, creating the need for educators to learn how to identify progressive cocaine abuse among adolescents, and prompting a *Time* magazine article, "Cocaine: Middle Class High" (Fortuna, 1983; *Time* magazine, 1981).

The coca plant is grown and harvested mainly in Bolivia and Peru, and the leaves are made into cocaine paste. This in turn is converted into cocaine base, and then into cocaine hydrochloride. Colombia is the major refiner and exporter of cocaine to the United States. It processes and distributes up to 70 percent of the cocaine entering this country, which is mainly through Florida (Cohen, 1982; DiCarlo, 1982). Once in the United States the drug is distributed through a hierarchical system similar to the heroin distribution system (see Chapter 10).* The fact that cocaine's potency deteriorates over time creates the necessity of a precise network of distribution, which increases the risk and also the profits.

Cocaine comes in three basic forms: the rock form, the flake form considered by connoisseurs to be a delicacy; and the most common "street coke," the powder form, which is usually diluted. Cocaine is almost always adulterated, being cut with synthetics such as Procaine, Benzocaine, and speed. United States street cocaine is reported to be of diminishing purity, sometimes as low as 6 percent (Cohen, 1981). It is more lucrative to buy larger quantities of cocaine, which tend to be considerably purer. However, the dangers of cocaine association increase with the quantities involved, thus driving the price even higher. As dealers rise up the network ladder, they buy larger amounts, which enables them to handle a purer quality, have greater turnover, and deal with fewer and more responsible clients.

---

* Briefly, this system consists of a few very wealthy importers at the top of the hierarchy and many, less important street dealers at the bottom.

Methods of Use

In its pure form, cocaine is a white crystalline powder that looks like sugar (hence the nickname "snow"). It is sniffed (snorted) in powder form, liquefied and injected, or made into "free-base" and smoked. Free-basing removes water-soluble adulterants in order to increase the drug's lipid solubility for better absorption, and to produce a substance that is more suitable for smoking (Holbrook, 1983). Smoking free-base produces a shorter and more intense "high" because the drug enters the blood more rapidly than with oral or nasal administration (NIDA, 1983). Trends in drug use change, and since sniffing cocaine leads to deterioration of the lining of nasal passageways and, eventually, of the nasal septum, smoking free-base is becoming increasingly popular as a method of taking cocaine into the body. Until about 1985 street market free base was produced almost exclusively via the ether method. This process was relatively quick but handling ether was quite volatile, and explosive accidents were not uncommon. Recently the free base distributed in the street has been produced using baking soda rather than ether. The product known as "crack" or "rush" appears as hard shavings similar to slivers of soap and is sold in small vials, folding papers, or heavy tin foil. It is smoked in a pipe or mixed with marijuana and gives an instant cocaine high which may last five to ten minutes or up to one-half hour. The street cost of one or two short-term intoxicating doses (about 300 mg) is between $5 and $10 per unit (NIDA, 1985). Crack is said to have originated in New York and spread to Miami, Los Angeles, Chicago, and other major U.S. cities.

Drug Action

Cocaine is a very powerful drug, capable of altering significantly the psychophysiological state of the user. Throughout history coca has been used as a physical energizer. The ability of coca to reduce hunger and fatigue and to stimulate muscular activity has been widely recognized. It was hypothesized that this effect may be due to the accompanying rise in acidity of the blood, freeing it of uric acid, and to the stimulation of the conversion of carbohydrates into tissue energy. Even if this metabolic action does occur, the effect on the user still depends on numerous factors. As with any drug, the effects of a minimal dose in particular varies with the mental state and the physical well-being of the individual user. The stimulation is much more profound if the user is physically below par, feeling fatigued or hungry. The effects are minimal if the normal euphoria associated with good health is present. Cocaine has been shown to have a positive effect on muscle activity in general and, more specifically, on reaction time and muscular strength. Researchers have not been able to demonstrate any direct effect of cocaine on motor nerves or muscle groups; thus they have concluded that its effect is probably indirect, acting to increase the general sense of well-being and preparedness for work.

Pharmacologically, cocaine produces two different and unrelated actions: First of all, it acts as a local anesthetic. After local application, cocaine will block impulse conduction in nerve fibers for about twenty to forty minutes, due to its ability to interfere with the movement of sodium ions through the nerve cell. Second, it is a powerful, central nervous system stimulant. This effect begins in the cortical, sympathetic nervous system, probably due to the competitive blocking of the reuptake of dopamine back into the neurons of the forebrain (Hammer & Hazleton, 1984).

The action on the central nervous system, creating euphoria and a feeling of excitement, represents the prime motivator for the use of cocaine. Cocaine reinforces the highest aspirations of initiative and achievement by providing the user with greater energy and optimism. Physiologically, cocaine causes an increase in pulse and respiratory rates, a rise in body temperature and blood pressure, constriction of the blood vessels, and dilation of the pupils.

Because cocaine is short-acting, it may be used repeatedly, and excessive amounts (up to 10 grams) may be taken within a single day. A lethal dose is approximately 1.2 grams (1,200 milligrams) for most individuals if the entire amount is taken orally at one time. After application to mucous membranes, cocaine can cause death with a dose as low as 30 milligrams. Death in this case is due to respiratory failure, although this occurrence is extremely rare. Large doses or chronic use may lead to anxiety, hallucinations, impotence, and insomnia. Large doses create a feeling of muscular and mental strength, as well as visual, auditory, and tactile hallucinations. Paranoid delusions, combined with the excessive sense of personal power, can make a person who is consuming large doses, especially by injection, very antisocial and dangerous. Quick changes in perception occur frequently; judgment is impaired; there is a release of inhibitions; and aggression, panic reactions, and eventual agitated depression are characteristic of the cocaine abuser.

Dependence

Early publications regarded cocaine as nonaddictive, that is, physical dependency and withdrawal do not occur. Today these views are being reassessed. Ronald Siegel, one of the contributors to both the 1977 and 1984 NIDA monographs on cocaine, says that cocaine patterns have changed so drastically since 1977 that he has completely reversed his thinking about the drug (Hammer & Hazleton, 1984). With the advent of the social-recreational user using more cocaine and with the free-base smoker, the effects of chronic use are becoming more apparent. Experts in the field now think that tolerance and withdrawal are definite entities in chronic cocaine use (Hammer & Hazleton, 1984).

In addition to a possible physical tolerance and dependence, cocaine is characterized by a strong tendency by its users to continue its use. It induces a high level of psychic dependence, and often results in a destructive type of drug abuse. This pattern is often hard to understand since many occasional users report no adverse effects, no craving or addiction. However, there are voluminous reports that follow this general pattern: Shortly following administration of the drug there is a loss of sensation in the oral cavity and often a feeling that the tongue is missing from the mouth. A pleasant sensation of warmth all over the body is followed by a sense of heightened excitement. The user feels strong and cheerful, capable of undertaking anything. Fatigue is reduced and often pleasant feelings of wealth and power are experienced. This sense of exhilaration lasts from about forty-five minutes to two hours, depending on the quality of the cocaine and the degree to which it has been cut. As the effects wear off, feelings of depression and fatigue often set in. Headache, discomfort, and depression often lead to a strong desire to get high once more. It is not difficult to understand the desire for continued use in this pattern of abuse. But, once again, as with every other drug use pattern described in this text, patterns of cocaine use depend on the individual. Some people use it occasionally with favorable results, while others get caught up in a vicious cycle of abuse. Hammer and Hazleton report that social-recreational users have about a 50-percent chance of controlling their intake of cocaine, while the other 50-percent chance escalates to more involved levels of cocaine use. Approximately 10 percent of regular users in a Los Angeles study became compulsive users (Hammer & Hazleton, 1984).

Research conducted by Dr. Arnold Washton using data from the 800-COCAINE hotline showed that of 458 drug users who had called in since crack had been on the market, 33 percent said that crack was their drug of choice and nearly half said that they experienced serious dependency problems within six months of first using the drug. Dr. Washton cautioned that this result should not be generalized to all crack users, but it did show that crack use appeared very suddenly, that large numbers are using it, and that it is causing rapid addiction and serious psychological and medical consequences in less than six months ("Crack," 1986).

Stages of Abuse

The euphoric state produced by cocaine and enhanced by feelings of confidence, by peer pressure, and by illusions of power perpetuate early cocaine use. Users may stay at the recreational or euphoric level, taking the drug infrequently. This kind of infrequent use (one to four grams per month per year) is usually not enough to produce the second or third stages as described below.

If a strong psychological drive motivates frequent and heavy use, the user goes into the second stage, called *cocaine dysphoria.* In this stage, the user experiences apathy, increased nervousness, insomnia, and increased weight loss from anorexia.

If the second stage proceeds unabated over a period of several months, the user will likely go into a third stage, the *psychotic state,* almost indistinguishable from acute paranoid schizophrenia. Hallucinations, hypomanic behavior (compulsive repetitive behavior), and delusional paranoia characterize this stage. Knowledge of these stages and their characteristics may be helpful in recognizing a cocaine problem in the home or school (Fortuna, 1983).

Help for Chronic Abusers

As cocaine dependence has emerged recently as a chronic, endemic problem, some attempts have been made to provide symptomatic withdrawal and psychological treatment for it (Cohen, 1982). Skilled psychotherapists, multiple and varied treatment contacts, and efficient selection of behavioral techniques have been found to increase the probability of drug abstinence (Van Dyke, 1981). In addition to psychotherapeutic and behavior modalities, the pharmacological approach to treatment of chronic cocaine use is also being studied. Tennant (1983) reported that desipramine, a tricyclic antidepressant, given every four to six hours for one to three weeks after the last dose of cocaine is taken, helps the chronic user to suppress drug craving, anergia, anorexia, and depression to the point where the patient can nearly always remain in long-term treatment. Desipramine and other drugs will continue to be researched now that neurotransmitter enhancement and antagonist administration are becoming treatment possibilities in stimulant and hallucinogen dependence.

Treatment for Acute Overdose

Treatment of cocaine toxicity is accomplished on a symptomatic basis. Drug-induced anxiety can be medically treated with sedatives such as diazepam (Cohen, 1982). Hospitalization with respiratory assistance is recommended for severe overdose. After recovery, psychological support is important. If the individual suffering from overdose is not breathing, immediate CPR is the only first aid that the lay person should administer. It is important that additional drugs be given only in a hospital setting. The cocaine user often has taken other drugs in addition to cocaine; administering additional depressants may exacerbate his or her condition. Signs of cocaine abuse may include gregariousness, hyperactivity, loss of appetite, rapid heart rate, racing thoughts, and euphoria. Anxiety and agitation may also be present.

Legal Restrictions

No legal control of cocaine existed in the United States until 1906, when the Pure Food and Drug Act was passed. The Act required accurate labeling of the contents of all over-the-counter preparations. In 1914, the Harrison Narcotic Tax Act was passed by Congress and cocaine was legally classified as a narcotic (even though it is pharmacologically categorized as a stimulant). The same penalties were imposed for illegal possession of cocaine as for the illegal possession of opium, morphine, or heroin. Persons authorized to handle or manufacture cocaine were required to register, pay a fee, and keep records of all narcotics in their possession.

As a result of the passage of the Harrison Narcotics Tax Act, cocaine lost much of its popular appeal, and the use of cocaine in medicine was largely superseded by a new group of synthetic drugs which were safer and more economical to produce. The recreational use of cocaine was somewhat limited to the underground, and by the 1920s, cocaine use was restricted almost exclusively to "jazz cultures" and to more affluent ghetto dwellers.

During the next forty years the abuse of cocaine was almost nonexistent. However, in the late sixties, cocaine reemerged as a popular drug among youth from all socioeconomic levels. Its use increased sharply and then leveled off.

The high abuse potential of cocaine led to its present classification as a Schedule II drug (high abuse potential with small recognized medical use) under the Comprehensive Drug Abuse Prevention and Control Act of 1970. Illegal possession, distribution, or manufacture of cocaine is punishable under federal law as a felony.

AMPHETAMINES

Amphetamines (Alpha-MethylPHenEThylAMINE) have been used as stimulant drugs for a number of years. In 1927 Alles (1927) synthesized an amphetamine

(Benzedrine) and learned of its stimulatory nature, which mimicked the action of the sympathetic nervous system. One of the first uses of Benzedrine was as a vaso-constrictor for nasal passageways—the Benzedrine Inhaler was introduced in 1932 by Smith, Kline, and French Laboratories of Philadelphia. Later, this inhaler was removed from the market because of its frequent abuse.

Further study indicated that there was an amphetamine closely related to Benzedrine (this was called Dexedrine), and led to the discovery of methyl-amphetamine ("speed"). Dexedrine is of greater potency than Benzedrine, with the effects of methylamphetamine somewhere in between. Of the three, Dexedrine is probably of greatest medical use because, even though its stimulatory effects on the central nervous system are greater than those of the other two, it offers fewer side effects. This is one of the main reasons that Dexedrine is the amphetamine most frequently used in diet pills today.

Amphetamines are quickly absorbed from the alimentary tract and also from other sites of administration. A relatively large proportion of an amphetamine taken into the body is excreted unchanged through the kidney; thus amphetamine is found in the urine soon after ingestion. And since metabolism of amphetamines is slow, the drug is found in the urine for several subsequent days.

Subjective effects of amphetamines include a feeling of euphoria, a sense of well-being, a reduced hunger for food (anorexia), loquaciousness, hyperactivity, and a feeling of increased mental and physical power. A single dose (5 to 15 milligrams) of amphetamine can produce these symptoms, and it has been found useful to administer the drug in emergencies when a person must keep awake and alert over a longer than usual period of time (for instance, in the case of the astronauts, upon reentry into the earth's atmosphere). If wakefulness is prolonged more than 1½ to 2 days, there is a high possibility that irritability, anxiety, and other undesirable effects will develop.

Therapeutic or medical use of the amphetamines is becoming very limited, and many people feel that there is little, if any, need for the further manufacture of these drugs. A decrease in physician prescription and adverse reports from the office of the Surgeon General led to the placement of amphetamines under Schedule II of the Controlled Substances Act (that is, drugs showing a high potential for abuse and limited medical use). In 1972 the Bureau of Narcotics and Dangerous Drugs set quotas for the production of amphetamines at 22 percent of the 1971 figure. In 1973 additional quotas imposed on amphetamine production reduced it to about 11 per-cent of the 1971 figure, reported to be 10.2 tons of amphetamines and 5.4 tons of methamphetamine in that year. In 1977, four million prescriptions were written for amphetamines (mainly for long-term weight control), and today amphetamine abuse is holding steady. The current supply is from both legitimate sources and illicit trade (Cohen, 1981).

The Use of Amphetamines

Therapeutic use of amphetamines is still accepted by the medical community mainly in the treatment of symptoms of narcolepsy (a sleep disorder), and hyperkinetic behavior in children with organic brain damage. Some medical communities encourage their clinicians to discontinue the use of these drugs to treat obesity, because of long-term ineffectiveness and because other nonamphetamine stimulants may suffice for short-term appetite suppression. Some physicians still find amphetamines useful in treating psychotic episodes and also in effecting a gradual withdrawal from high dosages. Amphetamine use is also defended by some clinicians who use amphetamine-narcotics mixtures for treatment of severe pain or disabling menstrual cramps. At one time amphetamines were used to treat depressive disorders, but since the advent of tricyclic antidepressants, this utilization has been almost completely discontinued. Still, a few patients who do not respond to other antidepressants may respond to amphetamines, so they may have their place in these rare cases (Morgan, 1981).

Misuse of Amphetamines

Since the use of amphetamines is of questionable value, the taking of these drugs, especially in situations other than those listed under medical treatment, may be considered misuse. The misuse of amphetamines generally revolves around the following.

1. Weight control
2. Increased physical performance
3. Increased mental performance, alertness, or relief from general lassitude

Weight Control. An exhaustive review of drugs used for weight control led Pennick to conclude in 1969 that amphetamines are of limited value in the treatment of obesity. Amphetamines do suppress appetite, but after a short time they lose their anorexic effect (Ellinwood, 1979). Controlled study has shown amphetamines to be of no greater value than placebos in treating obesity lasting more than four to eight weeks. The situations in which amphetamines would be of the most value include loss of small amounts of weight (ten to fifteen pounds, which can be safely accomplished in four to eight weeks), control of a sporadic, overwhelming craving for food, or the beginning of a long-term treatment regimen to "set" patterns and add motivation. The medical profession appears to be seeking nonamphetamine drugs that will affect food intake control centers in the brain.

Dangers of amphetamine use in relation to weight control include the pattern often referred to as the "housewife syndrome." Along with the "chemical willpower" they supply, amphetamines cause an elevation in mood. Gradually, the elevation in mood may become the main reason for taking the diet pill, with the user having a "perfectly good excuse" to take the drug. The user may find that he or she needs that "upper" before starting for work, cleaning the house, or merely facing another day. Then, to avoid depression, another pill or two must be taken during the day. Restlessness and insomnia often result in the increased use of depressants (alcohol, barbiturates, etc.) in the evening and a vicious cycle develops.

Physical Performance. There are constant reports of drug use among high school, college, and professional athletes (Burks, 1980). Previous to the 1980s, most of the cases of stimulant use by athletes involved amphetamines; however, cocaine is now the stimulant most often reportedly used. For example, the story of cocaine use by some members of the New England Patriots football team was aired the day after the 1986 Super Bowl, and prior to the 1986 baseball season seven major league baseball players were placed on suspension for their known drug involvement. These are only two of the many instances in which athletics and drug use have been linked.

Drug use to increase performance has resulted from a misinterpretation of historical use and scientific study, along with publicity and the basic human desire for achievement. Amphetamines were first used on a large scale by the major powers during World War II to keep soldiers, pilots, and factory workers awake when situations demanded that they operate with a minimum of sleep. Early scientific research verified this effect, showing that amphetamines were able to aid performance in certain endeavors. Breaking activity into such components as reaction time, steadiness of the hand, speed, and endurance, and studying each independently and in laboratory conditions has produced inconsistent results, ranging from no improvement in normal subjects to great improvement in subjects fatigued by the lack of sleep for twenty-four to sixty hours. The majority of laboratory studies conducted in the last ten years show no improvement in speed, strength, or endurance.

It is often difficult to determine whether the activities studied in performance experiments have great significance when compared to actual athletic performance, for what is involved in the latter is a complex set of coordinated actions and reactions based on learning, memory, and planning, as well as the all-important motivation. It makes more sense to test athletes during actual competition, and the numerous "dope testing" programs that have been initiated at various amateur athletic contests, such as the Olympics, gave researchers that opportunity. Studies of such contests showed greater validity than previous studies because both winners and losers were tested. In Winnipeg in 1967, testing a group of athletes with the same number of winners and losers revealed eight had used amphetamines, of whom three were winners and five were losers. In Rome during the same year, the cyclists who finished 11, 12, and 14 in a road race tested positive for amphetamines. In a more recent study, it was not until the later finishers were tested that evidence of drug use was found; none of the top six finishers had taken drugs, but at least six losers showed evidence of drug use (Wrighton, 1975).

Amphetamines act as a stimulant by releasing epinephrine and norepinephrine from the adrenal glands and central nervous system, respectively. The resulting increases in heart rate, blood pressure, glucose and fatty acid levels, accompanied by increased muscle tension and nerve impulses from joints, all bombard the brainstem (more specifically, the reticular activating system). Thus, the individual feels more alert, can resist sleep, and experiences less of the general feeling of fatigue. The athlete interprets these physiological symptoms as an indication of being more "up," more ready to play; it is more how one feels than what one does that perpetuates the amphetamine performance myth. Amphetamines produce an elevation in mood, a euphoria, a hyperoptimism that do not allow the performer to realistically evaluate his or her performance and alter it accordingly. Even in laboratory studies the drugged subject usually cannot believe his or her performance was not better than indicated by the results. One former professional football player stated that he had used bennies (Benzedrine) in only two games and that in both he had been thrown out for overaggressiveness and overzealous rough play. He thought at the time that he was the greatest defensive linebacker ever, but the feeling was subjective, for the grading films showed his many mistakes. In part, his aggressiveness came from getting to the action somewhat slower than usual.

Another problem with the relationship between amphetamines and performance is that of the variability of the drug and the complexities of administration. Dosage, purity, timing, solubility, and tolerance are examples of factors that can alter drug metabolism and an individual's reaction to it, which makes drug use, at best, a hit-or-miss affair.

One danger of amphetamine use during athletic performance is that it masks symptoms of fatigue; this may convince the athlete to perform longer than is safe. When accompanied by heat buildup, the result may be circulatory collapse. Amphetamines tend to make the body less efficient by increasing heart rate and blood pressure beyond what is needed to perform a particular task. Likewise, delays in pulse and respiratory recovery have also been shown. There are numerous examples of deaths among drugged athletes performing such endurance events as long bicycle races.

Mental Performance. One of the more widely recognized legitimate uses for amphetamines is to allay the feelings of fatigue and to fight the desire to sleep. As was previously mentioned, amphetamines became popular during World War II for this reason. The Japanese, Germans, British, and Americans gave out millions of energy pills to keep the machinery of war in high gear. Subsequent Army and Air Force studies show that amphetamines enabled soldiers and pilots to function for prolonged periods when drowsiness would have been hazardous. The astronauts used them to fight drowsiness when reentry into the earth's atmosphere unexpectedly took place at the end rather than the beginning of the day.

Although it has been shown that amphetamines will allay the feeling of fatigue and help fight drowsiness, they have not been shown to increase mental performance in the nonfatigued or rested state. The student needing extra time, the truck driver or salesperson fighting the highway hypnosis, all are making a trade; they are gaining hours, but giving up performance. It has been demonstrated repeatedly that the amphetamine-stimulated mind is able to resist sleep for all-night study sessions, but it is the opinion of most researchers that the fatigued mind (even when stimulated by more amphetamines) cannot learn or reason as well as the unfatigued mind. Furthermore, after the student has managed to stay awake all night, he or she must either take more of the drug for the testing session or risk the onset of fatigue. Either situation is likely to result in impairment of attention and loss of accuracy, judgment, and problem-solving ability. Just as in the case of the athlete, hyperoptimism does not allow the student to evaluate performance realistically and alter it accordingly. The student must make a decision based on the particular situation. For students who have not kept up their work during a semester, the material memorized in an all-night cram session might be worth the decrement in performance during the test. Likewise, truckers and others in similar situations must also realize that the gains in wakefulness and simple reaction time are usually offset by poor judgment and overreaction to stimuli, which often result in highway accidents.

Dangers of Amphetamine Abuse

The term *abuse* is usually reserved for a pattern of drug use that is viewed as productive of antisocial behavior or as detrimental to the health of the user. Various patterns of amphetamine use have emerged and reemerged over the last ten years, many of which can be labeled *abuse*.

One such pattern is chronic extension or exaggeration of the misuse patterns described in the preceding section. Low-dose oral amphetamines are taken compulsively on a daily basis in a desperate attempt to maintain a stimulated pace of life, to chemically reinforce an outgoing personality, to keep the mood elevated, and to hold back the inevitable depression that sets in as the body rebounds from the chronic stimulation. A common pattern usually emerges, uppers in the morning and afternoon, downers such as alcohol and barbiturates at night. In an attempt to reduce some of the nervous side effects of amphetamine stimulation, many commercial brands add sedatives, usually barbiturates, to the amphetamines, resulting in an unintentional barbiturate dependence.

Another pattern of amphetamine abuse lies in the intravenous use of high-dose methamphetamine. Unlike the chronic oral abuse, injected speed use is usually cyclical. Each episode or run may last from several hours to a few days and users are almost always motivated by the extreme euphoric effects (Senay, 1983).

The extreme physical effects of speed are the primary reason for its popularity. Within seconds after feeling the liquid flow into the vein, the user experiences an intense tingling sensation analogous to an electric shock; some appropriately refer to it as a "buzz." This is followed by more intense tingling sensations, some muscle contraction, and an immediate sense of extreme pleasure (Smith et al., 1979). It has been hypothesized that this feeling may be the result of rapid release of norepinephrine by amphetamine and subsequent replacement of norepinephrine by a breakdown product of the amphetamine. Numerous reports of orgasms, near-orgasms, and a vibrating feeling of the brain and spinal cord are indicative of intense stimulation of the sympathetic nervous system.

As tolerance develops, initial users progress from doses of around 10 to 40 milligrams several times a day to many times that amount as they become chronic users. These amounts are sufficient to activate the thalamus, hypothalamus, and reticular activating system to produce prolonged euphoria accompanied by feelings of extreme alertness, increased energy, and clever, insightful, and profound loquaciousness (Smith et al., 1979). Users in the group setting profess an ability to relate to the others in frank honesty and with extreme confidence. The excessive conversation is spurred by the belief that what one is saying is profound and that the others desire to listen rather than talk themselves (Ellinwood & Kilbey, 1975).

Amphetamine involvement with the limbic system and the hypothalamus seems to be responsible for many of the effects of speed, including the lack of appetite, insomnia, thirst, and hypersexuality (Holbrook, 1983). One who is high on speed exhibits extreme optimism as well as an overextended feeling of love; prolonged body contact with the opposite sex is common, but afterward, in most cases expression of love is either forgotten or regretted. This hypersexuality may result, at least in part, from accelerated tactile, auditory, olfactory, and visual impulses.

The initial sensations and activities of a speed experience are usually meaningful and purposeful. But as this hyperactive state is prolonged for several hours, the activity becomes progressively more compulsive and disorganized. The period of extreme hyperactivity may last for several days.

Because of amphetamine action on the hypothalamus, extreme anorexia occurs. A large weight loss is not uncommon on long runs. Despite the knowledge that large amounts of vitamins, liquids, and nutritional supplements are necessary, symptoms of malnutrition such as abscesses, ulcers, and brittle fingernails are often observed in speed users. Extreme pain in muscles and joints, accompanied by muscle tremors, often occurs after several days of prolonged use. Serious overdoses are uncommon, but high doses may result in unconsciousness, chest pain, heart throbbing, and a feeling of paralysis (Smith et al., 1979).

The longer the run persists, the more the scene changes from one of pleasant optimism and euphoria to one of hyperactive aggressiveness; this is not hard to understand, in light of the action of methamphetamine on the limbic and reticular activating systems. Accelerated and intermixed sensory impulses are combined with extreme fatigue caused by sleep deprivation. Unknown tactile, visual, and auditory stimuli appearing in the periphery trigger fear and aggressive responses. This effect is not necessarily inherent in the amphetamine reaction alone, but is a result of group interaction in a situation in which five or six people, hypersensitive to external stimuli, are all moving and talking at once. Psychoticlike characteristics begin to appear. Objects are observed in detail and the individual becomes overly concerned with attaching significance to even inanimate objects, such as cracks in the wall, dirt, etc. These are often mistaken for micro-animals and snakes, and adverse emotional reactions may occur. Also common to amphetamine psychosis is an inability to recognize faces, which leads to suspiciousness and a feeling of being watched. This paranoia often results in an acute psychotic reaction (Morgan, 1981).

Much has been written on the aggressiveness and violence associated with the speed scene. It should be repeated that this violence is the result of an excessively long run, and is especially likely to occur when all available speed has been used. The fatigued and irritated user then goes out in search of more speed or a safe place to crash (to come down off the drug). Both situations create an environment that can easily trigger potential hostility.

Likewise, the extreme irritability of the speed user during the post-high depression makes it difficult to find a place to crash. Friends, even those who use speed, do not want to expose themselves to an argumentative, potentially violent individual who is likely to attack with little provocation. This situation serves to augment the depression of the crash, which is so profound and intense that shooting up again is almost a necessity.

Paranoia and Violence. Intravenous, high-dose amphetamine inevitably leads to some degree of paranoia, but the user can prepare for it. But, as was described in the preceding section, long and intense runs usually result in a loss of rationality and as time goes on, the hypersensitivity, visual and tactile illusions, and fatigue state may cause paranoia. Once the user experiences extreme paranoia, a return to the same level of consciousness often triggers a similar experience. Extreme hyperactivity, fatigue, paranoia, and the social condition are all responsible for the increased violence associated with high-dose amphetamine use. The user changes moods rapidly and is irrational in the evaluation of a situation; thus coping behavior is overreactive and aggressive (Grinspoon & Hedblom, 1975).

Psychosis. Most psychoactive drugs have the ability to trigger a psychotic episode in psychosis-prone individuals, but study of chronic amphetamine users suggests that psychosis is not idiosyncratic, but rather an inevitable consequence of chronic high-dose amphetamine abuse (Holbrook, 1983). Acute psychotic episodes can be precipitated by an exaggeration of many of the conditions normally found in the amphetamine experience, i.e., lack of sleep, visual and tactile illusions, visual and auditory hallucinations, lack of food, extreme anxiety, paranoid delusions, aggressiveness, and irritability. Psychosis related to amphetamine abuse is acute and may recur with additional use, but usually is not chronic and does not carry over into the nondrug state unless the individual is psychotic-prone.

Overdoses and Death. Amphetamine overdoses, more often called "over-amping" (a term derived from the use of too many ampules containing liquid methamphetamine), are uncommon and not fatal. A user can develop a tolerance to the awakening effects of the drug, which often leads to use of amounts hundreds of times the clinical dose. Symptoms such as extreme chest pain, unconsciousness, aphasia, mental and/or physical paralysis, and erratically racing thought patterns often lead to shooting up again and hence an exaggeration of the problem that may require hospitalization.

Death is more often caused by chronic toxicity of amphetamines or by social conditions surrounding the user. Viral hepatitis is not an uncommon condition among those who share unsterilized hypodermic equipment. Hepatic damage as a direct toxic effect of amphetamines has also been suggested. If not properly cared for, infection from skin lesions and endocarditis may also cause death in extreme cases.

Treatment of Acute Overdose. It is important to ascertain a medical history and an accurate description of the drugs that were consumed by the individual suspected of amphetamine toxicosis. As poly-drug use is increasingly becoming the trend, one cannot assume that only stimulants were taken. The physician's attitude is as important as the physical treatment—it must be nonjudgmental and nonthreatening. The patient must be made to feel safe and secure. A benzodiazepine or phenothiazine can be given to reduce severe anxiety and, in the case of amphetamine poisoning or overdose, ammonium chloride can be given to acidify the urine, allowing for more rapid excretion of the amphetamines (Morgan, 1981).

Legal Restrictions

Although the abuse of prescription drugs was not a major problem in 1938, the Federal Food, Drug, and Cosmetic Act was passed to control prescription as well as over-the-counter drugs. This act drew attention to the misuse and abuse of drugs that were basically safe when used as prescribed. Subsequent amendments of this act provided stronger regulations against the manufacture, distribution, and possession of prescribed drugs, in addition to setting up penalties for illegal traffic. The Durham-Humphrey Amendment of 1951 provided even stronger control of prescribed barbiturates and amphetamines. These drugs are now controlled by the Comprehensive Drug Abuse Prevention and Control Act of 1970, in which they are classified as Schedule II drugs.

Penalties vary from state to state, but in most states possession of unprescribed pep pills or depressants is a misdemeanor, with a $1 to $3,000 fine and a prison term of up to one year, although conviction for sale can bring from ten years to life imprisonment.

CAFFEINE

Caffeine is the stimulant found in coffee, tea, and soft drinks labeled cola or pepper. It is a chemical that belongs to the xanthine group of drugs. Xanthines are powerful amphetaminelike stimulants that can increase metabolism and create a highly awake and active state. They also trigger release of the stress hormones which, among other factors, are capable of increasing heart rate, blood pressure, and oxygen demands on the heart.

It appears that caffeine interferes with adenosine, a naturally occurring chemical that acts as a natural tranquilizer in the brain. It attaches to sites on neurons and makes them less sensitive to other neurotransmitters that would normally excite them. Caffeine also attaches to brain cells and blocks adenosine from acting on them, making the recepting cells more sensitive to chemical stimulation (Rinzler, 1983).

Coffee (*Coffea arabica*) is the most frequently consumed source of caffeine in America, with those over the age of seventeen drinking six or more cups of coffee or tea a day (Cheraskin & Ringsdorf, 1978). The average brewed six-ounce cup of coffee contains about 108 milligrams of caffeine. Caffeine consumption of more than 250 milligrams per day is considered by many to be excessive, since it can have the adverse effects on the body that were mentioned above. In addition, Cheraskin and Ringsdorf (1978) reported that a significantly higher number of psychological complaints existed among persons drinking seven or more cups a day than among those whose intake was more moderate. A lethal dose of caffeine could be consumed in the form of twenty cups of coffee, if drunk all at once. Frequent side effects of excessive coffee are anxiety, irritability, diarrhea, arrhythmias (irregular heart beats), and the inability to concentrate. Coffee may also stimulate the secretion of the digestive enzyme, pepsin, within the stomach. In an empty stomach, this enzyme, combined with the natural oils in coffee, can irritate the stomach lining, a reason why those who already have ulcers should cut out caffeine products.

Research is not clear as to whether fibrocystic (benign) breast disease in women is improved with the elimination of caffeine from the diet, but it does appear that such elimination is associated with less premenstrual breast tenderness (Rinzler,

1982). Research is also investigating a coffee-cancer link. Perhaps because of these health hazards, coffee consumption fell by 20 percent in the United States between 1974 and 1980.

Additional sources of the xanthine stimulants are tea (*Camilia theca*), cola beverages, chocolate, cocoa, some over-the-counter drugs such as aspirin and other analgesics, and preparations to keep you awake, such as No-Doz. A six-ounce cup of tea contains about 90 milligrams of caffeine as well as the other xanthines, theobromine and theophylline. Yet, tea does not contain the irritating oils found in coffee, and will not antidote homeopathic remedies as does coffee. Table 7.2 contains examples of caffeine products.

Caffeine Toxicity and Withdrawal

The following neurological effects are seen following caffeine toxicity:

1. Significant increase in norepinephrine secretion
2. Sensitizing of CNS postsynaptic receptors to catecholamines
3. Possible change in acetylcholine and serotonin activity
4. Changes in calcium metabolism

Caffeinism is a recent clinical term that characterizes the acute or chronic overuse of caffeine, with subsequent caffeine toxicity. The symptoms of the syndrome include anxiety, mood changes, sleep disturbances, and other psychophysical complaints. Symptoms are usually dose-related extensions of caffeine's usual effects. The Diagnostic and Statistical Manual of the American Psychiatric Association gives the following criteria for caffeine intoxication:

Table 7.2   Common Sources of Caffeine*

Beverages	
Brewed coffee	80–150 mg per 5–6 oz cup
Instant coffee	85–100 mg per 5–6 oz cup
Decaffeinated coffee	2–4 mg per 5–6 oz cup
Tea (bag)	42–100 mg per 5–6 oz cup
Tea (leaf)	30–75 mg per 5–6 oz cup
Cocoa	5–50 mg per 5–6 oz cup
Cola drinks	25–60 mg per 8–12 oz
Chocolate bar	about 25 mg per oz
Nonprescription (OTC) Drugs	
Analgesics	
Anacin, Cope, Darvon Compound, Empirin Compound, Midol, Vanquish	32 mg
Excedrin	60 mg
Stimulants	
No-Doz	100 mg
Vivarin	200 mg
Caffedrine	250 mg
Many Cold Preparations	32 mg

*Greden, 1981; Holbrook, 1983.

Recent consumption of caffeine, usually in excess of 250 milligrams, and at least five of the following symptoms:

1. restlessness
2. nervousness
3. excitement
4. insomnia
5. flushed face
6. diuresis
7. gastrointestinal complaints
8. muscle twitching
9. rambling flow of thought and speech
10. cardiac arrhythmia
11. periods of inexhaustibility
12. psychomotor agitation

These symptoms cannot be due to any other mental disorder (DSM III, 1980).

Withdrawal from caffeine occurs when the drug is abruptly discontinued by those who have become tolerant to it. Symptoms of withdrawal include headache, irritability, lethargy, mood changes, sleep disturbance, and mild physiological arousal (Greden, 1981).

Caffeine and Children

In regard to colas, cocoa, and chocolate, favored dietary components of children, it should be noted that a child's body is far less tolerant of chemical agents than is the adult body. It has been clearly shown that such foods in excess can stimulate the child's system, increasing anxiety and decreasing learning effectiveness. Generally speaking, six to eight ounces of coffee can have a hypermetabolic effect on children, while anything in excess of three cups of coffee for an adult will adversely affect his or her behavior, as well as increase the potential for stomach upset and irritation.

REFERENCES

Alles, G. A. "The comparative physiological action of Phenylethanolamine." *Journal of Pharmacology and Experimental Therapy* 32:121–133, 1927.

Burks, T. F. "Drug use by athletes," in G. G. Nahas and H. C. Frick II, eds. *Drug Abuse in the Modern World.* New York: Pergamon Press, 1980.

Cheraskin, E., and W. M. Ringsdorf, Jr. *Psychodietetics.* New York: Bantam Books, 1978.

"Cocaine: Middle class high." *Time,* July 6, 1981, p. 68.

Cohen, Sidney. "Health hazards of cocaine." *Drug Enforcement,* Fall 1982, pp. 10–13.

Cohen, Sidney. *The Substance Abuse Problems.* New York: Haworth Press, 1981.

"Crack Can Hook Users in Six Months, Study Finds," *The Denver Post,* May 15, 1986, p. 6A.

Diagnostic and Statistical Manual (DSM) III. Washington, D.C.: American Psychiatric Association, 1980.

DiCarlo, D. L. "International initiatives to control coca production and cocaine trafficking." *Drug Enforcement,* Fall 1982, pp. 6–9.

Ellinwood, E. H. "Amphetamines/anorectics," in R. I. Dupont et al., eds. *Handbook on Drug Abuse.* Washington, D.C.: U.S. Government Printing Office, 1979.

Ellinwood, E. H., and M. M. Kilbey. "Amphetamine stereotype." *Biological Psychiatry* 10(1):3–16, 1975.

Fortuna, J. L. "Identification of progressive cocaine abuse among adolescents." *Health Education,* Sept./Oct. 1983, pp. 3–6.

Greden, J. F. "Caffeinism and caffeine withdrawal," in J. H. Lowinson and P. Ruiz, eds. *Substance Abuse: Clinical Problems and Perspectives*. Baltimore, Md.: Williams and Wilkins, 1981, pp. 167–184.

Grinspoon, L., and P. Hedblom. *The Speed Culture: Amphetamine Use in America*. Cambridge, Mass.: Harvard University Press, 1975.

Hammer, S., and L. Hazleton. "Cocaine and the chemical brain." *Science Digest*, October 1984, pp. 58–61.

Holbrook, John M. "CNS stimulants," in Gerald Bennett et al., (eds.) *Substance Abuse: Pharmacological, Developmental, and Clinical Perspectives*. New York: Wiley, 1983.

Miller, J. D., et al. *National Survey on Drug Abuse: Main Findings 1982*. Rockville, Md.: NIDA, 1983.

Morgan, J. P. "Amphetamines," in J. H. Lowinson and J. P. Ruiz, eds. *Substance Abuse: Clinical Problems and Perspectives*. Baltimore, Md.: Williams and Wilkins, 1981.

National Institute on Drug Abuse (NIDA). *Stimulants and Cocaine*. Washington, D.C.: U.S. Government Printing Office, 1983.

NIDA. "The Epidemic of Drug Abuse: Research, Clinical and Social Perspective." Washington, D.C. U.S. Department of Health and Human Services, 1985.

Pennick, S. B. "Amphetamines in obesity." *Seminars in Psychiatry* 1:144, 1969.

Rinzler, C. A. "The coffee war." *American Health*, Sept./Oct. 1982, pp. 44–47.

Senay, E. C. *Substance Abuse Disorders*. Boston: John Wright, 1983.

Smith, D. E., et al. *Amphetamine Use, Misuse, and Abuse*. Boston: G. K. Hall, 1979.

Tennant, F. S., Jr. "Treatment of dependence upon stimulants and hallucinogens." *Drug and Alcohol Dependence* 11:111–114, 1983.

Van Dyke, Craig. "Cocaine," in J. H. Lowinson and P. Ruiz, eds. *Substance Abuse: Clinical Problems and Perspectives*. Baltimore, Md.: Williams and Wilkins, 1981.

Wrighton, J. D. "Doping in sport." *Nursing Times* 71(1):35–39, 1975.

SUGGESTED READINGS

Britt, David. *The All-American Cocaine Story*. Minneapolis, Minn.: CompCare, 1984.

DEA. "The growth of cocaine abuse." *Drug Enforcement*, Fall 1982, pp. 18–20.

Dorociak, J. D., and M. L. Vincent. "Use and knowledge of diet pills among female college students." *Health Education*, June/July 1985, pp. 14–16.

Gold, Mark. *800 Cocaine*. New York: Bantam, 1984.

Langer, J. H. "Preventing cocaine abuse." *Drug Enforcement*, Fall 1982, pp. 27–28.

O'Brien, R., and S. Cohen. *The Encyclopedia of Drug Abuse*. New York: Facts on File, Inc., 1984.

Plasket, B. J., and Ed Quillen. *The White Stuff: The Bottom Line on Cocaine*. New York: Dell, 1985.

Stern, Bert, et al. *The Coke Book*. New York: Berkeley Books, 1984.

Stone, Nannette, et al. *Cocaine Seduction and Solution*. New York: Clarkson N. Potter, 1984.

Zinberg, Norman. *Drug, Set, and Setting*. New Haven, Conn.: Yale University Press, 1984.

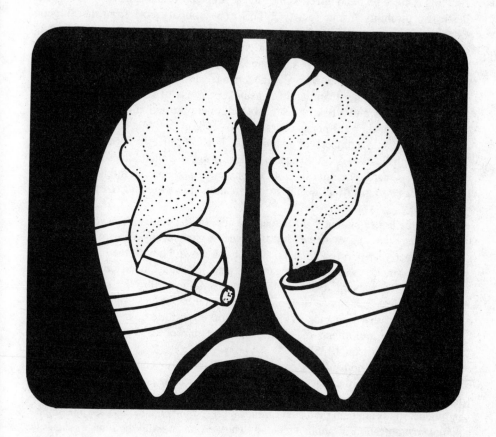

CHAPTER 8

SMOKING AND HEALTH

Next to caffeine, nicotine is the most widely used stimulant, despite its well-documented contributions to the national morbidity and mortality rates. "Cigarette smoking is currently recognized as the largest single preventable cause of premature death and disability in our society." This now familiar quote from the Surgeon General's report summarizes the voluminous research results that have clearly documented the health hazards of smoking cigarettes. The death rate for people who smoke two or more packages of cigarettes a day is twice as high as that for people who do not smoke. On the average, smokers have a risk of death from lung cancer that is ten times greater than that of nonsmokers; a risk of fatal heart attack that is two times greater; and a risk of death from chronic obstructive lung disease that is six times greater than for nonsmokers (Luoto, 1983).

Translated into numbers of individuals, it has been estimated that cigarette smoking contributes to 485,000 deaths each year in the United States from lung and other cancers, cardiovascular disease, emphysema, and chronic bronchitis. That is more than one-fourth of all deaths from all causes (*Smoking and Health Reporter,* 1985).

Nevertheless, apparently 40 percent of the adult population have chosen not only to disregard the evidence and continue to smoke but also to smoke more cigarettes per year (Gori, 1977). To subject one's own body to the harmful effects of tobacco smoke is generally regarded as an individual decision as well as a personal health problem. But not all the smoke is inhaled by the smoker. Smoke known as *sidestream smoke* may be inhaled by others in close proximity. Studies have indicated that nonsmokers living or working with smokers likewise suffer some of the harmful effects of tobacco smoke (Hinds et al., 1975; Iverson, 1975; Russell, 1975; Wilson 1975).

To protect the nonsmoker, ordinances have recently been passed that prohibit smoking in many public places, especially in enclosed areas such as elevators, and in many cities, it is "smokers to the back of the bus!" While smokers feel that their individual rights are being violated, groups representing nonsmokers are pushing for complete eradication of public smoking. Thus, even smoking the tobacco cigarette has become a controversial issue that has philosophical or moral overtones. One may choose to smoke, but does one have the right to alter the air that others must breathe?

The physiological consequences of smoking, the psychological and social forces for and against smoking, and the individual rights versus public safety controversy are issues that make the study of smoking and smoking behavior especially intriguing.

TOBACCO SMOKE CONSTITUENTS

At least 1,200 different toxic chemicals have been identified as products of tobacco smoke. Smoke is a mixture of hot air and gases that suspend small particles called *tars* in cigarette smoke. Many of the particles contain *carcinogens,* substances that are known to cause cancer. One such chemical, benzopyrene, is among the most potent carcinogens known. Also contained in the particulate matter are chemicals called *phenols,* which are thought to speed up or activate dormant cancer cells.

Normally, small particles that are inhaled are not problematic because the air passageways are cleansed constantly as millions of tiny hairlike whips (cilia) escalate mucus up the respiratory tract. If small particles get past the nasal trap (specially constructed wind tunnels that trap particles), they are snared by the sticky "mucal escalator" and are taken upward, there to be either swallowed or expectorated (see Fig. 8.1). If particles happen to get past this protective mechanism, there is a third line of defense within the lungs. Here white blood cells attack foreign particles and destroy or immobilize them. In an individual without constant overload on these protective devices, the lungs are normally cleared of dangerous materials. However, if a smoker constantly overloads this system, or if an individual works amid coal dust or other constantly inhaled particles, or if a person lives in an air-polluted environment, this system cannot remove particles effectively and there is danger of deleterious effects. Then as cigarette tar is deposited on normal respiratory tract cells, some chemicals in the smoke irritate the cells, some bring about the cancer process, and still others speed up this process.

Aiding the tars in their deleterious effects on the respiratory system is the action of various *gases* within cigarette smoke. The gases of importance here are ammonia, formaldehyde, acetaldehyde, and hydrogen cyanide (a strong poison in itself). These four gases combine to immobilize the cilia of the air passageways for six to eight hours, and it is obvious what happens to the mucal escalator when the ciliary movement ceases. No longer can particles be normally removed; hence, when they

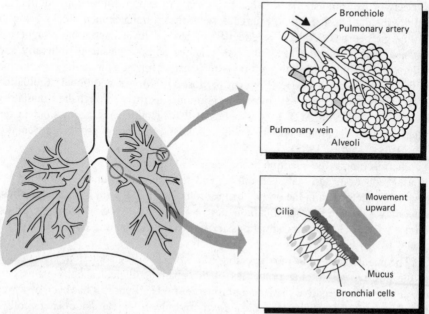

Fig. 8.1 The respiratory tree.

enter the respiratory tract, they can directly affect the mucus-producing and ciliary cells. It is as though two protective coverings have been removed and the underlying cells laid bare to the irritation of cigarette tars. Some of the cilia-producing and mucus-producing cells, then, are completely destroyed over a period of time. In an occasional smoker (e.g., one who smokes a pack or less a week) there may be sufficient time after each cigarette for the cilia to recover; however, a heavy smoker (a pack or more a day) rarely allows this recovery time, and permanent damage occurs. The absence of the cilia-mucus protective coating and clearing device makes the "smoker's cough" a necessity to clear phlegm, or particles large enough to affect the coughing mechanism, from the air passageways. The damage to these cells of the respiratory tract also makes the smoker more susceptible to upper respiratory infections and chronic bronchitis.

Another gas, carbon monoxide, produced by the incomplete oxidizing of carbon, is now being presented as perhaps the most hazardous of substances in tobacco. Physiological studies have shown the involvement of carbon monoxide in the atherosclerosis process, which will be discussed in the section on smoking and heart disease, while statistical studies have indicated that the concentration of carbon monoxide is the one factor most responsible for linking smoking and diseases of the cardiovascular system.

Another component of tobacco smoke is the drug, nicotine. Nicotine is a stimulant of the central nervous system which, like others in this class, produces distinct physiological and psychological changes in humans. While the behavioral effect attributed to nicotine has been observed for many years, more recently an intense research effort has been aimed at determining nicotine's mechanism of action. Nicotine has complex effects on the nervous system that are a result of its action on a variety of neurotransmitters. It has two phases of action, mimicking cholinergic activity in small doses, but with large doses it first stimulates then blocks firing of cholinergic neurons (Volle & Koelle, 1980). Several investigators have suggested that nicotine, mimicking acetylcholine, releases norepinephrine peripherally and perhaps centrally, and that this action is responsible for the stimulating effects that motivates smokers to smoke (Pradhan & Bose, 1978). An additional stimulating effect may result from a release of adrenal hormones, perhaps through the stimulatory action of nicotine on ACTH. It is believed that nicotine may also stimulate the release of beta endorphin and the enkephalins, and these may produce a tranquilizing effect (Karras, 1982).

Pharmacologically, nicotine seems capable of producing both stimulation and arousal reduction, and that such effects underlie the maintenance of smoking behavior. The determining factor may be the arousal state of the smoker. That is, those who smoke in high arousal situations derive a relaxing effect, whereas those who smoke mainly in low arousal situations are assisted in maintaining alertness (Myrsten et al., 1975).

The maintenance of a smoking habit, like any other drug addiction, is due partly to the positive reinforcing properties of the pharmacological agent, in this case nicotine, and the negative reinforcing properties of its absence. It has been observed that a variety of psychological, behavioral, and physiological disturbances follow the discontinuance of smoking. Among them are a craving for tobacco, irritability, restlessness, dullness, sleep disturbance, gastrointestinal disorder, drowsiness, headache, amnesia, anxiety, as well as impairment of concentration, judgment, and psychomotor performance (Jaffee & Jarvik, 1978). These effects seem to be primarily the result of the withdrawal of nicotine, although conclusive evidence is still lacking. Despite this lack of conclusive evidence, much of the research seems to be pointing in the direction of high nicotine involvement (Kuman & Lader, 1982). It has been well documented that smokers are able to sense the lack of nicotine in their systems and act to regulate that level. This phenomenon leads smokers to smoke more low nicotine cigarettes when they are substituted for their usual brand (if their original brand was higher in nicotine content) (Russell et al., 1975).

Nicotine seems to be the best candidate as the constituent in tobacco smoke that is most capable of producing central nervous system-mediated behavioral effects. Thus, smoking can be seen as a technique to self-administer the drug nicotine. The stimulation or high can result in a psychological dependence that may be a significant factor in habituation to cigarette smoking. Nicotine effects on the cardiovascular system are responsible for the strong statistical link between cigarette smoking and diseases of the cardiovascular system. The relationship between cigarette smoking and cardiovascular diseases will be considered in more detail later in this chapter.

The amount of tar and nicotine in tobacco is determined by such factors as plant strain, processing, origin of the plant, growth conditions, heat and humidity, and the aging process used. How much of the tar and nicotine gets into the system depends on how the tobacco is used: whether it is chewed, taken as snuff, or smoked, and of course, whether or not it is inhaled.

MOTIVATIONS FOR SMOKING

Most people start smoking for social reasons and continue out of habit or for satisfaction of a psychological need. Statistics reveal that most heavy smokers take up the habit before the age of twenty.

Smoking fits several of the most popular models designed to explain the use and abuse of drugs. The sociocultural model explains drug use from the meaning and significance a given society assigns to their use and users. It is obvious the initial use of cigarettes and smokeless tobacco by teen-agers has less to do with the pharmacology of tobacco and more with the sociocultural milieu surrounding its use. Smoking, at least in the initial stage of the habit, is a sociological phenomenon. Many people need oral gratification, but mainly those who have been oriented to smoking by family and/or friends will accept it as part of their lives. Research helps substantiate this by showing that ninth-graders exhibit smoking behavior identical to that of their best friends, and that children have a 50 percent greater chance of starting to smoke if their parents smoke. As students progress through high school and the sanctions against smoking are lessened, friendships among smokers and nonsmokers become commonplace. Even though high schoolers are better able to accept individual differences and are more internally motivated, parents, teachers, siblings, and peers still influence many to start smoking. Likewise, one cannot disregard smoking as a symbol of independence or of being grown-up.

The sudden disappearance of these motivators would still leave a very forceful one—that of advertising. Even without television advertising, cigarette manufac-turers spend more than 300 million dollars each year not only promoting one particular brand over another, but generally promoting the acceptance of smoking. A closer look at cigarette advertising clearly shows that very few facts about the cigarette are presented. The words are rather trite and meaningless, for few take the time to read them. The ads draw on the individual needs and memory of good feeling by presenting a picture of a pleasant and happy situation. Because there exists a universal need for love or at least for companionship, and a desire for escape and adventure, the scene often portrays an attractive couple obviously in love and enjoying themselves, or shows the rugged man out in the wilds of nature or the woman taking a much deserved minute of relaxation. The ads are designed to reduce one's anxieties about growing old, being alone, losing one's health, or one's sex drive. Or they may attempt to appeal to one's ego, by implying that he or she has something more than the next person. The impact of such advertising on potential smokers is substantial and it has been shown that sales are directly related to capital expenditure for advertising. Most smokers cannot even distinguish their favorite brand when blindfolded, which makes a taste factor highly questionable in choice of brand. A particular brand is chosen because of identification with the feeling portrayed by the advertisement or perhaps with someone who also smokes that particular brand.

But still the cigarette must deliver. Smoking must satisfy a need of the smoker, or smoking behavior would be extinguished. As previously mentioned, nicotine is a mild stimulant; thus a slight elevation in mood often results. This is usually interpreted as relaxation, a feeling of ease, of being in control of one's nervous energy. But usually it goes deeper than that. Smoking is abuse of a chemical substance and an abuse of oral gratification, and it usually develops into a habit. Although theories on the deeper psychological motivations are not well developed, studies on teen-age smokers suggest a relationship between the need to smoke and feelings of insecurity and low self-esteem.

The psychosocial model of drug use tends to put a major emphasis on the individual as the active agent in the drug-individual relationship. Drug use and drug users are a complex, dynamic interrelationship of psychological need and actual or perceived effects of the drug. Smokers continue to smoke primarily because of the perceived benefit derived from smoking. One theory postulates that smoking affects the stress-relaxation continuum. One group of smokers has been identified as the mood control group. It may be that these individuals possess certain personality variables that interact with nicotine and thus affect mood in a variety of ways (Golding & Mangan, 1982; Heinhold et al., 1982).

The relationship of stress to smoking has been frequently investigated. Smokers score consistently higher on nearly all anxiety measures than do nonsmokers (Williams et al., 1982; Rose et al., 1983). In addition, smokers are often seen as especially sensitive to stress because as a group they lack coping resources and resort to smoking in an attempt to cope (Billings & Moos, 1983). Subjective distress is one of the most frequently reported cues for smoking (Rose et al., 1983). Highly anxious smokers likewise have been found to have lowered expectations that they can produce desired outcomes, which translates into a lowered self-confidence.

Although failure to meet one's internal expectations is difficult to measure, it often results in low self-esteem, which has been observed more in smoking teen-agers than in nonsmoking ones. Since failure often results in diversion of efforts from assigned tasks, it is little wonder that teen-age smokers seem to experience more failure in school than do nonsmokers. Newman (1970; 1971) has found that smokers generally perceive themselves as not meeting the expectations of their parents. This perception gives rise to a certain amount of alienation, and it is not surprising that teen-age smokers are more apt to give "nonestablishment" responses to questionnaires. It has also been found that teen-age smokers tend to get lower grades, create more discipline problems, and participate less in school activities than do their nonsmoking counterparts. In a sociological milieu in which smoking is acceptable (in the teen-age world, often encouraged), smoking often becomes an unconscious attempt to gain acceptance.

Another classification of smoking behavior describes smoking as a dependence disorder. Such models as the addiction model and the maladjustive coping model view smoking as meaningless and as an unpleasant escape from withdrawal (Gottlieb, 1983).

The Horn-Waingrow Smoking Motives Questionnaire (pp. 159–160) addresses most schools of thought on motivations for smoking by assessing six factors identified as: sensory motor manipulation, stimulation, pleasure, tension reduction, habit, and addiction, with sensory motor stimulation being the weakest motivator and addiction the strongest.

Based on the motives for smoking, at least four different types of smokers have been identified. If you are a smoker, which type are you?

1. Do you smoke more in times of crisis? Have you frequently quit smoking, but seemed to lapse back into smoking behavior during particularly stressful times? Does your cigarette seem to be a sedative, reducing negative feelings of fear, anger, or nervousness? If so, you can be classfied as a *negative-effect smoker,* one who uses a cigarette as a crutch in times of crisis or as a sedative to relieve negative feelings such as nervousness, anger, shame, or disgust. This kind of need fulfillment offers tremendous reinforcement and smoking becomes a very pleasurable experience.

2. Do you find yourself lighting one cigarette before the other is completely out? Does the absence of a cigarette create an uncomfortable feeling? Do you constantly feel a strong desire to smoke? Then the chances are that you are an *addictive smoker,* one who uses cigarettes to satisfy needs or to solve problems, one who feels more normal with a cigarette than without one.

3. Do you really like to smoke and enjoy the taste of smoke? Does smoking relax you? Does it add enjoyment to a meal? Do you get pleasure from manipulating the cigarette, blowing smoke rings? Do you think you look older and more sophisticated when you smoke? If so, the chances are that you are a *positive-effect smoker,* often called a pleasure smoker.

4. If you are constantly running out of cigarettes, it is likely that you underestimate the amount you smoke. You are a chain smoker, but the habit is so automatic that the cigarette is out of the pack and into your mouth almost without conscious thought. You may find that cigarettes don't taste particularly good, but you seem to have one lit at all times. Often you light one up only to find one lit in the ashtray. If this behavior describes your smoking pattern, then what you have is a habit. The *habitual smoker* is an "automatic cigarette lighter-upper."

GIVING UP THE HABIT

There are more than 30 million former smokers in the United States and another 30 million people who have tried to quit but failed. The reasons why some people succeed and others fail is not well understood, but many researchers believe that success is a result of a combination of *personal motivation* and *an effective plan of action*.

There is not, nor is there ever likely to be, one model for a successful smoking cessation program. There are many examples of successful programs, but even the most successful program will not be effective for certain people in particular situations. Successful smoking cessation programs tend to include the following core elements (Girdano & Dusek, 1982):

Motivation or Commitment.   All effective programs focus on increasing the motivation of participants. Statistics show that 90 percent of smokers want to quit and 70 percent try to quit, but that is obviously not sufficient. Since the success rates of most programs are somewhere between 10 and 30 percent, program enrollment and financial commitment are not motivation enough. Motivation is an all-important factor, and can be increased via many strategies.

1. *Education about the harmful effects of smoking.* All smokers realize that smoking is harmful, but few know exactly why. Presentation of the basic physical effects in combination with related physiological mechanisms often help people to visualize the effects. However, research has shown that fear-provoking material is more likely to change the attitude of light and moderate smokers while alienating heavy smokers (Dyer, 1983). Strong fear-related messages work best when accompanied by a program that helps the smoker quit (Leventhal, 1973).

2. *Knowledge of psychological patterns of smokers.* Presenting information on how cigarettes satisfy psychological needs is often helpful. This can be accomplished in part by use of the quiz, "Why Do You Smoke?" which is distributed by the National Clearing House for Smoking and Health. For example, if this quiz reveals that smokers score high on the tension reduction section, they should concentrate on other more healthy ways of controlling the stress and tension in their lives. In addition, examination of the advertising/personal need interaction may also help the smoker understand how the habit developed.

3. *Examine intention.* Virtually everyone enrolled in a smoking cessation program wants to stop smoking, but that is usually not the only goal. Also, it is a negative type of motivation. It is usually better to have participants aspire to positive ends such as being more healthy (i.e., being without cancer, emphysema, or heart disease), having more energy and endurance, being more productive, being in control, more confident, more self-assured. Becoming a nonsmoker can be seen as a means to these ends. If participants want something positive and can see how their lives will be different when they achieve their goals, they are likely to be more motivated and committed to becoming a nonsmoker.

It also helps to examine barriers to becoming a nonsmoker, such as fear of weight gain, increase in nervousness, and absence of will power. These barriers can be reduced by providing the participants with specific information about how the program will help them to overcome these hurdles. It is also useful to identify the specific strengths of each participant that can be used to increase the likelihood of success. The motivation and commitment phase can be formalized by the signing of a contingency contract by the participant and the program leader. The contract should include a description of the reward the person will receive if he/she is successful. It can also be negatively based, including something the participant will have to give up if he/she is unsuccessful.

Breaking the Habit. No matter what the underlying psychological reason compelling an individual to smoke, a habit has developed, and a habit must be broken. A habit has been defined as a fixed behavior pattern, in this case, smoking; overlearned to the point of becoming automatic, accompanied by decreased awareness, not realizing how many cigarettes are smoked and not really being conscious of reaching for and lighting up a cigarette; and having an increased dependence on secondary gains, often relaxation or tension reduction (Glover et al., 1982). Smoking, like other addictions, has the following characteristics:

1. It acts as its own reinforcer
2. Tolerance is acquired
3. Physical dependence can develop
4. It produces contrasting moods
5. Arousal states can influence its use (Levison et al., 1983)

Programs that take these factors into account and provide opportunities to sufficiently and completely break the habit are usually more successful.

One of the key points is the diminished awareness. Smokers are seldom aware of how much they do smoke, so most programs include an initial record-keeping phase in which the smoker records all the cigarettes smoked and, in addition, usually provide information on the time, place, event, and mood. Self-recording increases awareness of how much is smoked and provides insight regarding the triggers to smoking.

A tapering-off process toward a targeted quitting date in three to six weeks is characteristic of many programs. During the tapering-off period, smokers try to create substitutions for the cigarettes not smoked and try to either avoid or otherwise diffuse triggers to smoking. Programs that do not deal with substitutions or do not teach skills to aid the smoker in handling triggers to smoking are less likely to succeed. Effective programs recognize that (1) it is easier to give up something if it is replaced with something else, and (2) smoking is an addiction similar in many ways to addictive patterns that develop with alcoholism, drug addiction, and overeating.

Programs often use behavior modification techniques associated with the buying, carrying, or handling of the cigarette. Many also attempt to move smokers progressively to cigarettes that are lower in tar and nicotine. The technique of moving to a lower tar and nicotine cigarette is the subject of concern for it has been found that if the number of cigarettes is not controlled, smokers tend to increase the depth of inhalation to compensate for the lower nicotine levels. The final result may be more harmful if more cigarettes are smoked because the smoker may be exposed to more tars and gases (Sepkovic et al., 1983).

A Healthy Life Style.   A third phase of an effective program is all too often not included in smoking cessation programs. This oversight undoubtedly contributes to the high failure rates reported in the literature. This phase focuses on psychological needs that smoking has traditionally satisfied. The goal is to extinguish these needs and develop life-style skills that will help the nonsmoker remain a nonsmoker. The basic components are:

   1. *Relaxation and stress management skills.* Part of almost every smoker's habit is the use of cigarettes to control one or more of the following factors:

1. Excess anxiety	4. Low self-esteem
2. Excess anger	5. Depression
3. Stressful life style	6. Inability to relax

   All of these factors can be aided by a good stress management program. It is difficult to imagine a smoking cessation program that does not include this component. Many programs double their duration in order to accommodate stress management skills and provide social support in the first three weeks after the last cigarette—the most likely period for relapse. The importance of these considerations to cessation success are emerging in the literature. A study by Gunn (1983) showed a high correlation between the number of recent stressful life changes and the frequency of dropping out of a smoking cessation program. This is not difficult to understand as it has long been known that life changes lead to increased anxiety and that many smokers use smoking as a means of alleviating anxiety.

   It is becoming increasingly obvious that motivation alone is not the only contributing factor in smoking cessation. Factors such as age, number of cigarettes smoked per day, length of years of smoking, number of prior attempts to quit, and a host of stress and life-style components should be considered when designing stress management programs (Garvey, 1983).

   2. *Diet.* This is an especially important life-style component for smokers, for many are nervous eaters who have substituted smoking for eating. Vacuums tend to be filled, so when smoking stops, eating and weight gain problems emerge. This has created a fear of success among weight-conscious smokers, many of whom are women. Paying close attention to diet and offering diet and weight management counseling is essential to the success of most smoking cessation programs.

3. *Exercise.* Exercise is not only an integral part of a healthy life style, it also may be an essential part of smoking cessation programs because it:

1. Builds confidence and self-esteem
2. Reduces anxiety and excess stress
3. Burns calories
4. Is antithetical to the physical deterioration caused by smoking

All these activities tend to help the smoker in his/her efforts to kick the habit.

After Support. The fourth phase is often neglected, but evidence shows that this phase can decrease the magnitude of recidivism. Most people who quit smoking and then start again do so within a few weeks of quitting (there is a 60–70 percent failure rate in the first three months after quitting). Follow-up data indicate that many programs lose 50 to 80 percent of their successful participants during this critical period. It makes little sense to allow this to occur when recidivism could be reduced through attention and support in the form of:

1. *Relapse training.* Two important factors are related to relapse. First, the need to smoke is still present. Even though the smokers have changed the overt smoking behavior, they either did not successfully eliminate the triggers, or cues, to smoke, or they did not establish a new behavior that acts as a substitute for smoking when the triggers occur. Secondly, the all-or-nothing attitude of smokers helps make them feel like total failures if they have one or two cigarettes after the program is over. This undermines their self-image, and a vicious cycle is initiated which further increases the motivation to smoke.

Relapse control consists of:

1. Not adopting an all-or-none attitude
2. Examining each relapse situation as a separate incident. Look for triggers, feelings, emotions, etc., and find new ways to handle them next time
3. Review the motivation and commitment portion of the program

2. *Support groups.* Successful programs often establish "smokers anonymous" meetings which offer ongoing support for ex-smokers for up to a year after the program ends. In addition to providing a forum for talking over common problems, these meetings encourage the development of positive life-style skills. They also create a new social circle, which fills the needs of many individuals.

Summary. The process of becoming a nonsmoker consists of these basic components:

1. Increasing motivation to become a nonsmoker
2. Breaking the habit
3. Conscious and subconscious substitution of more healthy behaviors for the smoking behavior
4. Building a healthy life style which is incongruous with smoking
5. Providing for relapse training and/or ongoing support which lasts, if possible, for one year after the program

Time, resources, and philosophy may dictate placing more emphasis on any one of the components outlined above. However, inclusion of all of them enhances the chances of success.

HEALTH CONSEQUENCES OF SMOKING

Heart Disease

Most of the excess deaths among smokers (deaths beyond the number encountered among nonsmokers) are due to the *drug effects of nicotine* on the circulatory system, which lead to heart disease. Coronary artery disease accounts for about 45 percent of the total excess deaths related to smoking; then, if one adds the excess deaths from other heart diseases, general arteriosclerosis, and hypertensive heart disease, the total of preventable deaths associated with heart disease accounts for more than 50 percent of all excess deaths in smokers.

Nicotine, as a stimulant, affects the human system in a manner similar to that of the amphetamines; that is, it increases heart rate and blood pressure, and other changes occur that are normally attributed to the sympathetic nervous system. However, nicotine works in a twofold manner to stimulate the system. First, it directly affects cholinergic nerve synapses by mimicking acetylcholine. This not only elicits great excitability but also blocks out meaningful impulses that would normally be directed by acetylcholine. After initially exciting these nerve fibers, nicotine "overloads" the ability of the nerve cells to respond, and a blocking effect takes place at the synapse (Astrup, 1974; Cellina et al., 1975).

The second way in which nicotine affects the nervous system is through its action on the adrenal glands. It causes these endocrines to release adrenal hormones, which circulate in the blood, creating excitation of the sympathetic nervous system. In addition to exciting the adrenals, nicotine releases these same hormones from other sites as well, thus completing its sympathomimetic action.

When a smoker takes nicotine into the lungs, the substance is quickly taken up by the blood and carried to all parts of the body. Then all these excitatory effects caused by nicotine combine to overwork the heart. If a smoker's heart is exposed to these events ten, twenty, or more times a day (often in rapid succession), it will almost certainly be adversely affected.

Nicotine is also thought to be responsible for the elevated plasma-free fatty acids found in smokers. The exact physiological mechanism has not been determined, but sympathetic nervous system and adrenocortical stimulation is known to be activated by nicotine, and must play an important role in the release of fatty acids from adipose deposits.

The carbon monoxide in the gaseous phase of cigarette smoke is thought to decrease significantly cardiac work capacity. Hemoglobin picks up the carbon monoxide from the lungs forming carboxyhemoglobin, which alters myocardial metabolism, interferes with oxygen delivery, and results in myocardial hypoxia (Castleden et al., 1974). The carboxyhemoglobin is a result of the incomplete combustion of the organic material in the cigarette. The carbon is oxidized to carbon monoxide gas and inhaled. The affinity of hemoglobin for carbon monoxide is approximately 245 times greater than its affinity for oxygen. Thus, carbon monoxide readily displaces oxygen from hemoglobin, which can harm cardiac tissue in several ways. Hemoglobin tied up with carbon monoxide cannot carry oxygen, so less oxygen will be delivered to the heart. Numerous studies have shown that this decreased oxygenation results in decreased work capacity. It should be noted that to the normal healthy heart this decrease in oxygenation is of minor consequence, unless the heart is functioning near capacity, as during exercise. However, the smoker's heart is not likely to be normal and healthy, and carbon monoxide has much to do with that cardiac deterioration as it significantly accelerates the atherosclerotic process. Carbon monoxide increases the permeability of the endothelial (inner lining) layer of the cardiovascular system. As a result, plasma leaks into the tissue causing edema, which widens the gap between endothelial cells. The edema sets in motion a buildup of mucopolysaccharides, which facilitates precipitation of lipoproteins and the eventual accumulation of lipids in plaques.

Carbon monoxide may be of more significance than nicotine in the development of cardiovascular disease among smokers and is also one of the dangerous elements of polluted air in our cities, which affects smokers and nonsmokers alike. It is of interest to note that the trend toward low-nicotine cigarettes is in reality not of much value in the prevention of cardiovascular disease, since it is impossible to reduce carbon monoxide content.

In summary, we can say that cigarette smoking is related to cardiovascular disease in the following areas:

1. Increased heart rate
2. Increased peripheral vasoconstriction, which in turn causes increased blood pressure
3. Release of fatty acids from adipose stores, thus elevating the level of circulating fats, which are known precursors of atherosclerotic plaques
4. Reduction of blood clotting time
5. Reduction of the amount of oxygen delivered to the tissues by the carbon monoxide content of smoke
6. Increase in edema, cell separation, and deposit of lipids in plaques

Lung Cancer

Serious chronic health problems other than heart disease that are related to cigarette smoking are due mainly to the particulate and gaseous contents of smoke rather than to the sympathomimetic action of nicotine.

The second major cause of excess deaths due to smoking is cancer, most of that being lung cancer. Lung cancer started to become increasingly apparent in the 1920s and 1930s and has grown into a full-blown epidemic since that time. This outbreak of lung cancer not so curiously followed the sharp rise in cigarette use in the United States during World War I—and it followed it by approximately twenty years, the average time involved in producing cancer. To support this temporal theory of lung cancer, it was found that Iceland produced the same pattern with a sharp rise in cigarette consumption during World War II, followed by a lung cancer "epidemic" about twenty years later. In 1974 approximately 40,000 people died of lung cancer in the United States, and for middle-aged men, cancer represents the second leading cause of death.

As is well documented now, cigarette tars or particulate matter (the particles enabling one to see smoke) that come into constant contact with the respiratory tract cause a slow change in cells of that system. In time, this change may cause the cell to reproduce a cell that is a modification of the original productive one. New cells without productive function are cancer cells—they multiply rapidly and compete with normal cells for nutrients, slowly killing off and replacing normal cells, and normal function of the system is affected.

Carcinoma of the bronchi accounts for approximately 95 percent of the malignant tumors found in the lung. Both lungs have an equal chance of being affected. About 65 percent of the bronchial tumors arise from the main stem or first bronchi division, the section that is the first to be exposed as the smoke enters the lungs. At this point the smoke is at its fullest concentration, but particles smaller than 0.4 micron will settle out and become deposited, especially on ridges and bifurcations, just as the sediment in a river forms a delta.

Lung cancer begins with the inhalation of carcinogenic material. The paralyzed cilia cannot function to remove particles; thus tar is deposited on the respiratory passageways and the tar and mucus buildup begins to attack the underlying epithelial tissues. Smoking alters the epithelium of the tracheobronchial tubes. Lesions consist of basal cell hyperplasia with alterations of the normal epithelial cells into a more atypical cell, sometimes indistinguishable from cancer cells. These atypical epithelial cells may be the site of cellular penetration of the constituents of smoke. Such lesions have been experimentally produced in smoking dogs and some have ultimately developed into cancer.

This entire process takes time, usually twenty to thirty years. Early symptoms may be a change in a chronic cough that the smoker may have had for years, fever, chills, an increase in sputum production, spitting of blood, or a wheeze. A worsening of these symptoms indicates that the bronchiole obstruction has increased and there is a loss of lung volume. Symptoms in the advanced stage include weight loss, anorexia, nausea, vomiting, and a generalized weakness. The longer the duration of symptoms, the more likely the lesion is not surgically removable; survival time for these cases varies from five to fourteen months after diagnosis. Thirty to fifty percent prove to be treatable; of those treated, about 20 percent survive for five years. In other words, if bronchogenic carcinoma is diagnosed in ten people, it is probable that six will die within fourteen months, and two within two to four years, while the last two will die during the fifth year.

Emphysema

Another lung ailment not well known at the turn of the century, but rapidly making its presence felt as a smoking-related disease, is emphysema.

Emphysema is characterized by the rupture of alveolar (air sac) walls; this reduces the surface area in which gas exchange can take place (see Fig. 8.1). Large pockets separated by scar tissue are formed, elasticity of the air sacs is lost, and the emphysema victim finds it very difficult to release the air taken into the lungs.

Here is the emphysematic process in more detail. In a healthy individual, when air is taken into the lungs, the bronchial passageways expand. Gas exchange (carbon dioxide from the tissues is exchanged for oxygen) then takes place in lung capillaries that perfuse the millions of tiny air sacs throughout the lungs. Then the stale gases are exhaled with the help of pressure exerted on the lungs by the rib cage and diaphragm and also by virtue of the elastic rebound of the air sacs and air passageways that were stretched upon inhalation. This process is normally a simple, automatic one; but in individuals with an accumulation of cigarette tars (or other particulate matter such as coal dust) in their bronchial tubes, air is allowed in by the normal expansion of the passageways and then is trapped because of the artificial blocking agent—the tar that has accumulated over a period of time. Pressure builds up in the blocked-off structures, and tissues rupture, making large areas out of many small ones. Scar tissue then develops, decreasing the elasticity of that area, so that it becomes even more difficult for the individual to exhale. It is not uncommon that an emphysema patient cannot blow out a match held only an inch or two in front of his or her mouth. Emphysema victims become barrel-chested as a result of labored exhalation, but gradually their increasing inability to exchange gases makes the remainder of their lives an agonizing effort.

In 1970, Hammond et al. ended any remaining doubts concerning the relationship between smoking and emphysema. Beagles were taught to smoke cigarettes and were exposed to various levels of tar and nicotine as they smoked every morning and afternoon for 875 days. The results clearly showed that fibrosis of the lung increased with exposure to higher tar and nicotine levels, as did the incidence and severity of emphysema. No emphysema was detected in the nonsmoking dogs. Another classic study was conducted by Auerbach et al. (1972), but this was an investigation of human lung sections from autopsies. They found that 90 percent of nonsmokers had no emphysema, 47 percent of pipe and cigar smokers had no emphysema, 13 percent who smoked less than one pack per day had no emphysema, and 0.3 percent who smoked more than one pack per day had no emphysema.

Chronic Bronchitis

Chronic bronchitis frequently precedes or accompanies emphysema. It is characterized by excessive mucus production in the bronchi of the lungs. The inflammation and hypersecretion of bronchi cells results in increased sputum and eventually a cough develops to remove the material that would normally be removed by ciliary action. Although chronic bronchitis has been found in persons exposed to extreme air pollution, coal dust, etc., the incidence in smokers is twenty times that in nonsmokers and is greater in smokers who leave their cigarettes dangling from the lips between puffs.

Smoking and Pregnancy

From the preceding discussions on the relationship between smoking and physiological functions, it should be obvious that a developing fetus would also be affected. It has been estimated that approximately one-third of the women in the United States of childbearing age are smokers. Although not definitely known, it is estimated that only 5 to 10 percent of these women quit smoking during pregnancy. Listed below are some of the most important findings related to smoking and pregnancy. Most are related to the effects of nicotine, but the polycyclic hydrocarbons (especially benzopyrene) have been found to reach the fetus (Colley, 1974; Colley et al., 1974; Meyer et al., 1974).

1. Cigarette smoking during pregnancy causes a reduction in infant birth weight.
2. Cigarette smoking is related to significantly higher fetal and neonatal mortality.
3. Cigarette smoking is associated with an increase in spontaneous abortions.
4. Preliminary study suggests that nicotine passes into the milk of lactating women; however, acute effects on the nursing infant have not yet been established.

Smoking and Peptic Ulcer

Statistical relationships have been established between smoking and the incidence of peptic ulcers. It has also been shown that smokers have a higher mortality rate from peptic ulcers than do nonsmokers. Nicotine has been found to inhibit pancreatic bicarbonate secretion, and it is believed that this mechanism is responsible for the potentiation of acute duodenal ulcer formation (Jedrychowski et al., 1974).

Pipe and Cigar Smoking

Mortality statistics show only a slight increase in health risk in pipe and cigar smokers when compared to nonsmokers. While this may give a sense of security to the pipe or cigar smoker, the feeling may be a bit premature. The ailments that seem to affect pipe and cigar smokers (cancer of the lip, oral cancer, cancer of the larynx, cancer of the esophagus, etc.) are easier to detect than cancer of the lung; treatment begins sooner, and thus, relatively fewer deaths occur than in lung cancer.

Only small differences exist in the tobacco of cigarettes, cigars, and pipes. The primary difference lies in how the tobacco is used—mainly in the inhalation. Nicotine is absorbed into the bloodstream from the lungs, but it can also be absorbed from the lining of the oral cavity (but in significantly smaller amounts). Tars that cannot be washed from the bronchial lining can be largely eliminated from the oral cavity. However, tars will mix with saliva and be swallowed, giving rise to the increased incidence of stomach and urinary bladder cancer found in smokers.

Contrary to common belief, cigarette smokers have a higher incidence of oral cancer than do pipe or cigar smokers. Cigarette smokers who smoke pipes and cigars are more apt to inhale the smoke of the latter and do so more often than those individuals who smoke a pipe and/or cigars exclusively.

Smokeless Tobacco

There has been a great resurgence in the use of all forms of smokeless tobacco in the United States. The sales of smokeless tobacco have increased about 11 percent each year since 1974, with an estimated 22 million users in the United States. There are several forms of tobacco which are either chewed or sniffed. One called *snuff* is a finely ground tobacco sold in circular cans. The most common method of ingestion is by placing a pinch of snuff between the lip and gum. Snuff is also placed on the back of the hand and sniffed through the nose. Chewing tobacco is loose leafed and sold in a pouch. It is also placed between the lip and gum for a period of time and then expectorated. Another type is the plug that is sold in brick form, from which the user cuts or bites off a piece.

The hemodynamic changes, primarily increase in heart rate and blood pressure, have been observed in three to five minutes. These physiological changes have not been shown to increase performance, contrary to claims by the leading proponents of its use (male athletes). A review of the literature reveals that the use of smokeless tobacco has the potential for causing cancer of the oral cavity, pharynx, larynx, and esophagus. Smokeless tobacco can produce significant detrimental effects on the soft and hard tissues of the mouth, causing bad breath, discolored teeth, gum recession, and periodontal destruction. Smokeless tobacco can contribute to cardiovascular disease in the same manner as smoked tobacco and is especially contraindicated in individuals with high blood pressure (Glover et al., 1984).

Passive Smoking

As was mentioned in the introduction to this chapter, smoking marijuana is not the only drug controversy now raging in our country. The use of tobacco cigarettes in public is now a disputed issue centering on individual rights: the rights of the smoker to smoke versus the rights of the nonsmoker to breathe air unpolluted by smoke. The scientific studies of the 1960s clearly showed that nonsmokers in the presence of smokers are also affected by the smoke. The smoking of one cigarette releases into the air surrounding the smoker approximately 70 milligrams of particulates and 25 milligrams of carbon monoxide. The level of carbon monoxide in smoke-filled rooms often reaches 80 parts per million and is considered to be hazardous by the Environmental Protection Agency, and to exceed the limits set for occupational exposure. Thus, very often, smoke-filled automobiles and smoke-filled rooms are in violation of pure air quality standards. To make matters worse, often the sidestream smoke is more potent than that inhaled by the smoker, since the sidestream temperatures are cooler and only incomplete oxidation of some constituents of the smoke occurs.

An increased knowledge of the hazards of smoking in general and the definitive studies of sidestream smoke, combined with an increased sensitivity for air pollution problems and the movement toward individual rights, have led to pressure against smoking in public. The nonsmoking public is armed, they have a bill of rights (see Fig. 8.2), and the war has begun.

CONCLUSION

Although 10 million Americans have quit smoking in the last five years, approximately 40 percent of adult Americans continue to smoke. Smoking is both a sociological and psychological phenomenon. It is a learned behavior, but satisfaction of psychological need and oral gratification create a positive reinforcement to continue. Reports have established beyond a doubt that smoking is harmful to the health

Fig. 8.2 Nonsmoker's bill of rights.

of smokers and suggest that it is harmful to the persons around the smoker. Smoking-related diseases are the most preventable known to our society, but knowledge of successful cessation methods still provides little competition against the seemingly strong motivation to smoke.

In his foreword to the *Research Monograph on Smoking Behavior,* William Pollin, director of the Division of Research, National Institutes of Health, emphatically stated that smoking is the largest preventable cause of premature death, illness, and disability. And to emphasize his point, he offered the following statistical comparisons, which provide a fitting conclusion to this chapter.

Most people, including health officials, are startled when the figures on smoking damage are put into perspective. For example, the number of people who annually die prematurely from smoking is estimated at 300,000. For comparison, annual automobile fatalities are estimated at about 55,000, overdose deaths attributed to barbiturates are estimated at about 1,400, and to heroin at about 1,750. Over 37 million people (one of every six Americans alive today) will die from cigarette smoking years before they otherwise would. If tobacco-related deaths were eliminated, there would be:

- 485,000 Americans each year who would not die prematurely;
- ⅓ fewer male deaths from 35 to 59;
- 85 percent fewer deaths from bronchitis or emphysema;
- ⅓ fewer deaths from arteriosclerosis;
- ⅓ fewer deaths from heart disease;
- 90 percent fewer deaths from cancer of the trachea and lungs;
- 50 percent fewer deaths from cancer of the bladder.

Self-Test: WHY DO YOU SMOKE?*

Here are some statements made by people to describe what they get out of smoking cigarettes. How often do you feel this way when smoking? Circle one number for each statement. Important: *Answer every question.*

		Always	Fre-quently	Occa-sionally	Seldom	Never
A.	I smoke cigarettes in order to keep myself from slowing down.	5	4	3	2	1
B.	Handling a cigarette is part of the enjoyment of smoking it.	5	4	3	2	1
C.	Smoking cigarettes is pleasant and relaxing.	5	4	3	2	1
D.	I light up a cigarette when I feel angry about something.	5	4	3	2	1
E.	When I have run out of cigarettes I find it almost unbearable until I can get them.	5	4	3	2	1
F.	I smoke cigarettes automatically without even being aware of it.	5	4	3	2	1
G.	I smoke cigarettes to stimulate me, to perk myself up.	5	4	3	2	1
H.	Part of the enjoyment of smoking a cigarette comes from the steps I take to light up.	5	4	3	2	1
I.	I find cigarettes pleasurable.	5	4	3	2	1
J.	When I feel uncomfortable or upset about something, I light up a cigarette.	5	4	3	2	1
K.	I am very much aware of the fact when I am not smoking a cigarette.	5	4	3	2	1
L.	I light up a cigarette without realizing I still have one burning in the ashtray.	5	4	3	2	1
M.	I smoke cigarettes to give me a "lift."	5	4	3	2	1
N.	When I smoke a cigarette, part of the enjoyment is watching the smoke as I exhale it.	5	4	3	2	1

*Test written by Daniel H. Horn, National Clearinghouse for Smoking and Health, Department of Health and Human Services.

Self-Test: WHY DO YOU SMOKE?* (continued)

		5	4	3	2	1
O.	I want a cigarette most when I am comfortable and relaxed.	5	4	3	2	1
P.	When I feel "blue" or want to take my mind off cares and worries, I smoke cigarettes.	5	4	3	2	1
Q.	I get a real gnawing hunger for a cigarette when I haven't smoked for a while.	5	4	3	2	1
R.	I've found a cigarette in my mouth and didn't remember putting it there.	5	4	3	2	1

SCORING

1. Enter the number you have circled for each question in the spaces below, putting the number you have circled to Question A over line A, to Question B over line B, etc.
2. Add the 3 scores on each line to get your totals. For example, the sum of your scores over lines A, G, and M gives you your score on Stimulation, lines B, H, and N give the score on Handling, etc.

TOTALS

___ + ___ + ___ =	
A G M	STIMULATION
___ + ___ + ___ =	
B H N	HANDLING
___ + ___ + ___ =	
C I O	PLEASURABLE RELAXATION
___ + ___ + ___ =	
D J P	CRUTCH: TENSION REDUCTION
___ + ___ + ___ =	
E K Q	CRAVING: PSYCHOLOGICAL ADDICTION
___ + ___ + ___ =	
F L R	HABIT

Scores can vary from 3 to 15. A score of 11 and above is high; a score of 7 and below is low.

REFERENCES

Astrup, P. "Tobacco smoking and coronary disease." *Acta Cardiologica* Suppl 20:105–117, 1974.

Auerbach, O., et al. "Relation of smoking and age to emphysema. Whole-lung section study." *New England Journal of Medicine* 286(16):653–657, 1972.

Billings, Andrew G., and Rudolf H. Moos. "Social-environmental factors among light and heavy cigarette smokers: a controlled comparison with non-smokers." *Addictive Behaviors* 8:381–391, 1983.

Castelden, C. M., et al., "Variations in carboxyhemoglobin levels in smokers." *British Medical Journal* 4(5947):736–738, 1974.

Cellina, G. U., et al. "Direct arterial pressure, heart rate, and electrocardiogram during cigarette smoking in unrestricted patients." *American Heart Journal* 89(1):18–25, 1975.

Colley, J. R. T., "Respiratory symptoms in children and parental smoking and phlegm production." *British Medical Journal* 9:201–204, 1974.

Colley, J. R. T., et al. "Influence of passive smoking and parental phlegm on pneumonia and bronchitis in early childhood." *British Medical Journal* 2:1031–1034, 1974.

Dyer, Nadien. "Smokers' luck: a shocking programme changes attitudes to smoking." *Addictive Behaviors* 8:43–49, 1983.

Garvey, Arthur, et al. "Smoking cessation in a prospective study of healthy adult males." *American Journal of Public Health* 73(4):446–449, 1983.

Girdano, Daniel, and Dorothy Dusek. *Becoming a Non-Smoker*. Winter Park, Colo.: Health Promotion Resources, 1982.

Glover, Elbert D., et al. "Cigarette smoking: addiction and/or habit?" *Health Values* 6(2):26–30, 1982.

Glover E. D., et al. "Smokeless tobacco research: an interdisciplinary approach." *Health Values* 8(3) May/June: 21–25, 1984.

Golding, J., and G. L. Mangan. "Arousing and de-arousing effects of cigarette smoking under conditions of stress and mild sensory isolation." *Psychophysiology* 19:449–456, 1982.

Gottlieb, Nell H. "The determination of smoking types: evidence for a socio-pharmacological continuum." *Addictive Behaviors* 8(1):47–51, 1983.

Gori, G. B. "Approaches to the reduction of total particulate matter (TPM) in cigarette smoke," in E. L. Wynder et al., eds. *Modifying the Risk for the Smoker*. Washington, D. C.: DHEW publication (NIH), 1977.

Gunn, Robert C. "Smoking clinic failure and recent life stress." *Addictive Behaviors* 8:83–87, 1983.

Hammond, E. C., et al. "Effects of cigarette smoking on dogs." *Archives of Environmental Health* 21:740–753, 1970.

Heinhold, Jerilyn W., et al. "Retrospective analysis in smoking cessation research." *Addictive Behaviors* 7(4):347–353, 1982.

Hinds, W. C., et al. "Concentrations of nicotine and tobacco smoke in public places." *New England Journal of Medicine* 292(16):844–845, 1975.

Iverson, N. T. "Smoke and heat." *New England Journal of Medicine* 293(1):47, 1975.

Jaffee, J. H., and M. E. Jarvik. "Tobacco use and tobacco use disorder," in M. A. Lipton et al., eds. *Psychopharmacology: A Generation of Progress*. New York: Raven Press, 1978, pp. 1665–1676.

Jedrychowski, W., et al. "Association between the occurrence of peptic ulcers and tobacco smoking." *Public Health* 88(4):195–200, 1974.

Karras, Athan. "Neurotransmitter and neuropeptide correlates of cigarette smoking," in W. B. Essman and Luigi Valzelli, eds. *Neuropharmacology: Clinical Applications*. New York: Spectrum Publications, 1982, pp. 41–66.

Kuman, R., and M. Lader. "Nicotine and the regulation of smoking behavior," in W. B. Essman and Luigi Valzelli, eds. *Neuropharmacology: Clinical Applications*. New York: Spectrum Publications, 1982, pp. 67–103.

Leventhal, Howard. "Changing attitudes and habits to reduce risk factors in chronic disease." *The American Journal of Cardiology* 31:571–577, 1973.

Levison, Peter K., et al., eds. *Commonalities in Substance Abuse and Habitual Behavior*. Lexington, Mass.: Lexington Books, 1983.

Luoto, Joanne. "Reducing the health consequences of smoking." *Public Health Reports* 98(1):34–39, 1983.

Meyer, M. B., et al. "The interrelation of maternal smoking and increased preinatal mortality with other risk factors." *American Journal of Epidemiology* 100(6):443–452, 1974.

Myrsten, A. L., et al. "Immediate effects of cigarette smoking as related to different smoking habits." *Perceptual and Motor Skills* 40:515–523, 1975.

Pollin, W. "Foreword." *Research on Smoking Behavior*. Washington, D.C.: National Institute on Drug Abuse Monograph, 1977.

Pradhan, S. N., and J. Bose. "Interactions among central neurotransmitters," in M. Lipton et al., eds. *Psychopharmacology: A Generation of Progress*. New York: Raven Press, 1978, pp. 271–281.

Rose, Jed E., A. Srijati, and M. E. Murray. "Cigarette smoking during anxiety-provoking and monotonous tasks." *Addictive Behaviors* 8(4):353–359, 1983.

Russell, M. A. "Blood and urinary nicotine in nonsmokers." *Lancet* 1(7905):527, 1975.

Russell, M. A. H., et al. "Plasma nicotine levels after smoking cigarettes with high, medium, and low nicotine yields." *British Medical Journal* 2:414–416, 1975.

Sepkovic, D. W., et al. "Cigarette smoking as a risk for cardiovascular disease." *Addictive Behaviors* 8:59–66, 1983.

Smoking and Health Reporter. Bloomington, Ind.: National Interagency Council on Smoking and Health, 2(2), April 1985.

Volle, R. L., and G. B. Koelle. "Ganglionic stimulating and blocking agents," in L. S. Goodman and A. Gillman, eds. *The Pharmacological Basis of Therapeutics*. New York: Macmillan, 1980.

Williams, S. G., A. Hudson, and C. Redd. "Cigarette smoking, manifest anxiety and somatic symptoms." *Addictive Behaviors* 7(4):427–428, 1982.

Wilson, D. G. "Mental effects of secondhand smoke." *New England Journal of Medicine* 292(11): 596, 1975.

SUGGESTED READINGS

Carney, R. M., and A. P. Goldberg. "Weight gain after cessation of cigarette smoking." *New England Journal of Medicine* 310:614–616, 1984.

Christesen, B. *Smoking: A Research Update, Part 1: The Facts*. New York: Pleasantville Media, 1984.

Christesen, B. *Smoking: A Research Update, Part 2: The Issues*. New York: Pleasantville Media, 1984.

Department of Health and Human Services. *Prevention in Adulthood: U.S. Surgeon Gener-*

al's Report on Smoking and Health. Washington, D.C.: Department of Health and Human Services, 1982.

Dicken, C. "Sex roles, smoking, and smoking cessation." *Journal of Health and Social Behavior* 19:324–334, 1982.

Jacobs, D. R., and S. Gottenborg. "Smoking and weight: the Minnesota Lipid Research Clinic." *American Journal of Public Health* 71:391–397, 1981.

Kannel, William B. "Update on the role of cigarette smoking in coronary artery disease." *American Heart Journal* 101:319–328, 1981.

National Cancer Institute. *Research Report: Lung Cancer.* Washington, D.C.: Department of Health and Human Services, January, 1985.

Prochaska, J. O., et al. "Self-change processes, self-efficacy and self-concept in relapse and maintenance of cessation of smoking." *Psychological Reports* 51:983–990, 1982.

Shiffman, Saul. "Relapse following smoking cessation: a situational analysis." *Journal of Consulting and Clinical Psychology* 50:71–86, 1982.

Strecher, Victor. "A minimal-contact smoking cessation program in a health care setting." *Health Promotion and Disease Prevention* 98:497–509, 1983.

Surgeon General. *The Health Consequences of Smoking: Cardiovascular Disease.* Washington, D.C.: Department of Health and Human Services, 1983.

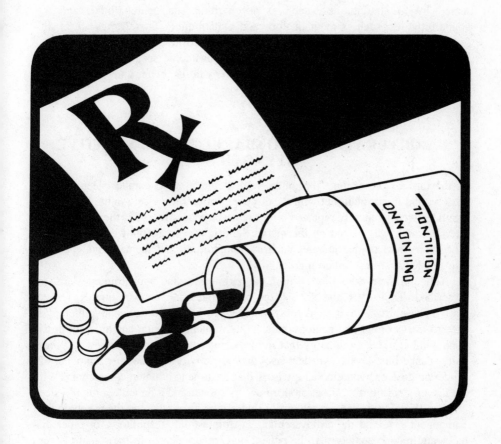

CHAPTER 9

SEDATIVE
HYPNOTICS

This chapter discusses two particular classifications of depressants, both of which in the popular pill form are commonly misused and abused. The first group is represented by the barbiturates, such as secobarbital and pentobarbital, and the nonbarbiturates, such as methaqualone and glutethimide. These drugs are of different chemical formulations, but all produce similar effects and problems.

The second group, although they are also considered sedative hypnotics, are commonly called *psychotherapeutic* or *antianxiety* drugs, better known as *tranquilizers*.

BARBITURATE AND NONBARBITURATE SEDATIVE HYPNOTICS

At the turn of the century, bromides were being used to combat sleeplessness, anxiety, and minor pain, but with the discovery of barbituric acid in the late 1800s, bromides were gradually replaced with the barbiturates. In 1903, the first barbiturate, Veronal, was placed on the market, and it was soon followed by Luminal. Since that time, nonbarbiturates such as glutethimide and memethaqualone have also flooded the prescription market.

Although their use is diminishing, the barbiturates and nonbarbiturates are still prescribed. Tables 9.1 and 9.2 list the barbiturates and nonbarbiturates, respectively. These drugs are used as follows: (1) Daytime, low-dose sedative therapy is used to treat normal and neurotic patients by reducing tension and anxiety; this is done without inducing lethargy that in turn could lower mental alertness to potentially dangerous levels, or decrease their reactivity to the environment. (2) Moderate-dose or hypnotic therapy is used at bedtime to counteract insomnia. With the use of a barbiturate, onset of sleep occurs sooner and a dreamless night's sleep ensues. These drugs are not analgesics, but often aid in reducing the psychological component involved in cardiovascular, gastrointestinal, respiratory, or other diseases and reduce anxiety that the patient may experience from the somatic symptoms of these diseases.

Because of the antianxiety and antitension qualities of the sedative hypnotics, their illegal use increased dramatically, and with their misuse and abuse, the dangers inherent in these drugs became apparent. It was found that they created tolerance (and cross-tolerance to other depressant drugs) and psychic and physical dependence, and that abrupt withdrawal after chronic abuse would bring on an abstinence syndrome more severe than that caused by any other drug mainly because of the life-threatening convulsions that accompany withdrawal. The dependence-producing nature of these drugs and their potential for respiratory depression stimulated medical research for safer substances. The drugs that emerged from this research were the tranquilizers, most of which possess potential dangers identical to the sedative hypnotics—tolerance, dependence, and overdose.

The barbiturate and nonbarbiturate sedative hypnotics produce their depressant effect by inhibiting the arousal systems of the central nervous system; that is they depress the reticular formation by interfering with oxygen consumption and energy-

Table 9.1   Barbiturate Classification

Drug	Action	Trade Name
Hexobarbital	Very short[1]	Sombulex
Methohexital	Very Short[1]	Brevital
Thiamylal	Very short[1]	Nonformulary
Thiopental	Very short[1]	Pentothal
Amobarbital	Short/Intermediate[2]	Amytal
Aprobarbital		Alurate
Butabarbital		Butisol
		Butazem
		Buticaps, Butal
		Sarisol
Pentobarbital		Nembutal
		Nebralin
Secobarbital		Seconal
Phenobarbital	Long[3]	Pheno-Squar
		Solfoton
		Luminal
		Eskabarb
Mephobarbital		Mebaral
Metharbital		Nonformulary

Note: The short- and intermediate-acting barbiturates listed here are the characteristic barbiturates of abuse, especially Seconal, Nembutal and Amytal.
[1] Very short-acting = under 3 hours
[2] Short/Intermediate = 3–6 hours
[3] Long-acting = 6 or more hours

producing mechanisms (Stimmel, 1983). The depression here reduces the nerve signals that reach the cortex, thus promoting sleep. A sedative dose makes one only slightly drowsy, but damps out enough incoming stimuli to reduce anxiety and tension.

The body eliminates these sedative hypnotics via the kidneys at varying rates,

Table 9.2   Commonly Used and Abused Nonbarbiturate, Nonbenzodiazepine Sedative Hypnotics

Chloral Derivatives	Carbamates	Bromides	Piperidinediones	Quinazolones
Chloral hydrate (Somnos)	Meprobamate* (Miltown, Equanil)	Sedamyl	Glutethimide (Doriden)	Methaqualone (Quaalude, Sopor)
Chloral betaine (Beta Chlor)			Methyprylon (Noludar)	Methaqualine HCl (Parest, Somnfac)
Triclofos sodium (Triclos)				
Ethchlorvynol (Placidyl)				

*Classified as a minor tranquilizer.

and it is mainly this rate of elimination that determines the duration effects of any one drug. There is an exception here in that short- and ultrashort-acting barbiturates rapidly redistribute themselves in adipose tissue, thus lessening their levels and effects in the brain. The intermediate- and long-acting drugs are metabolized more slowly and may produce some residual sedation (hangover) because they have not been thoroughly metabolized.

An interesting paradox with these drugs is that abusive levels in chronic users or normal doses in susceptible patients, especially the elderly, can produce excitation before the customary depressant action sets in. Another interesting effect of barbiturates is that when taken in the presence of psychological stress or extreme pain, they may cause delirium and other side effects such as nausea, nervousness, rash, and diarrhea (Goodman & Gilman, 1980). Another adverse effect of barbiturates, glutethimide, and other drugs of this classification is that they decrease the potency of certain other drugs, as seen in Table 9.3 (Cohen, 1981).

TRANQUILIZERS

The tranquilizers are divided into antipsychotic and antianxiety substances (Tables 9.4 and 9.5, respectively). The difference between these two groups of tranquilizers is of significance when speaking of drug abuse, because the antipsychotics hold no hazard of physical dependence and are not abused as street drugs. The antipsychotics are mentioned here merely to complete the tranquilizer picture.

Antipsychotics

The phenothiazines (aliphatic or Thorazine-type drugs, piperidine or Mellaril-type drugs; and piperazine or Stellazine-type drugs) are the standard antipsychotic agents (Table 9.4). It appears that all drugs in this category are equally effective drugs, but should be chosen on the basis of which will get the best results and cause the fewest side effects in each individual patient.

Every effective antipsychotic blocks dopamine receptor sites, which counteracts the excessive firing of dopaminergic neurons in the limbic system. Cohen (1981)

Table 9.3   Interaction of Barbiturates with Other Drugs

Drug	Effect
Alcohol (acute intoxication)	Increased CNS depression
Alcohol (chronic intake)	Decreased sedation
Anticoagulants	Decreased anticoagulant effect
Corticosteroid	Decreased steroid effect
Digitoxin	Decreased cardiac effect
Phenothiazines	Decreased tranquilizing effect
Phenytoin	Decreased anticonvulsant effect
Tetracyclines	Decreased antibiotic effect
Tricylic antidepressants	Decreased antidepressant effect

Table 9.4   **Antipsychotic Agents (Phenothiazines)**

Generic Name	Brand Name	Single Adult Dose	Duration
Chlorpromazine	Thorazine	10–25 mg	4–6 hr
Prochlorperazine	Compazine	10 mg	4–6 hr
Trifluoperazine	Stellazine	2 mg	4–6 hr
Rauwolfia	Reserpine	1 mg	4–6 hr

Note: These drugs are used for treatment of alcoholism, neurosis, psychosis, psychosomatic disorders, and vomiting. Their potential for psychological dependence is minimal and they hold no potential for physical dependence, thus making their overall potential for abuse minimal. Usual short-term effects are CNS depression, relaxation, relief of anxiety, and improved functioning, while long-term effects may be drowsiness, dryness of mouth, blurred vision, skin rash, tremor, and occasionally, jaundice.

suggests that the schizophrenia-type disorders may be due to excessive firing of these neurons.

Antianxiety Substances

The antianxiety substances, like the barbiturates and nonbarbiturates, are common drugs of misuse and abuse. The rise in consumption of tranquilizers began in the 1960s with Miltown and Equanil (generic name, meprobamate) as the prototypes, and these were later replaced by Librium and Valium. In 1968, 40 million prescriptions were written for the latter two drugs. Five years later the number was 80 million, in 1976 the figure had increased to 91 million, comprising about 8 percent of all prescriptions written by physicians in the United States. More prescriptions are written for tranquilizers than for any other psychoactive drug. In 1983 Dalmane (flurazepam) was reported to be the most commonly prescribed sleeping pill, accounting for more than one-half of all sedative-hypnotics prescribed (Parker, 1983). The implications here are that many Americans are trying to solve their problems through the use of psychotropic drugs, and that American physicians feel that tranquilizers are the most efficient manner in which to deal with their anxiety-ridden patients. The all-out prescribing of tranquilizers has its impact on the street-drug scene in two ways—directly, by supplying legitimate drugs (via theft) to the black market system, and indirectly, through parental example of attitudes toward drugs. Use of illicit drugs by teen-agers has been shown to parallel their parents' use of tranquilizers, with children being especially influenced by their mothers' use of these drugs.

The action of the benzodiazepines on the central nervous system is quite dissimilar to that of the barbiturates and nonbarbiturates. Rather than suppress activity of the reticular activating system, the tranquilizers appear to act on brain tissue at special benzodiazepine binding sites. The receptors are widespread throughout the brain, accounting for the multiple levels of benzodiazepine action. The benzodiazepines appear to affect all of the known neurotransmitters, but their major interaction appears to be with GABA, a major inhibitory neurotransmitter whose effects are increased by these tranquilizers. The particulars of drug-neurotransmitter interaction are still unknown, but it is thought that these drugs alter the postsynaptic GABA response (Gallagher, 1978).

The drugs that appear in Table 9.5 have been selected because of their incidence of abuse. If taken in excessive doses over a long enough period of time, all of the drugs listed will create tolerance and physical and psychological dependence.

DANGERS OF SEDATIVE HYPNOTIC ABUSE

Policy makers of federal drug abuse organizations have called for a reevaluation of barbiturate use. The very fast-acting barbiturate anesthetics and the slow-acting phenobarbital have escaped this evaluation, however, due to their low abuse potential. The major reason for reevaluation is the misuse and abuse potential of the other barbiturates, such as secobarbital and pentobarbital. Some of the problems seen with these drugs (along with nonbarbiturate sedatives such as methaqualone) include the following:

1. Barbiturates are used more frequently as the means of suicide than any other drug.
2. Accidental death occurs from sublethal levels of barbiturates when they are used in conjunction with alcohol.
3. The barbiturates have been consistently abused since the arrival of these drugs on the market. Their abuse has been linked with death by overdose, violent behavior, and accidents due to motor clumsiness.
4. Withdrawal from barbiturate dependence is a serious medical consideration, and life-endangering to the dependent individual.

In addition to these life-endangering aspects, barbiturates also radically change sleeping patterns by decreasing REM sleep, and then cause sleeping problems when the drug is no longer used. Another disadvantage of barbiturate use is that they stimulate hepatic (liver) enzyme production, which in turn causes other substances (such as anticoagulants or antibiotics, as seen in Table 9.3) to be broken down more quickly than expected, thus diminishing their effectiveness. Finally, because the barbiturates depress the respiratory center, they pose a danger to those with respiratory problems.

Table 9.5   Commonly Used Benzodiazepines (Antianxiety Agents)

Generic Name	Trade Name
Chlordiazepoxide	Librium
Clorazepate	Tranxene, Azene, Tranzene SD
Diazepam	Valium
Flurazepam	Dalmane
Lorazepam	Ativan
Oxazepam	Serax
Prazepam	Verstran, Centrax
Ketazolam	Halcion
Temazepam	Restoril

Although the nonbarbiturates and the antianxiety substances may not possess all of the inherent dangers seen in the barbiturates, all of them share the dangers of dependence, tolerance, withdrawal, and abuse potential; and some of them may possess all of the dangers cited above for barbiturates. Where there are exceptions or specific indications of certain drugs in this classification, they will be noted as some of the dangers are more fully discussed throughout the chapter.

Alteration of Sleep Patterns

Insomnia is a common condition and can arise from numerous underlying causes:

1. Situational (e.g., jet lag, being in unfamiliar surroundings)
2. Medical (e.g., pain)
3. Psychological (e.g., anxiety, inadequacy, neurosis)
4. Drug intake or withdrawal (e.g., alcohol, caffeine)

The sedative hypnotics have been used as sleeping aids for various difficulties in sleeping—inability to fall asleep, early morning awakenings, inability to stay asleep, and combinations of these. For whatever purpose the sleeping aid is taken, it is important to know that the sleep that it produces is not "normal" sleep.

An important drawback of prescribing the sedative hypnotics for relief of insomnia is that many of these drugs reduce REM (rapid eye movement) sleep time. These include chloral hydrate, barbiturates (especially pentobarbital, secobarbital, and amobarbital), glutethimide, and methaqualone. The benzodiazepines, diazepam, and chlordiazepoxide produce quantitatively less depression of REM both acutely and chronically (Cohen, 1981). It appears that REM sleep is necessary, for if individuals are deprived of this period of sleep in which dreams occur, they grow irritable, anxious, and even neurotic. In a normal night's sleep, five or six periods of orthodox sleep occur broken up by short periods of REM sleep, with the first period occurring about an hour to an hour and a half after onset of sleep and lasting varying lengths of time. Normally, REM sleep makes up 20 to 25 percent of one's total sleep time (Holbrook, 1983).

Unfortunately, the use of a barbiturate as a sleeping aid creates an initial reduction of REM sleep, which occurs during the first week of nighttime hypnosis. Subsequent nightly use of barbiturates for as little as two weeks brings about some tolerance; it takes longer to fall asleep and total sleep time is shorter, but REM sleep time rises to normal levels again. Even though one regains a normal level of REM sleep, a serious situation has arisen with the REM sleep that was lost initially. It has been found that there is a large increase in REM sleep after one discontinues using sleeping pills (Cohen, 1981; Wesson & Smith, 1981). When this increase occurs, patients experience nightmares, restlessness, and nighttime awakenings. They feel they do not get a full night's sleep and become anxious about their poor sleeping behavior. This situation is very likely to induce patients to return to barbiturates to "cure" the problem. Study has shown that it takes a month or more to repay this REM sleep debt (Cooper, 1977) but if the patient can withstand the transition period, he or she can escape the barbiturate-induced sleep routine.

Diazepam and antihistamines have been suggested as substitute drugs for barbiturates in cases of insomnia and other neurotic symptoms because these drugs appear to have fewer adverse effects (Cohen, 1981).

Suicide and Accidental Death

Other dangers in the use of sedative hypnotics are suicide and accidental death (Shader, 1982). Over the last few years the number of barbiturate-related deaths has been declining, but it still remains at a quantitatively high level. Recent figures from DAWN (the Drug Abuse Warning Network) show that barbiturates and nonbarbiturate sedatives account for about 20 percent of all drug-related deaths. This nearly equals the proportion of deaths related to heroin. DAWN figures also show that the sedative hypnotics accounted for over 15 percent of drug-abuse emergency ward episodes and there is growing evidence that acute overdoses involving tranquilizers have been increasing at an alarming rate (NIDA, 1980).

The National Center for Health Statistics examined all 1974 death certificates and found that there were 286 barbiturate-related accidental deaths among those over twenty years old, and 144 accidental deaths were related to the nonbarbiturate sedative hypnotics. It was estimated in that year that 13 million people over the age of eighteen used barbiturates (both medically and nonmedically) and an estimated 24 million used nonbarbiturates. Combining this information, we see that of every one million users of barbiturates, about twenty-two people die accidentally; and of every one million nonbarbiturate users, about six die accidentally (Cooper, 1977).

It is apparent that there is a group of patients complaining about the symptoms for which these drugs are prescribed who demonstrate a considerable degree of psychopathology. In addition, a large population of users, the elderly, may be more vulnerable to life crises, making them a high-risk group for misusing these drugs. Therefore, before prescribing CNS depressants, it is important for physicians to examine the relative toxicity required to produce illness or death.

As we can see from Table 9.6, the benzodiazepines show a considerable margin of safety between their therapeutic dose and the dose required to produce serious overdose or death. The barbiturates, nonbarbiturates, and nonbenzodiazepine sedative hypnotics demonstrate a much narrower margin of safety than do the benzodiazepines such as Valium and Librium (Greenblatt et al., 1977). Due to its high lipid solubility and anticholinergic action, glutethimide presents special difficulty in the treatment of overdose, as does methaqualone.

In many cases of barbiturate-related death, it is difficult to determine whether death was accidental or planned, because the effects of drug poisoning occur gradually. Termination of life is not instantaneous. Thus, insomniacs who take one or two sleeping pills and find that these do not work immediately may take more. If the second dose added to the first exceeds the lethal dose for the individual, death will occur. Another way in which suicide or accidental death occurs is through self-administration of sedative hypnotics or tranquilizers after ingesting a large amount of alcohol. The lethal dose of these depressants is markedly reduced in such a case because alcohol has already depressed vital cell action. Similar effects occur with any multiple drug use that is a combination of depressant drugs: for example, barbiturates and opiates, methaqualone and alcohol, or alcohol and methadone.

Table 9.6   Relative Therapeutic and Toxic Doses of Common Sedative Hypnotics*

	Usual Therapeutic Dose
Nonbenzodiazepine Nonbarbiturates	
Chloral hydrate	0.5–1.0 g
Paraldehyde	4–8 g
Glutethimide	500 mg
Methaqualone	150–300 mg
Barbiturates	
Amobarbital	100–200 mg hypnotic
	20–30 mg sedative
Secobarbital	100 mg hypnotic
	30–50 mg sedative
Pentobarbital	100 mg hypnotic
	30–60 mg sedative
Phenobarbital	100 mg hypnotic
	15–30 mg sedative
Benzodiazepines	
Chlordiazepoxide	5–25 mg
Diazepam	2–10 mg

*Cooper, 1977.

Another hazard is that of operating dangerous machinery, especially an automobile, while under the influence of sedative drugs. Barbiturates and similar drugs cause a type of intoxication that is much like alcohol intoxication; the individual initially experiences a relaxed feeling, and release of social inhibitions occurs, just as in the first stages of alcohol intoxication. Further use of the drug brings on sluggishness, lack of motor coordination, slurred speech, and eventually sleep. However, large doses of these drugs in the stomach do not affect the vomiting mechanism as large amounts of alcohol do (rescuing the drunk from death); thus, large doses of barbiturates, for example, are more dangerous than alcohol.

All the dangers described here (loss of REM sleep, death by accident or suicide, potentiation of other drugs) stem from misuse of barbiturates or barbituratelike drugs. There is the additional danger that misuse will lead to an ever-increasing *abuse* of these drugs; that is, instead of misusing legal prescriptions, individuals may buy these drugs illegally purely for psychological gratification. There are three factors that lend support to the idea that misuse is the forerunner of abuse. First, without these drugs of increasingly dubious medical value, there would be no overflow of the drug itself into channels of abuse. Current production of all sedatives exceeds medical needs by a considerable margin. Granted, a drug alone does not create drug abuse; but in addition, these drugs are prescribed mainly to individuals who are in a weakened psychological condition. Misuse during this low period may lead to future abuse. Finally, the widespread medical use of these drugs gives them an air of universal acceptance (such as that given to alcohol), thus aiding the development of our whole drug culture.

Taking all three factors (the drug, the individual, and the culture) into consideration, one might conclude that these drugs should not be so freely manufactured or prescribed.

Dangers of Dependency

In 1976 about 11,000 patients were admitted to federally funded treatment centers for primary abuse of barbiturates, and 75 percent of those admitted were under twenty-five years of age. The 1982 Survey on Drug Abuse (Miller et al., 1983) showed that of the youth ages 12–17, 5.8 percent had used sedatives nonmedically and 4.9 percent had used tranquilizers nonmedically at some time in their lives. In the young adult group ages 18–25, 19 percent had used sedatives and 15 percent had used tranquilizers for nonmedical purposes; and in the older adult group (those over 26), 4.8 percent had used sedatives and 3.6 percent had used tranquilizers for nonmedical reasons at least once in their lives. These figures represent a growing population of drug abusers, and the concern these figures have generated is reflected in the stricter control of some of these drugs, such as methaqualone, in the last decade.

Abuse of the sedatives is a more intense problem than their misuse because of the more serious physical, psychological, and social dangers involved. Goodman and Gilman (1980) say that persons with a tendency to become addicted to barbiturates have some basic personality disorder or psychoneurosis. They also feel that this type of addiction presents a greater public health and mental health problem than heroin addiction because it produces more severe emotional, mental, and neurological problems and withdrawal is more dangerous.

The American Medical Association provided a breakdown or categorization of the different types of individuals who abuse sedative drugs. It is easy to recognize that these individuals differ from the common misuser described earlier in the chapter, the difference being mainly the *intensity* of motive and dosage. The categories are as follows:

1. Those who seek sedative effects to deal with emotional stress. This sedation may be carried to extremes when the person seeks almost total oblivion and stupor, moving about only to answer nature's call or to take more drugs.
2. Those who seek the paradoxical excitation that has been seen to occur, especially after one can tolerate large doses of the drug. Now instead of depression, the person feels exhilaration—much like the initial effect of amphetamines—and uses the drug for typical stimulatory reasons.
3. Those who take the drug to counteract the effects of abusive use of stimulants and LSD. This kind of use may set up a cycle of ups and downs that eventually leads to addiction.
4. Those who use sedatives in combination with other depressant drugs, mainly alcohol and heroin. Alcohol plus the sedative gives a more instant "high" but is especially dangerous because of the double depressant action. Heroin users may resort to barbiturates if their heroin supply is cut off.

The four categories given above probably overlap very little and give a fairly good picture of the various types of abusers. The solution for all these individuals has to be realignment of values based on factual knowledge.

Tolerance and Physical Dependence

Two of the most dangerous aspects of hypnotic-sedative abuse are physical and psychological dependence. If an individual takes these drugs as prescribed, dependence is not likely to occur (however, tolerance to even small doses may develop). For various reasons, though, the individual may increase the dose of barbiturates and build his or her tolerance to an incredible level. When this occurs and the barbiturate or tranquilizer is taken regularly, true addiction will develop (see Fig. 9.1).

It is commonly recognized that three factors, *tolerance, physical dependence,* and *psychological dependence,* are necessary for true addiction to occur, and although they have been intensely studied for over half a century, their precise mechanisms of action are not understood. Nonetheless, their existence is an inescapable fact for all too many abusers of depressant drugs.

It has been widely observed that development of physical dependence on barbiturates is a relatively slow process requiring weeks or months before withdrawal symptoms are manifested. Doses of 200 to 400 milligrams of pentobarbital or secobarbital can be taken daily for a year with little or no physical dependence. It would take daily doses between 900 and 2,000 milligrams for one month to produce withdrawal symptoms. However, it has been demonstrated more recently that large doses of short-acting pentobarbital can produce some mild withdrawal symptoms after only twenty-six hours of intoxication, with symptoms increasing in severity as the length of intoxication increases (Jaffe, 1977). Taking 300 to 600 milligrams of Librium per day for five months will produce physical dependence with serious withdrawal; Doriden, secobarbital, and pentobarbital at around one gram per day for a month or more may make the user physically dependent. Miltown at 1.5 to 2.5 grams per day for a prolonged period, or methaqualone at two to three grams per day for a month will produce a similar dependence (Wesson & Smith, 1981; Woolf, 1983).

Treatment

The treatment for withdrawal from these drugs is one of intensive care and should be carried out in a hospital, where every medical advantage may be gained over the

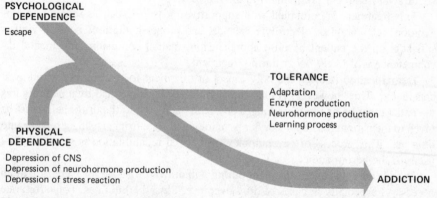

PSYCHOLOGICAL DEPENDENCE
Escape

TOLERANCE
Adaptation
Enzyme production
Neurohormone production
Learning process

PHYSICAL DEPENDENCE
Depression of CNS
Depression of neurohormone production
Depression of stress reaction

ADDICTION

Fig. 9.1   The pattern of addiction.

possibly fatal withdrawal symptoms. Many addicts who enter a hospital for treatment are also addicted to heroin. In such cases, withdrawal from the barbituratelike drug is the major focus, with heroin treatment following.

Addicts seek treatment when they can no longer cope with the sedative-induced depression, when they are arrested, when they can no longer afford their drug habits, or for a number of other reasons. Upon commencing treatment, if withdrawal has begun, the individual will appear weak, anxious, nauseous, and/or tremulous. These symptoms signal the danger of convulsion and/or psychosis. If the patient does not yet show these symptoms, a careful vigil is kept so that they can be treated immediately upon their onset.

In the first eight hours after abrupt withdrawal, signs of intoxication decline and the patient's condition actually appears to improve. However, after eight hours the symptoms described above occur, perhaps accompanied by muscle twitches, impaired cardiovascular responses, headaches, and vomiting. These signs and symptoms increase in intensity for the next eight hours (until about sixteen hours after withdrawal from the drug) and become quite severe after twenty-four hours. Untreated, these conditions will likely develop into *grand mal*-type seizures between the thirtieth and forty-eighth hours. These convulsive seizures have been seen as early as the sixteenth hour and as late as the eighth day after abrupt withdrawal (Stimmel, 1983).

During and following these two days there may be recurrences of insomnia culminating in delirium (much like the delirium tremens), hallucinations, disorientation, and marked tremors. The delirium typically lasts about five days, ending with a long, deep sleep. The whole withdrawal process is self-limiting, even if untreated. However, death is a real danger in uncontrolled, untreated withdrawal (Woolf, 1983).

Treatment usually consists of administering an initial short-acting barbiturate to allay the first symptoms of withdrawal and then tapering off with either the same drug, or more often with decreased doses of a long-acting drug such as phenobarbital. Because there is a cross-tolerance with many of these drugs, theoretically any of them could be administered during the withdrawal process. Since phenobarbital provides a low fluctuation level of barbiturate and is not usually accompanied by euphoria as are the short-acting barbiturates, it is the drug of choice in many withdrawal treatment programs (Stimmel, 1983).

This treatment is combined with supportive measures such as vitamin administration, restoration of electrolyte balance, and proper hydration. A close vigil is still kept on the patient because apprehension, mental confusion, and mental incompetence will likely occur during treatment.

Detoxification is often the only aspect of treatment for barbiturate withdrawal considered. This, however, is only the beginning. After medical treatment assures the patient that he or she is no longer physically addicted to the drug, help must be given to the patient to keep his or her psychological state from causing a relapse into drug use. This process of psychological and social rehabilitation is similar to that used for the heroin addict (see Chapter 10).

In addition to hospital treatment during withdrawal, first-aid measures are often necessary, especially in cases of drug overdose. Since barbiturates, nonbarbiturate sedatives, and the tranquilizers are often abused, because the various kinds may be taken at the same time and because they may be taken with alcohol, overdoses are not uncommon. In a victim of barbiturate overdose, for example, coma, flaccidity of the muscles, and respiratory depression would likely be apparent. The treatment to follow would be to (a) open the airway and clear out the oral cavity, (b) give mouth-to-mouth resuscitation if breathing has stopped, and (c) check the pulse. If there is no pulse, one should perform cardioresuscitative procedure (Stimmel, 1983). Perhaps the most important help one can give is to call for emergency medical assistance as fast as possible.

LEGAL RESTRICTION OF THE SEDATIVE HYPNOTICS

Just as the 1938 Federal Food, Drug and Cosmetic Act and the Durham–Humphrey Amendment of 1951 put legal control over the amphetamines, so did they control the barbiturates and nonbarbiturates. Subsequent amendments placed even stronger control over prescribed drugs. All of the drugs listed in this chapter are now placed in Schedules II, III, or IV of the Comprehensive Drug Abuse Prevention and Control Act (see Chapter 6 for the various classifications).

REFERENCES

Cohen, Sidney. *The Substance Abuse Problems.* New York: Haworth Press, 1981.

Cooper, J. R., ed. *Sedative–Hypnotic Drugs: Risks and Benefits.* Rockville, Md.: NIDA, 1977.

Gallagher, D. "Benzodiazepines: potentiation of a GABA inhibitory response in the dorsal raphe nucleus." *European Journal of Pharmacy* 41:133–143, 1978.

Goodman, L. A., and A. Gilman. *The Pharmacological Basis of Therapeutics.* New York: Macmillan, 1980.

Greenblatt, D. J., et al. "Acute overdose with benzodiazepine derivatives." *Clinical Pharmacology and Therapeutics* 21(4):497–514, 1977.

Holbrook, John M. "The autonomic and central nervous systems," in G. Bennet et al., eds. *Substance Abuse.* New York: Wiley 1983, pp. 3–16.

Jaffe, J. "Hypnotic and sedative agents," in M. Jarvik, ed. *Psychopharmacology in the Practice of Medicine.* New York: Appleton-Century-Crofts, 1977.

NIDA. *Project DAWN Annual Report.* Rockville, Md.: The Institute, 1980.

Miller, J., et al. *Student Drug Use in America 1982.* Rockville, Md.: NIDA, 1983.

Parker, J. M. *Valium, Librium and the Benzodiazepine Blues.* Phoenix, Ariz.: D.I.N. Publications, 1983.

Shader, R. I., et al., eds. *Emergency Room Study of Sedative-Hypnotic Overdosage.* Washington, D.C.: U.S. Government Printing Office, 1982.

Stimmel, Barry. *Pain, Analgesia, and Addiction: The Pharmacological Treatment of Pain.* New York: Raven Press, 1983.

Wesson, D. R., and D. E. Smith. "Abuse of sedative-hypnotics," in J. H. Lowinson and P. Ruiz, eds. *Substance Abuse: Clinical Problems and Perspectives.* Baltimore, Md.: Williams and Wilkins, 1981, pp. 185–190.

Woolf, Donna S. "CNS depressants: other sedative hynotics," in G. Bennett et al., eds. *Substance Abuse.* New York: Wiley 1983, pp. 39–56.

SUGGESTED READINGS

Folsom, J. P., Gen. Mgr., *Physicians' Desk Reference to Pharmaceutical Specialties and Biologicals*. Oradell, N.J.: Medical Economics, 1984.

Glatt, M. M., and J. Marks. *The Dependence Phenomenon*. Ridgewood, N.J.: George A. Bogden & Sons, 1982.

Krivanek, J. A. *Drug Problems, People Problems*. Sydney, Aust.: George Allen & Unwin, 1982.

Nahas, G. G., and H. C. Frick II. *Drug Abuse in the Modern World*. New York: Pergamon Press, 1980.

O'Brien R., and S. Cohen. *The Encyclopedia of Drug Abuse*. New York: Facts on File, Inc., 1984.

Senay, Edward C. *Substance Abuse Disorders in Clinical Practice*. Littleton, Mass.: John Wright, 1983.

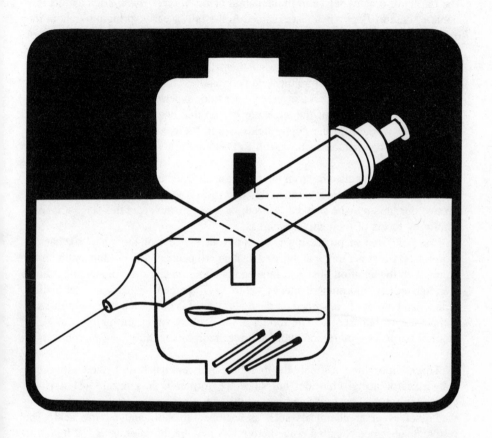

CHAPTER 10

THE OPIATES

THE OPIUM HARVEST

The family of opiates derive from the parent plant *Papaver somniferum* and its raw exudate, opium. Poppy fields are planted in the fall or early spring throughout the belt that reaches from Turkey's Anatolian plateau through Pakistan and northern India to the "Golden Triangle" of Burma, Laos, and Thailand. About three months later the plants flower and, when the petals drop, the poppy pod is exposed. It is at this precise time (before the seed pod matures) that laborers score the pod in a manner proscribed by centuries of ancestral experience. The result of this procedure is the release of the white milky sap that oozes out, to be scraped off patiently by workers of the poppy fields within the next twenty-four hours. It is estimated that one person spends a full forty-hour work week to collect one pound of opium.

After opium is collected from the field it is air-dried until its water content is at an acceptable level for purchase. In this raw form it is brown in color, possesses a strong odor, and may be smoked, sniffed, or eaten; however, at this stage it is used mainly by locals of the cultivation areas.

The next step in processing is to cook out the rest of the water so that the morphine content per unit weight rises to about 10 percent. By soaking and filtering opium with the addition of slaked lime and ammonium chloride, organic impurities are removed and morphine content rises to 50–70 percent. This is an intermediate product and not easily absorbed by the body; thus it is converted into morphine salt compounds or into heroin. The former is the form in which morphine is used for medical purposes—morphine hydrochloride, morphine sulfate, and morphine acetate.

Diacetylmorphine is simply the morphine base that has been treated with acetic anhydride (or acetyl chloride, but since the former is less hazardous, it is the compound most often used) and passed through a process of heating and filtering that involves other chemicals such as acetone, alcohol, and tartaric acid. The resultant substance is called crude heroin and may be the same as No. 2 heroin in the heroin number code of Southeast Asia.

The natives of Southeast Asia use crude heroin to manufacture purple or No. 3 heroin, which is smoked. The process is one of heating, crushing, and drying plus the addition of strychnine, caffeine, and barbitone (which offsets extreme intoxication), to the extent that heroin content is lowered to around 15 percent. It is tan to gray in appearance and granular or coarse in composition.

Crude heroin is also precipitated, dried, and crushed to form white or No. 4 heroin, the injectable drug seen in the United States. It resembles talc or flour in consistency and may have a heroin content of 95 percent or more before it is adulterated. The color varies from white to creamy yellow unless it comes from Mexico, in which case its color is brown due to a chemical process differing from that used in Europe and Asia. The supply of heroin from Mexico has risen and dropped over the last decade. At times, Mexico has been a significant source of heroin to the United States market.

PHARMACOLOGICAL EFFECTS

Heroin and the other opiates are narcotic sedatives that exert their effects by depressing the central nervous system, especially the sensory areas of the thalamus and cerebral cortex. This depressant action works to relieve pain and, in large doses, to induce sleep. Overdose causes death because of the narcotic's selective depressant action on the respiratory center in the medulla.

Heroin has a rapid onset of action and proceeds with its analgesic effect. The results are a flush of euphoria, elevation of mood, and a feeling of peace, contentment, and safety as the drug offers relief from the environment, both internal and external. This is one of the most significant reasons for heroin's highest addiction potential of all the illicit drugs. Its analgesic effect is about three times that of morphine—2 to 5 milligrams of heroin via intramuscular injection has about the same effect as 8 to 16 milligrams of morphine administered in the same manner or 300 to 600 milligrams of opium given orally. Heroin is still used in Britain as a medicine and proves to be an efficient tranquilizer, cough suppressant, and short-acting pain reliever. It also counteracts diarrhea and has been used in the treatment of cancer patients.

Common effects of the opiates (see Table 10.1) are respiratory depression (both rate and depth), constipation, pupillary constriction, postural hypotension, libido suppression, and release of histamine (which causes the itching that may accompany heroin use). Nausea and vomiting also often accompany heroin use, especially in the neophyte. Contrary to common belief, high-dose users of the opiates can function quite adequately, and aside from the danger of unsterile needles and other catastrophes inherent in the life style of the heroin user, the addict does not suffer the physical deterioration resulting from chronic use of other drugs such as alcohol. Diseases such as hepatitis, septicemia, and endocarditis accompany the use of unsterile needles, and abscesses are common among heroin addicts, also. Another cause of fatality in heroin addicts is cardiovascular collapse due to allergic reaction to the injected substance.

Heroin's pharmacological action is that of morphine because it is converted back into morphine in the body. Thus, both drugs are eliminated through the urine as morphine, which becomes the basis of urinalysis. It is also eliminated in the breast milk of a lactating mother, and in sweat and saliva. Because it easily crosses the placental barrier, infants born of heroin abusers come into the world as narcotic

Table 10.1   Opiate Drugs: Their Origin and Potency

Drug	Origin	Potency
Laudanum	Alcoholic solution of 10% opium	0.10 × opium
Paregoric	4% tincture of opium	0.04 × opium
Morphine	Natural alkaloid	10 × opium
Codeine	Natural alkaloid	0.50 × opium
Heroin	Semisynthetic	3 × morphine
Dilaudid	Semisynthetic	3–4 × morphine
Meperidine	Semisynthetic	0.1 × morphine
Methadone	Synthetic	Equals morphine

addicts, too. They are given paregoric, tincture of opium, or methadone in decreasing dosage until the physical dependence is alleviated.

The adult heroin user's perils parallel the infant's need to allay withdrawal. As the effects of an injection of heroin wear off, the addict generally has four to six hours in which to find his or her next supply. If a strong depressant is not taken within this time, withdrawal symptoms begin to appear—runny nose, dilation of pupils, stomach cramps, chills, and the other symptoms of the classic abstinence syndrome. Barbiturates, nonbarbiturate sedative hypnotics, cough syrup with codeine, or other such depressants may be used by the addict to postpone withdrawal if heroin or the money to purchase it is not available.

In cases of overdose, addicts are given narcotic antagonists such as levallorphan, nalorphine, or naloxone that will reverse the acute, life-threatening respiratory depression. Using such antagonists counteracts the pharmacological action of narcotics and, in essence, induces "cold-turkey" withdrawal. The severity of withdrawal symptoms differs with the user and is dependent on numerous factors. In a study of heroin users who ranked withdrawal symptoms by severity, it was found that the most severe were: insomnia; aching bones and joints; anxiety; irritability; excessive sweating; muscle cramps; lack of energy and restlessness (Cohen et al., 1983).

The heroin user's preferred form of administration of the opiates is intravenous because of the immediate rush that is felt. Experienced opiate addicts can discern heroin from morphine because its acetylated form assists its entry into the central nervous system. Other forms of administration include snorting (sniffing), intramuscular injection (skin-popping or joy-popping, or as used in a hospital setting), and smoking. Many of the American GIs who experienced heroin use in Vietnam smoked it in tobacco cigarettes. The heroin available there was extremely more potent than American street heroin because it was sold in almost pure form; but when smoked, it was rapidly reduced in potency because the high burning temperature of the cigarette (around 850°C) destroys about 80 percent of the effect of the heroin. Thus, a milder dependence would develop from smoking almost pure heroin than from other modes of administration (Gay & Way, 1972).

TRADE ROUTES

Four principal networks of opiate harvest and heroin production smuggle heroin into the United States. The primary network is that of Turkey, France, Western Europe, South America, Canada, and the United States. The second network involves the opium harvested in the "Golden Triangle" area of Burma, Thailand, and Laos. This travels through shipping points in Hong Kong, Malaysia, Bangkok, and the Philippines into Canada and the west coast of the United States. The third network is that of Afghanistan, Pakistan, Iran, and India, referred to as the "Golden Crescent." The journey of the opium to the United States is a long and convoluted one through Western Europe, South America, and sometimes Canada. It should be noted here that India is the prime producer of licit opium (about 85 percent of total world exports of opium). About 90 percent of the opium produced for medicine is used for morphine, most of which is converted into codeine. About 35 percent of licit morphine is extracted from the crushed stems and pods (called poppy straw) of the plant. This is the most efficient way to produce morphine, since the whole process can be mechanized.

Upon serious curtailment of the entry of French heroin into the United States, Mexican brown heroin appeared on the American scene, thus completing the list of major networks of illicit import (Fig. 10.1).

HISTORY OF THE OPIATES

Historically, opium and its derivatives have single-handedly generated the deep fear of addiction and the drug addict in American society. Although history has not contributed an answer to our heroin problem, it can ease the understanding of how the problem developed. This understanding then might be instrumental in developing a new and workable approach to our dependence problem.

The history of opium begins centuries before the birth of Christ (circa 3500 B.C.) in the country of Sumeria (now Iraq), where opium was used to treat dysentery. The Sumerians carried this drug to Egypt and Persia, and in time, Portuguese sailors carried it to India. In the tenth century, it found its way to China. Throughout this time it was taken orally, as medicine, and generally not abused; but in the seventeenth century the Western custom of smoking came to Asia and opium smoking became popular. Abuse of the drug first occurred on a large scale in India during the seventeenth century, when the drinking of alcohol was forbidden. Opium smoking soon became a Chinese custom and vice, in spite of governmental edicts against its use and sale. Thus, when the East India Company of England monopolized the Indian opium trade, China no longer asked for gold and silver in exchange for tea and silk—in return, they imported opium. In 1729 (when the emperor imposed an edict against opium) China was importing around fifteen tons of opium per year, but by 1790 imports had reached nearly 400 tons, due mainly to the involvement of the East India Company.

The opium wars were fought in 1839 and 1856 because China wished to enforce an 1800 edict that banned opium importation, and European countries (suppliers of opium) fought with them for better trade conditions, The outcome was that China was economically forced to legalize the opium trade, a factor leading to widespread opium smoking and addiction.

The use of opium gradually increased in the United States, and it became the analgesic property in many patent medicines such as Dover's Powder or Dr. Barton's Brown Mixture. The opium derivative, morphine, was also heavily relied on for treating wounded soldiers during the Civil War. During this time, heroin was produced by the Bayer pharmaceutical company in Germany; soon after, heroin was found to prevent withdrawal in morphine addiction, a condition that was present in about one out of 400 Americans by the turn of the twentieth century. Many soldiers treated by morphine in the war continued their dependence, the general citizenry became dependent on their favorite patented cure-all, and a limited number of individuals were abusing heroin.

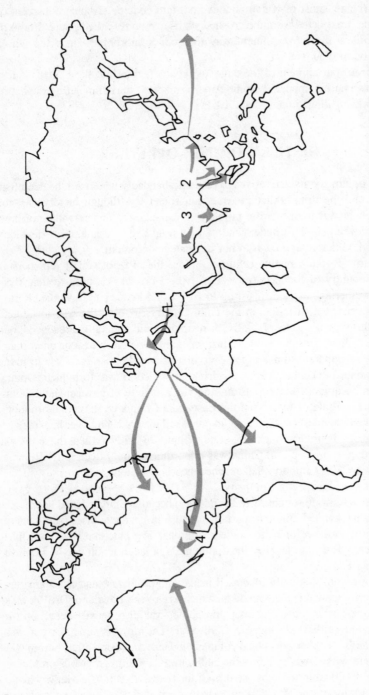

Fig. 10.1 Major opiate smuggling networks and routes: (1) Turkey, France, Western Europe, South America, Canada, and the United States; (2) Burma, Thailand, Laos, Hong Kong, Malaysia, Bangkok; Philippines, Canada, and the United States; (3) Afghanistan, Pakistan, Iran, and India; and (4) Mexico and the United States.

Except for a tariff imposed in 1842 on imported opium in order to regulate its entry into the United States, the first step that the government took to regulate the opiates was the passage of the Pure Food and Drug Act in 1906. This act demanded that all drugs containing opiates be labeled as such, so that consumers would know precisely what they were buying.

Growing concern for the addiction problem was made manifest in the time-honored tradition of the government: cut off the supply. This was attempted with the 1909 meeting of the International Opium Commission in Shanghai, where the United States pressed for such stringent control of opium production and trade that the other twelve countries present could not support the request. The goal of the United States was total prohibition of opium in all countries in which it was culti-vated, to be effective immediately. Since many of these countries depended on opium exports in their balance of trade, the American position was less than tenable to them. Because the 1909 meeting did not produce a treaty, the same group met in the Hague in 1911 and agreed that governments should control narcotics at both national and international levels. In the United States, the Harrison Narcotics Act naturally followed these international events; there is even speculation that these conferences were staged to persuade the passage of the Harrison Narcotics Act in 1914 (Kramer, 1972).

Historically, it appears that the United States was strongly affected by the problems of addiciton, and throughout the Geneva Conference in 1924 and 1925, all participating countries were urged by America to honor the agreement of the Hague Convention. It was obvious by this time that America could not control its addiction problem and that the task entrusted to law enforcement had too many ramifications to be treated simply with a total prohibition policy. The Harrison Narcotics Act limited the legal supply of opiates to users, so they had to go "underground" to get their drugs. This is highly consequential, since it marked the begining of the illicit, street-drug culture that terrifies America today. Individual physicians attempted to aid their addicted patients, but in 1915 the Treasury Department (in charge of enforcing the Harrison Narcotics Act) declared that physicians who were treating narcotics users had to show decreasing doses over a period of time. Noncompliance was considered a violation of the Act. Subsequent court decisions against maintaining an addict, along with pressure on physicians from the American Medical Association Drug Committee to accept the police policy and stay out of the morphine-prescribing business, took most physicians out of the picture.

The government attempted to help heroin users who were shut off from legal drug supply through the establishment of morphine clinics, which opened in some of the large cities. Here morphine was provided in order to curb antisocial behavior and to aid the user in withdrawal from his or her drug habit, but crime rates rose as users from outlying areas came in droves to the city for free morphine, thus con-tributing to the poor living conditions already there. After several years all these clinics had closed down in failure. They had not conquered the problem—in fact, addiction had increased. In 1970, the Drug Abuse Prevention and Control Act was passed, which for the first time provided a combination of prevention, treatment, and research, and also made available financial support for drug education in schools.

In 1972, the Special Action Office for Drug Abuse Prevention was created to strengthen prevention and rehabilitation efforts of the government. Effectiveness of this program is still to be tested, but it was a positive step in treating the addiction problem, since a social dimension was added to law enforcement.

A positive aspect about opium was the discovery in the last fifteen years that the human brain produces a natural opiate similar to the pain-relieving drug. The discovery that opiumlike substances are present in normal brain tissue has led to new research and information on how reward and reinforcement mechanisms may operate in the brain. This discovery also helps to explain scientifically and to understand the ancient techniques of natural anesthesia such as acupuncture. An exciting possibility for medicine is the potential of being able to utilize natural compounds in the body for treatment of pain instead of synthetic opiates which lead to physical dependence and tolerance.

The history of the pharmacological discovery of opiates is as interesting as the history of its use. Eighteenth-century Chinese physicians searched for a substance that had the analgesic properties of opium without producing the unwanted physical dependence. Modern scientists searched for a natural substitute and were successful in producing synthetic or semisynthetic substitutes. As a result, opium was refined into morphine, which was later synthesized into heroin, and finally resulted in substances such as methadone and dilaudid. Each new discovery was heralded as "the breakthrough." However, in time it was found that each new substance also produced tolerance and physical dependence.

One of the most important discoveries in the search for opiate substitutes came in the 1950s with the development of narcotic antagonists. Narcotic antagonists are substances that countered the effect of opiates. These antagonists work by competing for binding sites on the cellular membranes and thus rendering the opiate substance inactive. Narcotic antagonists (e.g., nalaxone, nalorphine) were found to reverse the effects of respiratory depression from high doses of morphine and thus became a useful first-aid treatment in overdose cases.

Another equally important discovery about opiates was that there appeared to be specific binding sites for opiates within the central nervous system. Therefore, it was reasonable to assume that if such binding sites would not exist if there were no naturally occurring (endogenous) opiates similar to substances in the brain. In the mid-1970s, it was found that large, naturally occurring protein substances that were bound to specific opiate receptor sites would produce behavioral and physiological effects similar to those of the opiates. Peptides including B-lipotropin, mez-enkephalin, and leu-enkephalins were shown to produce opiatelike activity (Seiden, 1983).

The pharmacologists have been joined by the psychopharmacologists and other professionals interested in understanding how these natural opiatelike substances are released, under what conditions, and how this knowledge may change what we now know about the science of behavioral reinforcement, reward, and maturation. Also at hand may be an explanation of ancient healing arts, such as acupuncture and other similar techniques. It is predicted that by the end of this century the mystery of the opiates that has intrigued scientists for hundreds of years will be solved.

In the last decade, several pharmacological discoveries have started to unravel the mystery of opiates. The most significant was the discovery of the natural binding sites for opiates and the existence of naturally occurring opiatelike substances in the body. More recent research has concentrated on the density of these sites in specific CNS structures for which the behavioral response is known. Some of the highest densities of opiate receptors were found in the limbic system. Fewer but still significant densities have been located in the hippocampal cortex and the hypothalamus. The function of these areas of the CNS is generally described as being behavioral and emotional, and may be responsible for many of the often observed behavioral effects of opiates that include euphoria, mental cloudiness, memory changes, and drowsiness.

Another line of research has described the structural similarities between the naturally occurring opiates, the enkephalins and endorphins, and the opiate molecules. These structural similarities allow for an easy displacement of the natural compounds by the opiates. The final line of research which helps shed light on the action of the opiates is centered around their ability to block the release of natural neurotransmitters. One of the best examples of this exists in the primary afferent fibers of the spinal cord which are so important in the transmission of pain sensation. Opiates have been found to block the release of the neurotransmitter Substance P, and this may explain the analgesic action of opiates (Atweh, 1983, Bromage et al., 1980).

DEPENDENCE

According to one school of thought, there are three major factors that create dependence: life situation, personality, and pharmacology of the drug. It has often been said that people start to use drugs for one reason but often continue using them for very different reasons. This is particularly true in the case of the heroin user. This is because opiates can "create" a personality that is complete with specific drives, needs, and values which may be entirely different than those possessed by the individual when not addicted. Recent research has added credence to this long-held hypothesis.

The discovery of the endogenous opiatelike neuropeptides has led to the identification of an endocrine system within the CNS. ACTH neuropeptides are active in the processes of motivation and attention; B-endorphin neuropeptides are involved with pain perception, pathological pain, and psychopathological disorders; and vasopressin is active in memory processes. These findings suggest that because of the opiates' ability to mimic and displace natural brain endocrines, they can influence pain and reward responses and subsequently are self-reinforcing. Thus, opiates have the ability to "control" behavior which leads to their continued use. This is one definition of dependence.

A definition of dependence includes several criteria such as physical dependence, behavioral dependence, the negative reinforcing abstinence syndrome, and the positively reinforced conditioning factors. The complex interaction of personality, environment, and drug effects can be understood best as a continuum along which these different factors contribute in varying degrees to the dependence behavior.

Opiate dependence represents a classical model of conditioning. A specified antecedent condition elicits a response which becomes reinforced. The opiate becomes an effective positive reinforcer and the environmental context in which the drug is self-administered becomes one of the antecedent conditions in addition to being a conditioned secondary reinforcing stimuli. Successful treatment and rehabilitation of drug-dependent individuals must take into consideration the behavioral paradigm outlined above.

Examining past histories of heroin users, Chein (1964) describes not an addictive personality per se, but an underdeveloped personality, one that is retarded in development by pathological social conditions. This may account for the high incidence of drug experimentation in the ghettos. It is difficult to pinpoint the initial factor, but the slums are basically places of high anxiety and frustration, with little development of competence to handle these problems. Broken homes are commonplace, and children and parents all suffer the obvious disadvantages. Even in homes in which the parents have managed to stay together, the fatigue and preoccupation with life struggles allow little time for gaining insight into the child's role and human individualism. Expectation as well as discipline are sporadic, based on mood. Goals are often unrealistic dreams. Graduating from this impoverished preschool environment, these individuals are often seen as unteachable and incorrigible misfits by inexperienced teachers. On the street, an aimless delinquent subculture develops as the only sympathetic diversion to a hostile home and school environment.

Superficially, there is nothing mysterious or obscure about the conflicts that develop in these situations, but researchers have been a bit overzealous in reasoning that these conflicts are responsible for a lifelong desire to withdraw. More realistically, these may be powerful motivators for initial experimentation, for few examples of consistent psychopathological personality have been observed when the drug cycle has been blockaded in programs such as methadone maintenance (Dole & Nyswander, 1966).

Since Chein's classic work in the late fifties and early sixties, the heroin scene in the United States has changed, not by the elimination of the underprivileged user, but by the addition of more users from the middle and upper socioeconomic classes. Even though these individuals are more privileged, they possess some of the same developmental problems as their less fortunate counterparts. In this light, the heroin user is regarded as being abnormally high in externalization and abnormally low in ego development. The result is a particular susceptibility to social and environmental reinforcers and influences. In the case of dependence, drugs as well as many other environmental influences become powerful determinants of behavior. Current psychological literature is saturated with research suggesting a trend toward the increased externalization of society in general. Certainly an abuser of anything, be it TV, food, smoking, or drugs, has surrendered some of his or her inner power to the external object, substance, or in many cases, to another person. The heroin-dependent individual however, has relinquished his or her power to a more destructive force, a potent drug that can reduce anxiety, relieve pain, and bring the external world more ''in line'' with the inner world (McAuliffe & Gorden, 1974).

This destructive nature of heroin and the hazards to which a chronic heroin user is subjected led Khantzian (1977) to hypothesize a theory of self-disregard associated with impairments of ego function designated as self-care and self-regulation. There is little evidence of the addict's fear, anxiety, or realistic assessment of the dangers inherent in his or her life style.

There is no universal agreement as to the cause of addiction. Consequently, there has been no agreement on the most effective methods of rehabilitation. The life of addiction has been a total life to the addict. Heroin is not just a chemical taken at intervals; it is a social life, a psychological life, a physical life—in fact, the addict's life is totally centered on that necessary chemical. This totality contributes to the difficulty of rehabilitation. To the heroin-dependent person, only money and heroin count. In the process of rehabilitation something must be substituted for heroin, and the first step in this substitution is that of filling up time. The ex-user has all the time in the world—time formerly spent in the cycle of hustling and shooting up. Now that time must be filled with nondrug-oriented behavior, and the absence of supportive aid, this sick, disoriented person who continually has the feeling that "something is missing" will go back to the old drug life for lack of anything better to do.

Because of this need for multidimensional reorientation, only a small percentage of heroin addicts up to this time have been "cured." Treatment and rehabilitation attempts must strive for this goal, and the closer they come, the higher the cure rate will be. With this in mind, we will examine the current treatments and rehabilitation programs available in the country today, and point out in what ways they serve the addict.

TREATMENT AND REHABILITATION

The current dominant modalities used singly or in combination for treatment of opiate dependence include acute withdrawal, pharmacological intervention, behavioral intervention, social group support, therapeutic communities, and social service approaches.

Since dependence on the opiates has existed for centuries, one might assume that knowledge of causative factors and methods of rehabilitation would be well advanced. Unfortunately, program after program has been theorized, tried, and shelved in the attempt to control addiction and the sociopathology surrounding it. The difficulty lies in the psychosocial components of addiction. Even though there are no preaddictive personality traits that can be used to predict which members of our society will become influenced and subsequently driven by heroin, there are any number of traits that are shared by the majority of heroin addicts. Reiteration of psychosocial traits of the addict, as reported by Chein in 1964 and continually validated by subsequent research, are given in Table 10.2.

The traits listed in Table 10.2 do not describe every user, nor does every individual with many of these traits become a heroin dependent. But knowing they are shared by a large number of individuals should be helpful in devising programs of treatment.

The first serious attempt to rehabilitate the heroin user became a reality with the opening of the two federal hospitals at Lexington, Kentucky, and Fort Worth,

Table 10.2   Psychosocial Traits of Heroin Users

Social	Psychological
Impoverished	Weakness of character
Pathological social conditions	Self-indulgent quest for euphoria
Broken homes	Need to escape reality
Poor parental guidance in discipline or goals	Emotional preoccupation with self
Poor family cohesiveness	Fearful
Criminal	Lacking self-assurance, self-confidence
	Underdeveloped personality
	Retarded development
	Feeling of futility
	Feelings of negativism

Texas, in 1936 and 1938, respectively. The emphasis was on the withdrawal procedure, followed by an attempt at psychological and vocational rehabilitation. With major emphasis on the medical aspect and minor emphasis on those traits outlined in Table 10.2, success was not to be expected, and the absolute failure of these federal narcotics hospitals is well known. The return rate varies from report to report, but approximately 95 percent of those treated eventually returned to drugs, 90 percent within six months after their release. Supporters of this program were quick to point out such obvious factors as forced confinement and quick release as major contributors to failure. While not denying that these built-in pitfalls were significant, one must also consider the methods and underlying philosophies of the program, which in retrospect seem to have been based more on legal detoxification than on psychosocial support. Being unable to rationalize the support of a heroin habit, hospital authorities gave primary consideration to abrupt and absolute withdrawal; thus, little attention was given to prewithdrawal support, sensitizing, or the building of incentive.

The socially conscious and enlightened 1960s did produce many programs that seemed promising, for they are based on more realistic theories. Dole and Nyswander (1967) have been responsible for the inception of several programs based on drug maintenance, centering their rehabilitation efforts on the idea that the symptoms of the addictive personality are a *result* of the completely life-engrossing drug habit and not the *cause* of it. In regard to the traits listed in Table 10.2, the theory of Dole and Nyswander (1966) (as a prototype for maintenance programs) is based on eradication of social factors that keep the user down, while the "third-community" approach (with Synanon as the prototype) focused more on the psychological aspects. The theory behind the type of rehabilitation exemplified by Synanon revolved around personality growth and the development of self-confidence, self-concept, and self-reliance. Each of these basic approaches is preceded, however, by medical treatment or withdrawal from heroin, which takes place before rehabilitation is attempted.

Withdrawal

This represents the simplest approach to treatment and consists of a supervised period of opiate withdrawal. The heroin-dependent person is usually given methadone for a short period of time and then that drug is gradually withdrawn. If the patient has been on a methadone maintenance program for a prolonged period, the gradual withdrawal may consist of gradually reduced dosages over a period of weeks. The pain and discomfort of abstinence symptoms can be reduced through the use of other drugs, such as clonidine, tricyclic antidepressants, and benzodiazepines.

Available data suggest that a withdrawal strategy alone is usually not effective in that after discharge from the hospital the individual is likely to return to a pattern of drug use. Simple withdrawal does little to reduce the strength of conditioned behaviors.

MAINTENANCE PROGRAMS

Much research in medicine centers on identification of the cause of a disease, and subsequent elimination of the cause usually eliminates the problem. However, in the case of heroin dependence, there are two basic areas with which one must deal. The first is a *psychosocial circle* of conditions and events leading to experimentation with heroin; the other is a *psychophysiological circle,* which necessitates continuation of heroin use. If all the psychological and social conditions mentioned earlier in this chapter were responsible for drug use, then we would have to rid the user of these factors so that stronger, more adaptive personalities would develop. Although this is not a realistic short-range goal for our society, "third communities" rehabilitation are evidence that a change in environment will support drug abstinence.

Since American scientific technology has advanced more rapidly than have social conditions, it would appear that the psychophysiological circle would be the more profitable of the two on which to work, even if such work were only a stopgap measure. Programs based on this premise are called *maintenance programs.* Although they are now being used in many countries of the world, the program in use in England has received the most publicity and is known as the "British system." In this program, the heroin user receives a regular daily supply of opiates free or at minimal cost. He or she is under the supervision of a knowledgeable and ethical physician who supplies the maintenance needs. The program is in the hands of a specialized individual in each area, thus reducing the corruption that once plagued the system. While the British have not legalized heroin possession, its use under a physician's care is legal. The drug culture there remains basically stable, and little crime is attributed to opiate addicts (Kramer, 1972). When involved in this program, the user does not spend his or her life seeking sources of heroin or the goods to pay for it.

Methadone Maintenance

A similar system in the United States is the use of methadone maintenance. Methadone (diphenyl-dimethylaminoheplanone—trade and generic names include Methadone hydrochloride, Adanon HCl, Dolophine HCl, Althose HCl, and Amidone HCl), like morphine, is an analgesic drug, but is dissimilar in chemical structure. This completely synthetic substance does possess pharmacological characteristics much like those of morphine but has many practical advantages over the opiates:

1. It can be taken orally, mixed with drinks such as orange juice, in doses from 40 milligrams to 120 milligrams; most average around 50 milligrams per day.
2. Its metabolism is sufficiently slow to prolong its action for twenty-four hours.
3. It is less likely to cause toxic side effects, such as the menstrual irregularities suffered by most female users, than is morphine.
4. Most important, it suppresses the desire for heroin primarily by blocking heroin euphoria and abstinence symptoms.

Methadone is a narcotic, and does produce tolerance and physical dependence. Although the mechanism of its action is poorly understood, the theories resemble those put forth for morphine. One of these theories hypothesizes a selective depression of interneurons of the spinal cord and postganglionic neurons of the autonomic system. Although its primary involvement seems to be with the cholinergic system (the system of nerve fibers activated by acetylcholine), findings of both increases and decreases in acetylcholine obscure exact evidence of its depressive mechanism. Depression of selected reflexes indicates action on the spinal cord, decreases in respiration rate indicate action on the medulla, and decreases in body temperature indicate action on the hypothalamus. Involvement with the hypothalamic-pituitary-adrenal axis may be indicated by suppression of the release of ACTH (adrenocorticotropic hormone, the pituitary hormone responsible for initiating the stress response in the body), and could be responsible, therefore, for generally suppressed stress reactions. The suppressed production of sex hormones could also be responsible for the menstrual problems of the female and the loss of libido experienced by both sexes (Cushman et al., 1970).

Aside from constipation, patients have not shown any major ill effects from taking methadone. Both mental and neuromuscular functions appear to be normal. Patients perform well at jobs and in the classroom. In fact, researchers have not been able to find a medical or psychological test, except urinalysis, that can distinguish methadone patients from normal individuals.

In the methadone maintenance program, the user's cycle of hustle, fix, hustle, fix is broken and the search for drugs is ended. In essence, he or she is stabilized in a state of blockade, between euphoria and withdrawal. Patients have shown that they soon begin to tolerate frustrating situations without feeling the hunger for heroin. Their dreams and conversations about drugs begin to subside and often, when busy, they even forget periodic medication (Dole & Nyswander, 1966).

Methadone blocks the physical need for heroin, thus removing physical behavior from the heroin pattern (Fig. 10.2) With this removal, changes in social and psychological behavior are evident, but depend solely on the maintenance drug. Unlike some of the self-help programs to be discussed later, methadone maintenance per se does little for psychological and social development. Indirectly, however, it does allow ex-users to stay off heroin, to get steady jobs, to support their families, and to get a start on the way to becoming productive members of society. In this way methadone maintenance contributes not only to social factors but to psychological factors as well.

However, at this time there are a number of drawbacks to and criticisms of the methadone maintenance program:

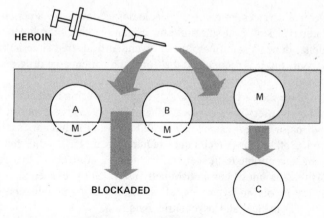

A Psychological behavior
B Sociological behavior
C Physical behavior
M Methadone treatment

Fig. 10.2 Methadone blocking the physical need for heroin.

1. Even though the daily cost to the addict is roughly that of a cup of coffee, the total treatment costs to society are substantial.
2. Doctors are justifiably reluctant to start young patients on a treatment that could keep them dependent for life.
3. It ties the patient to a daily ritual of receiving the medicine at outpatient clinics.
4. Methadone maintenance is at best an incomplete cure.
5. The giving of an addicting drug to drug users is contrary to prevalent morality.
6. Some methadone eventually finds its way into the street market.

Paradoxically, the most severe criticisms of methadone clinics stem from problems peripheral to the heroin problem. Many heroin users are also alcoholics and pill users. Methadone clinics can be gathering places for boisterous drunks, drug dealers, and unemployed loiterers. Yielding to the community's concerns, many clinics have closed and funding reduced. This, of course, is like the old saying of throwing out the baby with the bath water. For no other program, drug-free or maintenance, has had better results than the methadone maintenance in long-term care of chronic heroin users. Tens of thousands of previously intractable heroin addicts, most of whom had previously failed in various abstinence-directed treatments, have been restored to living normal lives (Dole & Nyswander, 1983).

Methadone Detoxification

The two major modalities that use methadone, detoxification and maintenance, are often confused. The methadone regulations issued by the FDA define detoxification treatment and maintenance as follows.

Detoxification treatment using methadone is the administering or dispensing of methadone as a substitute narcotic drug in decreasing doses to reach a drug-free state in a period not to exceed twenty-one days in order to withdraw an individual who is dependent on heroin or other morphinelike drugs from the use of these drugs.

Maintenance treatment using methadone is the continued administering or dispensing of methadone, in conjunction with provision of appropriate social and medical services, at relatively stable dosage levels for a period in excess of twenty-one days as an oral substitute for heroin or other morphinelike drugs, for an individual dependent on heroin. An eventual drug-free state is the treatment goal for patients but it is recognized that for some patients the drug may be needed for long periods of time.

Since the early 1950s various techniques using methadone for the detoxification of heroin users have evolved. Chambers (1973) has grouped these techniques into two major categories: inpatient withdrawal and ambulatory (or outpatient) detoxification. Both of these techniques require certain basic adjustments to make the treatment appropriate to the patient, including modifications that take into consideration (1) the amount of heroin habitually used; (2) the existence of multiple-drug dependency involving hypnotics, alcohol, or minor tranquilizers; and (3) the patient's overall physical and psychiatric condition.

Proponents of inpatient methadone withdrawal generally assert that users present themselves not only with a drug-dependency problem, but with a multiplicity of psychosocial disorders as well. These external conditions are often regarded as the major underlying causes of the drug-dependency problem and figure importantly in the high relapse rates seen in patients following withdrawal. The goal of inpatient withdrawal is, therefore, to help an individual reach a drug-free state in a supportive and closely supervised environment which, for a limited time at least, protects him or her from the adverse pressures of the street. During this process it is hoped that the program will be able to provide adequate ancillary services (such as counseling, job placement, and so on) and that, once drug free, the patient will be more likely to become a productive member of society.

The philosophy of ambulatory withdrawal programs shares many characteristics with that of the inpatient technique. The first major goal is to stabilize the addict on a low to moderate dose of methadone (20 to 40 milligrams per day) and then to gradually reduce the dose until the patient no longer requires the administration of a narcotic to allay withdrawal discomfort. During the treatment process a great deal of emphasis is placed on helping the addict to learn new or to reestablish old productive behavioral patterns. However, the ambulatory methadone detoxification technique, more than any other, requires the patient to assume the largest share of responsibility for treatment and rehabilitation success. The physician's role is decidedly more passive than in inpatient detoxification; he or she can only administer medication and provide supportive services if the addict-patient decides to come to the clinic. During the course of withdrawal, the patient must, in fact, make a series of decisions to come back for treatment. In this sense, ambulatory detoxification becomes a social-interaction and motivational process, whereas inpatient withdrawal is more of a medical process.

Opiate Antagonists

Other pharmacological substances have also been tried in an attempt to find a more practical pharmacological deterrent to heroin dependence. Nalorphine, naloxone, cyclazocine, and naltrexone are a few of the drugs classified as *opiate antagonists*.

These are less objectionable than methadone from a moral standpoint, for they are antinarcotic and block the effects of morphine. Because of their toxic effects and their inability to relieve the craving for heroin, however, the antagonists are not as popular as methadone with patients. The mechanism of their action is not definitely known, but it is thought to be associated with increased acetylcholine levels at specific sites (Harris, 1970).

Treatment with cyclazocine first necessitates withdrawal from heroin. Then cyclazocine is administered in increasing doses until tolerance develops. The usual dose at which tolerance develops is about 4 milligrams per day. This level will block the subjective effects of 20 to 25 milligrams of heroin for a period of twenty to twenty-six hours. The user is usually tranquil and free of anxiety, without any appearance of sedation or mental disturbance. Most important is the absence of the drive to find heroin, which allows for social rehabilitation and increased productivity.

Nalorphine is too short-acting to be of much clinical value; it is used more to detect the use of heroin and to counteract the effects of overdose. Naloxone must be administered in massive doses to achieve heroin blockage, and since its supply is limited, its use is also limited. At this time there is very limited use of the antagonists in treatment programs because (1) they have unpleasant and disturbing side effects, (2) they must be administered daily, and (3) heroin addicts do not find these drugs helpful (Select Committee on Crime, 1971).

Naltrexone is the experimental antagonist drug that has demonstrated the best potential for usefulness in the treatment of heroin dependence. In the presence of a sufficient dose of naltrexone, heroin and other opiate drugs will have no effect. It is currently theorized that naltrexone's blocking effect is created as a result of its structural similarity to the opiates. It is believed that naltrexone molecules, through a process that is poorly understood, competitively displace opiate molecules at opiate receptor sites in the body. Through this displacement, the narcotic effects are blocked by an agent that itself is essentially neutral.

Naltrexone is nonaddicting and there are no withdrawal symptoms associated with its discontinuance. It is a nearly pure antagonist with no euphoric effects, and therefore it has no street value and does not stimulate any illicit activities in the community. Naltrexone's side effects are minimal. For many individuals there are no side effects, but in some cases relatively minor reactions occur. These include nausea and mild stomach pain, and a slight increase in blood pressure. Gastrointestinal reactions are usually relieved by taking the medication after eating a meal. Elevations in blood pressure are generally not clinically significant; blood pressure tends to return to normal as treatment progresses (Brahen et al., 1977).

Naltrexone is taken orally (it has an extremely bitter taste) in a variety of different dosage patterns. Individuals who are physically dependent on opiates must first be detoxified before induction to naltrexone. A dose of 50 milligrams normally lasts for about twenty-four hours, and doses of 110 milligrams and 150 milligrams last forty-eight hours and seventy-two hours, respectively. Induction usually begins at 10 milligrams and increases by 10 milligrams per day until the maintenance dosage level is achieved. One of the more common treatment regimens is 50 milligrams daily for an initial period of several weeks followed by a routine of three doses a week—100 milligrams, 100 milligrams, and 150 milligrams, on Monday, Wednesday, and Friday, respectively. In certain cases, twice-a-week doses of 150 milligrams on Tuesday and Friday may also be prescribed (Landsberg et al., 1976).

Drug delivery systems providing for the sustained, long-acting effect of naltrexone are being experimented with. Such systems utilize a variety of techniques ranging from microcapsules, tubes, and solid balls, to implanted discs and gelatinous masses injected intramuscularly. These vehicles will provide for effective antagonist blocking effects for periods of a month or longer (Willette, 1976a, 1976b).

THERAPEUTIC COMMUNITIES

Therapeutic communities are residential treatment programs that attempt to deal with the psychological causes of addiction by changing the addict's character and personality. The techniques used were modeled after those of Alcoholics Anonymous which involved repeated confessions, group interaction, and mutual support among the members. During the late 1950s and early 1960s, the concept of group therapy was growing in popularity throughout the country, and as therapeutic communities developed, they too adopted the concept as a major technique. The growth of therapeutic communities also paralleled the growth of communes, and some of the cooperative spirit of the communes were incorporated into the therapeutic communities. The idea of a group of people living and working together for their mutual benefit was, and still is, a basic tenet of the therapeutic community.

Although therapeutic communities are often managed by former users, and do not usually have mental health professionals on their staffs, the treatment method is based on two techniques of group psychotherapy. The first technique is confrontation, or encounter group therapy, in which the addict is forced to confess and acknowledge his or her weakness and immaturity. The second technique is milieu therapy, in which the addict lives and works within a hierarchical social structure and may progress upward in status as he or she demonstrates increased responsibility and self-discipline. The principles of behavior modification, or conditioning, are constantly applied within the community in the form of reinforcement of good behavior and punishment of bad behavior. The time period for treatment varies from one therapeutic community to another. Synanon is a permanent community in which residents may remain for life. Most therapeutic communities require members to stay for one or two years. The programs also vary in selectivity. The older programs screened applicants rigorously, accepting only the most highly motivated individuals. These programs also continue to be completely drug-free, whereas some of the newer programs use methadone maintenance or both methadone and drug-free therapy.

The problem with therapeutic communities as a treatment method is that they appear to be suitable for very few people. In fact, about 75 percent of those who enter them drop out within the first month. Some critics feel that the treatment of residents in a demeaning or punitive way, which is characteristic of many communities, is contrary to the principles of supportive psychotherapy. Because they are residential, therapeutic communities are more expensive to operate than drug-free outpatient programs, even though many are operated entirely by members. In terms of results, however, therapeutic communities do not appear to be more effective than other drug-free methods of treatment. Since Synanon served as the model for such programs, a few specific words on that program are warranted.

Synanon: The Early Model

Endore (1968) has stated that society prepares the crime, while the criminal merely executes it; he goes on to say that Dederich, the founder of Synanon, has designed a new society for drug addicts in which they no longer *have* to be junkies.

In recent years the reputation that Synanon once enjoyed has eroded substantially, as it has been referred to as a religious cult and a private army. The Synanon family structure has as its patriarch the charismatic figure, Dhuck Dederich. Devotion to him was a crucial element in the rehabilitation program. This transference to and absolute reverence of Dederich served to keep the addict at Synanon. One of Synanon's key ingredients was a powerful reward system that provided jobs, status, and recognition in a step-by-step, achievable pattern analogous to society at large. A basic strategy of Synanon is behavior shaping. The approach is the use of confrontation, frustration, and attack. A great deal is said about the small-group sessions in Synanon, but even its founder cannot fully explain them. They are dynamic encounters in which all the fury, frustration, and other deep emotions of one individual are pitted against all the others in the group. The only restraint is the basic rule of no physical violence. No one can hide from the truth, for other members turn their full vehemence on anyone who even appears to be deviating from the truth or hiding behind a lie. Since Synanon members live together within the organization's community, they relate with each other constantly, with all participants learning more and more about themselves, others, and the nondrug life in general.

Drug users have been likened to children who have not had a chance to mature or learn to live in a loving, caring, protecting world. Nearly every user has lacked these qualities in his or her life, and at Synanon each is finally given the experience of knowing them. One cannot rule a child with punishment and hostility, because a child does not come into this world equipped with a sense of moral responsibility. To continually punish children for a reason that they do not understand is to place on them a guilt for which they know no cause, and thus their development is arrested. At Synanon, residents are given the rest of their lives—if they wish to stay that long—to develop these missing characteristics. No specific time can be set on a cure for addiction. Some members move out of the Synanon community when they feel confident enough about their new nondrug life, but a large majority of the ex-addicts remain within the organization (Deitch & Zueben, 1981).

Therapeutic communities have claimed the highest cure rate of any rehabilitation program to date. Many people argue that this is due to the high degree of motivation of the members of these communities—people who voluntarily enter a program that they know will involve difficult problems of readjustment are obviously motivated toward cure—and perhaps this is an important variable. But the most important fact is that addicts have been transformed into complete human beings once again. This transformation has involved a change in all the factors of addiction—social, psychological, physical—and the chemical has been eliminated. We have seen that other treatment programs may attempt to change one or more of these factors, but unless all are ministered to, cure rates will continue to be low. The ex-addict must live a totally new life, totally different from the life of drugs, or he or she may be led back to the drug by old drug-conditioned reflexes.

Through the aid of therapeutic communities, a completely new environment is substituted for the old heroin environment; thus, our basic diagram of addiction can be revised to show all behavior moved outside of heroin into a new, drug-free world (see Fig. 10.3).

Halfway Houses and Other Rehabilitation Centers

There are other programs in the United States that offer the opiate-dependent individual a place to reconstruct his or her life. The services offered by halfway houses range from full-time residency, as at Daytop Village, to mere visits for counseling. These various programs throughout the nation are supported by many different institutions or organizations, and management and philosophy differ from program to program. Most of these programs treat users who have come to them from the courts, and the program is designed to enable each participant to reenter society. Halfway houses will most likely enjoy limited success because of their inability to minister to all of the many factors that cause addiction.

Legislative Programs

Civil commitment programs have been in existence in some states (led by California and New York) for about twenty years. Their primary purpose is to keep the heroin user off the street and away from the public. In comparison with programs such as therapeutic communities and methadone maintenance, which have had some measure of success in rehabilitation, these civil commitment programs may seem a step backward, but they are a temporary measure to protect society. Even if the heroin

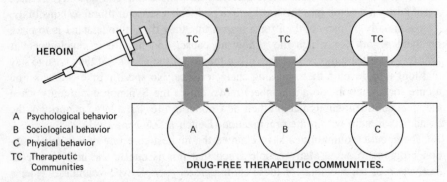

Fig. 10.3 Drug-free therapeutic communities.

user is no more inherently criminal than anyone else, once on the heroin cycle his or her involvement with crime increases significantly. It has been shown that one user can be directly responsible for starting at least thirty additional users. Though not all users are this prolific, most have been introduced to the drug by friends; thus, every user removed from the street reduces the number of potential users.

The particulars of these programs vary from state to state, but in general, when a person is convicted of heroin possession or of a civil crime related to heroin use, he or she may be sent to a rehabilitation center rather than to prison. The systems have been notable for their inflexibility and some centers are considered little better than prisons, but the courts have realized the drug-compulsion motivation for the crime and often dismiss criminal charges after several years of successful parole.

In most cases the user is sentenced to a specific period of time, which may vary from three to ten years depending on the offense. The first six months are spent in the rehabilitation center for withdrawal and for determination of psychological and vocational aptitude. After a brief stay at a regional center, the individual is discharged on parole and is supervised as closely as possible. Some centers ask the parolee to report regularly to a clinic for Nalline tests, which detect the presence of opiates. If he or she remains drug-free for the period of parole, the individual is discharged from commitment, and often criminal charges are completely dropped.

Drug-Free Outpatient Treatment

The treatment method that offers drug-free services on an entirely outpatient basis is referred to as either drug-free outpatient, ambulatory drug-free, or outpatient abstinence treatment. There are many differences among programs as to the scope or level of treatment they provide, but they usually include some or all of the following services: group or individual psychotherapy, vocational and social counseling, family counseling, vocational training, education, and community outreach. Programs also differ in the degree of patient involvement in treatment. Some programs are social or "rap" centers where patients drop in occasionally. Others are free clinics providing a wide range of health services. Some programs provide structured methadone detoxification and monitor patient drug use by urinalysis throughout treatment. Little evaluation has been done on this method of treatment since program records often omit data on patients who drop out of treatment early. Most experts believe that these programs do help some people but that the attrition rates are very high. It appears that drug-free outpatient treatment may be more effective with youths who are experimenting with drugs than with hard-core addicts.

Multimodality Treatment

Some treatment programs have adopted a multimodality approach by providing more than one method of treatment. This approach has the advantage of offering the patient a choice among alternative treatment regimens. Some patients respond better to a particular method of treatment than to another, and in a multimodality program patients can be transferred easily from one type of treatment to another. The larger multimodality programs may include methadone maintenance, detoxification services, inpatient and outpatient drug-free treatment, and a therapeutic community. The federal government today strongly supports the community-based, multimodality approach to drug-dependence treatment.

SUMMARY

The wide diversity of treatment methods reflects the present lack of precise knowledge about the nature of drug addiction and abuse. Uncertainty still exists regarding the causes, whether or not it is an illness, and the degree to which the condition is physical or psychological. Policy makers continue to debate these issues while research is attempting to increase our knowledge of this complex social problem. Meanwhile, even though treatment programs across the country are not "curing" some patients of their drug dependence, nonetheless, for the majority, these programs are providing support and a marked degree of social rehabilitation for better functioning and a better life.

Because no one method of treatment has proved to be the answer to the drug abuse problem, research and experimentation are being conducted on a wide variety of potential treatment methods. Some researchers are working with behavioral techniques such as aversive therapy, or negative conditioning, in which electric shocks or nausea-producing substances are administered simultaneously with narcotics. Others are using biofeedback techniques to train people to control internal states and body processes. Transcendental meditation has been investigated as a possible method of reducing soft drug use, particularly among college students. Much attention is currently directed toward developing alternatives to drug abuse, which may include any meaningful activity or pursuits in which young people can become involved rather than resorting to drugs.

REFERENCES

Atweh, Samir F. "Characterization and distribution of brain opiate receptors and endogenous opioid peptides," in J. E. Smith and J. D. Lane, eds. *The Neurobiology of Opiate Reward Processes*. Amsterdam: Elsevier Biomedical Press, 1983, pp. 60–85.

Brahen, L., et al. "Naltrexone and cyclazocine: a controlled study." *Archives of General Psychiatry* 34:1181–1184, 1977.

Bromage, P. R., et al. "Epidural narcotics in volunteers: sensitivity to pain and to carbon dioxide." *Pain* 9:145–160, 1980.

Chambers, C. D. "A description of inpatient and ambulatory techniques," in C. D. Chambers and L. Brill, eds. *Methadone: Experiences and Issues*. New York: Behavioral Publications, 1973.

Chein, I. *The Road to H: Narcotics, Delinquency and Social Policy*. New York: Basic Books, 1964.

Cohen, A. J., C. J. Klett, and W. Ling. "Patient perspectives on opiate withdrawal." *Drug and Alcohol Dependence* 12:167–172, 1983.

Cushman, P., et al. "Hypothalamic-pituitary-adrenal axis in methadone-treated heroin addicts. *Journal of Clinical Endocrinology* 30:24–29, 1970.

Deitch, David A., and J. E. Zueben. "Synanon: a pioneering response in drug abuse treatment and a signal for caution," in J. H. Lowinson and P. Ruiz, eds. *Substance Abuse: Clinical Problems and Perspectives*. Baltimore, Md.: Williams and Wilkins, 1981.

Dole, V. P., and M. E. Nyswander. "Narcotic blockade." *Archives of Internal Medicine* 118, 204–209, 1966.

Dole, V. P., and M. E. Nyswander. "Heroin addiction—a metabolic disease." *Archives of Internal Medicine* 120:19–24, 1967.

Dole, Vincent, and Marie E. Nyswander. "Behavioral pharmacology and treatment of human drug abuse—methadone maintenance of narcotic addicts," in J. E. Smith and J. D. Lane, eds. *The Neurobiology of Opiate Reward Processes*. Amsterdam: Elsevier Biomedical Press, 1983.

Endore, G. *Synanon*. Garden City, N.Y.: Doubleday, 1968.

Gay, G. R., and E. L. Way. "Pharmacology of the opiate narcotics," in D. E. Smith and G. R. Gay, eds. *It's So Good Don't Even Try It Once*. Englewood Cliffs, N.J.: Prentice-Hall, 1972, pp. 45–58.

Harris, L. S. "Central neurohormonal systems involved with narcotic agonists and antagonists." *Federal Proceedings, Federation of American Societies for Experimental Biology* 29:23–32, 1970.

Khantzian, E. J. "The ego, the self, and opiate addictions: theoretical and treatment considerations." *Psychodynamics of Drug Dependence NIDA Research Monograph 12*. Washington, D.C.: U.S. Government Printing Office, 1977.

Kramer, J. C. "A brief history of heroin addiction in America," in D. E. Smith and G. R. Gay, eds. *It's So Good Don't Even Try It Once*. Englewood Cliffs, N.J.: Prentice- Hall, 1972.

Landsberg, R., et al. "An analysis of Naltrexone use—its efficacy, safety, and potential," in D. Julius, and P. Renault, eds. *Narcotic Antagonists: Naltrexone Progress Report, Research Monograph 9*. Rockville, Md.: National Institute on Drug Abuse, 1976.

McAuliffe, W. E., and R. A. Gorden. "A test of Lindesmith's Theory of Addiction: the frequency of euphoria among long-term addicts." *American Journal of Sociology* 79(4): 795–840, 1974.

Seiden, Lewis S. Foreword to *The Neurobiology of Opiate Reward Processes*, J. E. Smith and J. D. Lane, eds. Amsterdam: Elsevier Biomedical Press, 1983.

Select Committee on Crime (House Report 92–678). *A National Research Program to Combat the Heroin Addiction Crisis*. Washington, D.C.: U.S. Government Printing Office, 1971.

Willette, R., ed. *Narcotic Antagonists: The Search for Long-Acting Preparations, NIDA Research Monograph 5*. Washington, D.C.: U.S. Government Printing Office, 1976a.

Willette, R. "The development of sustained action preparations of narcotic antagonists," in D. Julius and P. Renault, eds. *Narcotic Antagonists: Naltrexone Progress Report*. Rockville, Md.: National Institute on Drug Abuse, 1976b.

SUGGESTED READINGS

Bellis, D. J. *Heroin and Politicians*. Westport, Conn.: Greenwood Press, 1981.

Bourne, P. G., ed. *Addiction*. Orlando, Fla.: Academic Press, 1974.

Courtwright, David. *Dark Paradise*. Cambridge, Mass.: Harvard University Press, 1982.

Kaplan, John. *The Hardest Drug*. Chicago: The University of Chicago Press, 1983.

Kaufman, E. The psychodynamics of opiate dependence: a new look." *American Journal of Drug and Alcohol Abuse* 1(3):349–370, 1974.

Khantzian, E. J. "Opiate addiction: a critique of theory and some implications for treatment." *American Journal of Psychotherapy* 28(1):59–70, 1974.

Krantz, J. C. "The fate of heroin in man." *Current Medical Dialog* 39:296–297, 1972.

Latimer, Dean, and Jeff Goldberg. *Flowers in the Blood.* New York: Franklin Watts, 1981.

Maddux, J. F., and D. P. Desmond. *Careers of Opiod Users.* New York: Praeger, 1981.

Milby, Jesse. *Addictive Behavior and Its Treatment.* New York: Springer, 1981.

Smith, D. E., and G. R. Gay. *It's So Good Don't Even Try It Once.* Englewood Cliffs, N.J.: Prentice-Hall, 1972.

Trebach, A. S. *The Heroin Solution.* New Haven: Yale University Press, 1982.

Westermeyer, Joseph. *Poppies, Pipes and People.* Berkeley: University of California Press, 1982.

Wishnie, H. "Opioid addiction: a masked depression," in S. Lesse, ed. *Masked Depression.* New York: J. Aronson, 1974.

Wurmser, L. *The Hidden Dimension: Psychopathology of Compulsive Drug Use.* New York: J. Aronson, 1978.

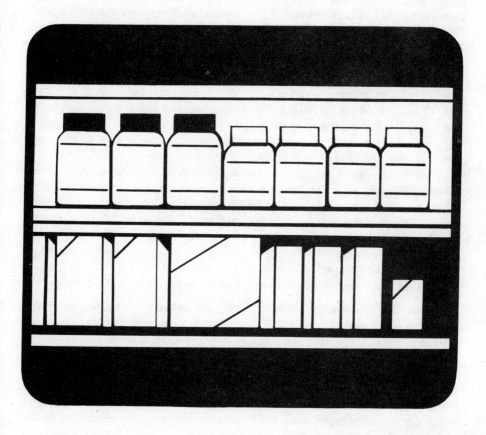

CHAPTER 11

NONPRESCRIPTION
DRUGS

Americans are basically independent and like to take care of themselves, and professional medical care is rapidly pricing itself out of the reach of the majority of our population. The persuasive television announcer outlines symptoms and assures us that we are not alone, that millions have insomnia or simple nervous tension, and either can be easily remedied by simply, inexpensively, taking brand X or Y or Z. Thus the foundation is laid for a rapidly expanding multimillion-dollar industry that produces virtually thousands of different nonprescription (or over-the-counter) drugs. It is not that Americans have that many ailments, but hundreds of millions of dollars in advertisements have convinced us we do. We are encouraged toward self-diagnosis and self-medication for everything from falling hair and fallen arches to the condition of one's breath, stomach, or bowels. We are so convinced of the need for self-medication that in the average American household thirty different drugs can be found, twenty-four of which are nonprescription.

While the average American does not buy over-the-counter (OTC) drugs in the pursuit of pleasure, he or she does seek and expect the drug to relieve some of life's painful reality. It is often said that we are a drug-using society, but more important, we are a drug-*mis*using society. If you define misuse as the taking of a substance for an effect other than that which the substance was intended to produce or can produce, then you must add the multitudinous proprietary medicines to the list of America's misused drugs.

How can the taking of nonprescription drugs be justifiably labeled misuse?

1. Nonprescription drugs, for the most part, are ineffective and almost never live up to their advertising claims. It should be noted that the advertising is based more on underlying wants, needs, fears, and desires to escape, than on medical cures. Senate investigations over the last decade have been looking not only at basic misrepresentation but also at the often unrelated psychological gimmicks used to promote these products.

2. Nonprescription drugs can be quite dangerous. There are dangers inherent in the chemical itself: dangers presented by personal idiosyncrasies (numerous deaths of individuals who did not know they were allergic to the substance have been reported), and the potential dangers of any drug used by persons who are unqualified to handle it. Ineffectiveness often leads to overdoses, and since most people are somehow convinced that all dangerous drugs are regulated by prescription, they do not consider an overdose of a nonprescription drug as dangerous. It should be pointed out that only the *most* dangerous drugs are regulated by prescription.

3. Nonprescription drugs are diversions of both time and money.

4. Nonprescription drugs give a false sense of security by masking symptoms; hence, proper medical aid is not sought.

5. Perhaps the most important factor is that the "better things for better living through chemistry" idea encourages the notion that there is a chemical cure-all for everything. This could be at the very root of America's drug problem.

This chapter presents only a few of the many classes of over-the-counter drugs; this discussion should serve as a model and be applied to the overwhelming majority of other drugs that need to be approached with extreme caution.

REGULATION OF NONPRESCRIPTION DRUGS

The fact that America is a chemical society can be understood in its fullest sense when viewing the thousands of advertisements and commercial messages that promote self-diagnosis by outlining symptoms. Although many suggest that one should see a doctor, they proclaim loudly that their product will do the job and at much less expense.

The public is also lulled into complacency by thinking that the legality of these substances ensures their effectiveness and safety. A brief look at the major legislative acts affecting over-the-counter drugs will indicate good intention, but a general lack of results. The first attempt at regulation came in 1906 with the passage of the Pure Food and Drug Act, which prohibited interstate commerce of adulterated or misbranded food and drugs. However, drugs did not have to be proven safe for human consumption until the passage of the Food, Drug, and Cosmetic Act of 1938. All *new* drugs coming onto the market had to be proven safe by the manufacturer and more carefully labeled. Still, old drugs were not covered by this law. Also in 1938, the Wheeler-Lea Amendment to the FTC Act provided additional control over false advertisement of drugs and cosmetics and over other deceptive practices not specified. In 1952, the Durham-Humphrey Amendment to the Food, Drug, and Cosmetic Act divided drugs into two classes: prescription and nonprescription. Finally, the Kefauver-Harris Amendment to the 1938 Food, Drug, and Cosmetic Act provided that the drug be proven not only safe, but effective. Again, only new drugs came under the law's jurisdiction.

Thus, it would appear that the public is well protected; however, some problems still exist. For example, the National Academy of Sciences-National Research Council evaluated drugs introduced between 1938 and 1962 for effectiveness, and in relation to label claims, the panel concluded that of the drugs evaluated, only 15 percent were effective. Twenty-seven percent were probably effective, but evidence was not conclusive; 47 percent were possibly effective (again, the evidence presented was not conclusive); and 11 percent were definitely ineffective. However, the major inadequacy of this study was that only 400 of the estimated 100,000 to 500,000 OTC drugs were studied by this panel. The past decade has produced thousands of new drug products, far too many for the Federal Food and Drug Administration to test. The government has initiated a program of self-testing by pharmaceutical companies and depends on their integrity for control. These companies, while basically honest, naturally accentuate the positive and eliminate the negative. In recent Senate hearings, testimony indicated that in case after case pharmaceutical companies have been guilty of misrepresenting, distorting, and even withholding information about their products.

Because of the growing concern regarding the safety and effectiveness of OTC drugs, in 1971 Senate committee hearings were held focusing on the promotion and advertising of OTCs as they affected competition, small business, and the health and welfare of the public. Due to the flourishing research regarding possible health dangers of the OTCs, the undeniable ineffectiveness of most of these preparations, and misleading labeling and advertising claims made by the manufacturers, the FDA decided to study, in an organized fashion, the safety and effectiveness of the OTC drugs. This monumental task involved categorizing the OTCs into twenty-seven classes,

establishing sixteen panels to investigate these classes, and then printing a conclud-
ing monograph regarding the safety, effectiveness, and labeling of the products
involved (see Fig. 11.1 for the FDA panel process). Basically, each panel looked
at two things: (1) the active ingredients (it is estimated that only 200 different active
ingredients make up the hundreds of thousands of OTC drugs), and (2) what these
ingredients could do for the consumer. Thus, each panel identified only those active
ingredients that were safe and effective and limited the labeling claims regarding
what those ingredients could be expected to do at a certain recommended dosage.

In organizing the investigation process, the panels set up were to study the
following categories:

Antacids and antiflatulents	Vitamins/minerals
Cough and cold products	Antidiarrheal products
Laxatives	Antiperspirants
Emetics	Sunburn prevention and treatment
Antiemetics	products
Dandruff products	Oral hygiene aids
Dentifrices and dental products	Hemorrhoidal products
Hematinics	Bronchodilator and antiasthmatic
Analgesics	products
Stimulants	Sedative and sleep aids
Allergy treatment products	Antitussives
Ophthalmic products	Antirheumatic products
Miscellaneous dermatologic products	Contraceptive products
Antimicrobial products	Miscellaneous internal products

When all investigations have been completed, the public will have greater
assurance that OTC drugs are properly labeled, safe, and effective at recommended
dosage levels. All were to be completed by 1975, but the process continues. As each
panel reports its findings, a press release is issued to inform us of the "recent

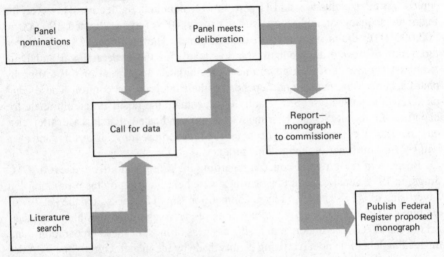

Fig. 11.1   The FDA drug review process.

findings'' regarding the use of laxatives, or mouth washes, or antacids. And although millions of Americans have learned that their favorite OTC drugs may not be effective, they continue to use them anyway.

When the FDA panel verifies that some products are not safe and effective or are mislabeled, the manufacturer of that product has a limited time in which to make it safe and effective and/or to change the label. The manufacturer might also choose to make a new-drug application, thereby gaining time to prove a particular product safe and effective.

Although the panels have found some ingredients to be safe and effective, they have at times concluded that a particular product in general might be unnecessary and could prove to be unhealthful for the consumer. The laxatives are an example of this, with the panel opining that there is widespread overuse of self-prescribed laxatives and that their prolonged use can seriously impair normal bowel function.

New regulations concerning the deceptive advertising and labeling of OTC drugs have also been adopted. Advertising is considered deceptive if an attempt is made to conceal the active ingredient or if the manufacturer attempts to create new markets by creating new diseases. A product is inadequately labeled if (1) all the ingredients and amounts are not listed, (2) the label makes exaggerated therapeutic claims, (3) warning statements are not prominent, and (4) the warning statements are not easily understood by lay people.

The following pages discuss some of the categories of OTC drugs and the findings of the FDA panels regarding the safety, effectiveness, and labeling of the products within the particular category.

ANTACIDS

Americans spend well over $100 million annually on antacid preparations, which are available in every conceivable size, shape, and form to fit the needs and convenience of the users. There are over 300 different brands of tablets, pills, gums, and lozenges, about 150 liquids, and over 100 different powders.

The first FDA panel to meet was the antacid review panel, and some of the pertinent guidelines brought out in this review process were as follows (1974).

1. Antacid manufacturers could make only three therapeutic claims on their labels—that their product was safe and effective for the symptomatic relief of ''heartburn,'' ''acid indigestion,'' and/or ''sour stomach.'' The label was also to include warnings of side effects that could be expected to occur in 5 percent or more of the consumers taking the product. Virtually all antacid labels one sees in the drugstore now comply with these early rulings.

2. The panel determined that there were only thirteen acceptable ingredients or groups of ingredients for antacids (these are given in Table 11.1). Manufacturers who did not comply with this ruling could continue to market a product if the ingredients were changed to comply with the panel's standards.

3. Maximum safe and minimum effective dosage levels were established for each of the active ingredients.

Table 11.1   FDA-Acceptable Active Ingredients in Antacids

Aluminum-containing ingredients	Citrate-containing ingredients
Bicarbonate-containing ingredients	Magnesium-containing ingredients
Bismuth-containing ingredients	Phosphate-containing ingredients
Calcium-containing ingredients	Potassium-containing ingredients
Sodium-containing ingredients	Tartrate-containing ingredients
Sodium bicarbonate	Glycine (aminoacetic acid)
Dried milk solids	

The Disease

The stomach is equipped with cells that make and secrete hydrochloric acid (HCl) so that a proper pH can be established for digesting food, especially proteins. The stomach also has cells that produce mucus so that the stomach lining is protected from its own acids and enzymes. The ingestion of food becomes a stimulus for secretion of HCl into the stomach; certain foods especially stimulate this production (for instance, coffee and spicy foods). Nervousness can also cause hypersecretion of HCl. Gulping air while eating may also cause the heartburn or sour stomach that calls for an antacid. All of these problems then can singly, or in combination, result in acid indigestion.

Active ingredients in the nonabsorbable antacids are usually combinations of magnesium and aluminum hydroxide, but a wide variety of ingredients may be encountered. Antacids are usually considered effective if used properly; however, overuse can cause problems. Many of these preparations use aspirin, and individuals suffering from gastric ulcers, gastritis, and other stomach disorders should limit their intake of any product containing aspirin. Even for those without stomach disorders, antacids containing aspirin are not recommended for upset stomach, for aspirin is the single most ingested gastric irritant. In fact, the most-often cited reasons for the use of antacids (that is, heartburn, upset stomach, and acid indigestion) represent situations in which aspirin should have no place in the treatment. Also, alcohol and unbuffered aspirin exert a synergistic effect in promoting augmented blood loss from gastric mucosa.

Antacids are used by sufferers of gastritis and ulcers to keep acidity levels from doing further damage to the stomach or intestinal lining, but because of the ''overshoot'' phenomenon (when stomach pH is reduced by an antacid, the stomach's reply is to produce more acid), popping Tums or Rolaids may be as much a cause of the problem as it is a cure. Antacids are usually safe and effective when taken as directed; however, the stomach empties rapidly and the neutralizing effect is lost within thirty minutes. If the condition persists, additional antacids must be consumed. Food, especially protein from lean meat or milk (skim milk is as good as whole), provides good natural neutralization of the gastric environment and produces less constipation than do antacids.

If stomach neutralizing is needed, sodium bicarbonate (good old baking soda) may be the best bet—it is inexpensive and contains no aspirin or other ingredients, but the sodium contained in it and in many of the other antacids may cause possible side effects. Sodium promotes water retention and is contraindicated in those individuals with hypertension. Individuals on low-sodium diets should avoid sodium bicarbonate. Neither aluminum, magnesium, nor calcium should be taken with the antibiotic tetracycline, since they interfere with the absorption of this antibiotic from the gastrointestinal tract.

LAXATIVES

It has been suggested that laxatives are the most overused and misused OTC products in America. Hundreds of different laxatives are on the market and Americans spend several million dollars yearly on them. There are *bulk-forming* laxatives that may contain cellulose derivatives, polycarbophil, or dietary bran. These create bulk so that water will be absorbed into the intestines, thus easing the passage of fecal material. The FDA panel stated that bulk-forming laxatives are among the safest, since they work naturally. These laxatives require the ingestion of eight ounces of water with each dose to ensure that obstruction does not occur in the digestive tract. Dietary bran was given top billing by the panel—6 to 14 grams per day plus liquid is considered safe and effective. Bran-rich breakfast cereals and whole-wheat bread are good sources of wheat bran: 100 grams of bran flakes contain between 2.7 and 6.5 grams of crude fiber; one slice of whole wheat bread contains from 1 to 2 grams. Bran tablets were not given safe and effective status by the panel.

Another kind of laxative is the *saline* (salt-containing) *and other hyperosmotic* agents. It was assumed that they act by drawing water into the gut due to osmotic attraction to the salt or other osmotic agent, but the mechanism of action appears now to be a complex series of exchanges in the GI (gastrointestinal) tract (DHEW, 1975a). The panel concluded that saline laxatives should be restricted to occasional use only, as serious electrolyte imbalances have been reported with long-term or daily use. Examples of these laxatives are products with magnesium and phosphate salts. Sodium warnings must appear on the labels of these products, as must warnings against prolonged use or use by those with kidney disease or other ailments.

A third type of laxative is one that exerts its effects through *stimulation* of the gut. The ever-popular Ex-Lax and castor oil are included in this category. These laxatives should be used only occasionally and the label on such a laxative must read: "Prolonged or continual use of this product can lead to laxative dependency and loss of normal bowel function. Serious side effects from prolonged use or overdose may occur" (DHEW, 1975a). The mechanism of action of these laxatives is to move intestinal components through the tract more quickly by stimulating peristalsis in the gut.

Lubricant laxatives (mineral oil, for instance) make up another category designated as safe and effective in amounts usually administered orally. These laxatives are to be taken at bedtime only. The drawbacks to the use of mineral oil are that fat-soluble vitamin absorption is impaired, prothrombin levels may be lowered, and regular use in pregnancy may predispose to hemmorhagic disease in the newborn. Also, with chronic use (particularly with excess dosage), anal leakage and skin reactions may occur (DHEW, 1975a).

Since constipation is of such concern to Americans, greater knowledge concerning its cause should be sought. Definition is generally given as "difficult or infrequent evacuation of the large bowel," but many people have their own definition of "infrequent." The panel recognized as normal, three bowel movements a week to three bowel movements a day; information indicating that the low fiber content in refined foods common in the American diet may contribute to the high prevalence of diverticular disease, irritable bowel syndrome, appendicitis, and cancer of the colon suggests that regular emptying of the bowels is of importance to our health.

However, when the causes of constipation are reviewed, we can deduce that laxatives are not the answer to the problem. Constipation is caused by

1. Inadequate water intake
2. Inadequate bulk in the diet
3. Inadequate physical activity
4. Not listening to Mother Nature when she calls

Therefore, it follows that to avoid constipation, one should first of all drink plenty of water. Some authorities suggest ⅓ ounce of water per pound of body weight: In other words, a 120-pound person would drink 40 ounces (five 8-ounce glasses) of water a day. Also, fiber content in the diet—raw fruits, vegetables, nuts and wholewheat grains—should be increased. Besides the fiber content, these foods are full of vitamins and minerals beneficial to the body. Exercise, even walking, is another curative element that has fringe benefits here: Not only does it help to tone the smooth muscle of the gut, but it also has the possibility of increasing endurance, strength, agility, flexibility, and skill—not to mention the release of mental stress that may accompany, or may even be a causative agent of, constipation. And finally, keep in mind that it's not healthy to fool with Mother Nature—when she calls, answer. Try to establish a time of day when you will not be hurried out of the bathroom and develop a habit. Generally, the entire GI tract is stimulated by food, so become aware of the gut and its signals after a meal.

It is healthier and safer to treat your body naturally to prevent constipation, but if circumstances cause this problem, a natural laxative (bulk-forming or lubricant) is better for you than a stimulant or hyperosmotic laxative.

NIGHTTIME SLEEP AIDS AND DAYTIME SEDATIVES

Until the FDA panel reported on the safety and effectiveness of sleep aids and daytime sedatives, most of the OTC sleep aids contained antihistamines, scopolamine compounds, bromides, and/or miscellaneous compounds such as aspirin. The action of most of these substances was derived primarily from their anticholinergic properties, that is, they blocked acetylcholine at nerve synapses. The effects of the anticholinergic agents were variable and unpredictable, and often a bizarre combination of excitation and depression of the central nervous system occurred in users. Most brands contained some combination of several substances, and this often compounded the confusing symptomatology. Prior to 1979, OTC sedatives still containing scopolamine posed a potential problem known as "atropinic psychosis." Users of these sedatives frequently developed CNS toxicity (Moore, 1983).

The conclusion of the FDA panel regarding OTC sedatives was that the ingredients mentioned above (bromides, scopolamine compounds, and antihistamines) were not generally recognized as safe and effective as nighttime sleep aids or daytime sedatives (DHEW, 1975b). The bromides were considered unsafe in therapeutic doses as OTC nighttime sleep aids or daytime sedatives because of toxicity and possible teratogenic effects. Similarly, the scopolamine products were pronounced unsafe at doses high enough to be possibly effective. The antihistamines were listed as "probably safe and may be effective," but could not be considered safe and effective by the panel, since additional data were required before the marketing of sleep aids with these ingredients could be sanctioned.

Presently, the main OTC sedatives sold in the United States rely on either pyrilamine or doxylamine (both antihistamines) for their sedative quality (see Table 11.2). Drugs of similar chemical configuration are sold as antihistamines, commonly used to treat allergies and symptoms of the common cold. (As the name implies, antihistamines block the vasodilation action that histamine exerts on the capillaries, thus decreasing fluid loss and congestion in the nasal cavity.) The drowsiness or hypnotic side effects were, in the past, considered undesirable; today, it is the side effect that is being marketed in sedatives.

At recommended doses of the two antihistamines mentioned here, most people will develop some sedation. Other side effects include tremors, dry mouth, diplopia (double vision), weakness, paradoxical insomnia, and a "feeling of heaviness." At this time there is no long-term research on the safety and effectiveness of these drugs (Moore, 1983).

One problem inherent in the ineffectiveness of the OTC sleep aids is that when they do not give the desired results, users tend to overmedicate themselves. Two or three times the recommended dose may produce disorientation and hallucinations. The toxicity of these newer formulations is not expected to be of the degree seen in the past with combinations that included scopolamine, but since they have anticholinergic properties, large doses could produce confusion and impairment of memory. In acute toxicity, there may be fever, excitement, fixed and dilated pupils, and hallucinations (Moore, 1983).

Americans have become aware of and, to some extent, preoccupied with the

Table 11.2 **Active Ingredients in Some Selected
OTC Sedatives**

Sedative (Brand Name)	Sedative Ingredients
Compoz	Pyrilamine maleate, 25 mg
Nervine	Pyrilamine maleate, 25 mg
Nytol	Pyrilamine maleate, 25 mg and 50 mg
Quiet World	Pyrilamine maleate, 25 mg
	Acetaminophen, 162.5 mg
	Aspirin, 227.5 mg
Sedacaps	Pyrilamine maleate, 25 mg
Sleep-Eze	Pyrilamine maleate, 25 mg
Sominex	Pyrilamine maleate, 25 mg
Somnicaps	Pyrilamine maleate, 25 mg
Unisom	Doxylamine succinate, 25 mg

detrimental effects of arousal caused by the stress and tension of modern society. It has been estimated that as many as one-half of the patients crowded into physicians' waiting rooms have ailments that are either entirely emotional or that have significant emotional overtones. Solomon and colleagues (1979) reported that nearly one-third of Americans over 18 say that they have had at least one incident of not being able to get to sleep in a given year. Consequently, it can be seen that tranquilizers rank just behind antibiotics as the most-often prescribed drugs. In a large sample of nonpsychiatric patients who used psychotropic drugs, 23 percent of those who used hypnotics used OTC sedative-hypnotics (Greenblatt et al., 1975).

After studying the effects of an OTC tranquilizer (Compoz), prescription tranquilizers (Librium), and a sugar pill placebo on patients showing mild to moderate symptoms of anxiety and tension, Rickels and Hesbacher (1973) concluded that in terms of clinical efficiency, Compoz did not differ from the placebo. The prescription tranquilizers proved most effective.

As more research on sleep is conducted, it is hoped that the treatment approach to sleep problems will change. It is becoming increasingly apparent that sleep requirements differ from one individual to the next, and that as we age, we need fewer hours of nightly sleep. However, many people hold to the old concept that everyone must have eight hours of undisturbed sleep. No hypnotic drug can produce a natural, normal night's sleep, as all drugs change sleep patterns, and not many drugs continue their original sedative effect for more than a few nights in a row.

While recognizing that the experiencing of occasional sleep problems is a valid indication for OTC medication, the FDA panel warned that people with severe or chronic insomnia are not candidates for self-medication. If insomnia is serious enough to interfere regularly with a person's normal waking activities, the need for clinical treatment and/or prescription is indicated. Insomnia is not a disease, it is the symptom of a problem (worry about something or someone), so the only conclusive way to cure insomnia is to go to the heart of the problem and deal with it. Professional therapeutic help in the form of psychological counseling may be indicated.

ANALGESICS

It should come as no surprise that the most common analgesic in the world is aspirin (acetylsalicylic acid). Although this acid was not synthesized as aspirin until the nineteenth century, natural sources of its active ingredients have been used for thousands of years. Thanks to the stress and strain of our modern society (or to effective advertising), the "ailing" United States population's daily ingestion of aspirin tablets is rapidly approaching 50 million. There are hundreds of products that have acetylsalicylic acid as their primary ingredient. Pharmaceutical manufacturers have buffered it, colored it, sugar-coated it; they have made it fizz, given it a round or oblong shape, and put it in time-release capsules. As the packaging changes, so does its use. One shape is advertised for use on the good old-fashioned headache, another shape for nervous tension. Of course, the ones for nervous tension caused by screaming children are different from the ones for nervous tension caused by missing a bus! If it is pretty enough and has a feminine-sounding name, women can use it for menstrual pain; and if it is candy-coated, children will enjoy it. Symptoms such as headache, upset stomach, and nausea constitute to millions of Americans a signal for the ingestion of aspirin. If one is looking for an example of drug misuse, aspirin consumption in the United States today is as good an example as any.

Acetylsalicylic acid is truly a wonder drug. Its adverse effects are minimal compared to its beneficial pharmacological action. Still, aspirin follows only barbiturates, alcohol, and carbon monoxide in the number of fatal poisonings attributed to it annually. Excess use of aspirin has also been linked with certain kinds of kidney disease. Approximately two out of every 1,000 persons are hypersensitive to aspirin and approximately 16 percent of asthmatic patients are allergic to it. Young children whose systems cannot withstand the dehydration and acid-base change are most affected. It should come as no surprise that the flavored compounds are responsible for 62 percent of the salicylate poisonings (Dipalma, 1981). Also, since two aspirins can have an adverse effect on blood-clotting time for up to two weeks, women who use them immediately before or during their menstrual periods may increase the blood volume lost, thus adding to their menstrual problems. Likewise, aspirin should not be taken before surgery or by a blood donor before giving blood. One of the more publicized dangers of aspirin, especially nonbuffered aspirin, is possible gastrointestinal bleeding.

Administration and Absorption of Aspirin

The rapid absorption of aspirin from the gastrointestinal tract is one of its most attractive features. Fifty percent of the normal dose of 650 milligrams (usually two 325-milligram tablets) is absorbed within thirty minutes. The convenience of analgesia over an eight-hour period has prompted many pharmaceutical houses to develop time-release capsules. It was noted in one recent study, however, that the convenience of the time-release capsule may be overshadowed by decreased effectiveness. In a comparison of aspirin and Bufferin with (time-release) Measurin, it was found that both aspirin and Bufferin produced higher early concentrations of salicylate and unhydrolyzed acetylsalicylic acid. The equal disappearance rate of the unhydrolyzed acetylsalicylic acid in the three cast some doubt on the benefits of prolonged-action preparations.

Primary Pharmacological Effects

Analgesic Action. Empirical evidence would seem to indicate that acetylsalicylic acid is effective in the relief of pain. The evidence is still empirical, for researchers have not developed quantitative measures of pain or pain relief. Pain produced by pricking the skin, applying heat to the skin and teeth, sending electric current through metal dental fillings, etc., has produced varying levels of pain in different people. Some studies have shown aspirin to be more effective than morphine and codeine in relieving pain, while others show aspirin as being no more effective than a placebo.

There is still some controversy as to the site of the analgesic action of aspirin.

Some researchers feel it is central in the hypothalamus, while others feel the action is peripheral. Still others believe the action to be purely psychological (the placebo effect).

It bears mentioning that even though the advertisements insinuate that aspirin will relieve the pain of a headache, they do not state this fact directly, for there is no evidence to support such a claim. Although headache is the most "popular" ailment in the United States, not a great deal is known about its causes and cures. It would stand to reason that the most common type of headache, the tension headache, thought to be caused by the pain of tense muscles of the head and neck being referred to subcutaneous pain receptors around the head, would be predominant in fast-paced technological societies. Not all headaches are psychological, just most of them. Many are psychosomatic—the pain is as real as that caused by muscle tension. These headaches perhaps result from psychological stress and worry for which aspirin may offer some relief by dulling the perception of the pain. In Africa, Asia, and the Antarctic, headache is almost completely unknown. In industrialized South America and Europe, headaches are a minor nuisance of life and are not a topic of conversation, a convenient excuse, or an indication that the individual is important enough to have something to worry about. In the United States, however, advertising has elevated the headache to a national institution. Symptoms are outlined, throbbing pain is vividly described, and most important, the social situations that might cause a headache are mentioned continually. An artificial ailment can usually be cured by a substance that is *perceived* as being effective. It is little wonder that forty cents of each dollar spent on such products is allotted to advertising.

Antipyretic (Anti-Fever) Action. Infectious disease often causes the body to produce and contain increased amounts of heat. Body heat is elevated by increasing body metabolism and through muscular activity, usually shivering. The delicate temperature regulator, or thermostat, in the hypothalamus, although functional, becomes set at a higher level. Body temperature in relation to the thermostat is cool; thus, shivering is initiated while heat dissipation processes are decreased.

Although the exact pharmacological mechanism is not well understood, aspirin seems to lower the thermostat and allow for dissipation of heat through normal process, such as dilation of cutaneous vessels. Aspirin is effective in the treatment of fever, but it will not lower temperature in individuals with normal body temperature.

Anti-Inflammatory Action. Acetylsalicylic acid has become one of the most-used therapeutic agents in the treatment of rheumatoid arthritis. Neither the pharmacology nor the mechanism of action is known, but aspirin seems to be effective in reducing the inflammation by decreasing the leakage of fluid from capillaries in the inflamed sac directly, or indirectly by action on the anti-inflammatory hormones produced by the adrenal cortex. Aspirin has also been shown to reduce fever associated with rheumatoid arthritis and to raise the pain threshold by interfering with the brain's interpretation of the pain or through interference with peripheral transmission.

Alternatives to Aspirin

Although aspirin is still the leading OTC analgesic, two newer drugs are gaining some of the market. These drugs are acetaminophen (Tylenol, Panadol) and ibuprofen (Advil, Nuprin). Along with aspirin, these drugs work by inhibiting the prostaglandins (natural hormonelike substances in the body) that trigger fever, inflammation, and pain. It appears that aspirin works to inhibit the prostaglandins that set off these three responses in the body, while acetaminophen inhibits only the prostaglandins that cause pain and fever. Ibuprofen works against an array of prostaglandins, especially those in the uterus, making this drug effective in relieving menstrual cramps (Buying Guide: Pain Relievers, 1984).

Acetaminophen, like aspirin, is reported to have analgesic and antipyretic action, but seems to be less toxic to the gastrointestinal system, resulting in less gastric blood loss, and does not seem to affect blood coagulation. It, however, does not have the anti-inflammatory properties of aspirin. Acetaminophen is not without potentially harmful side effects, especially fatal hepatic necrosis that may result from acute overdose (Flowers et al., 1980). Ibuprofen causes fewer side effects and allergic reactions than aspirin, but it also has some drawbacks (as shown in Table 11.3). Table 11.3 compares the indicated use, allergic reactions and other side effects, and contraindications of aspirin, acetaminophen, and ibuprofen.

In summary, aspirin is highly effective (and inexpensive, especially the generic brand) for pain, fever, and inflammation for those people who can take it safely. Acetaminophen is probably not as effective as aspirin or ibuprofen in relieving pain or fever, but it is useful for those who cannot take aspirin. Ibuprofen has fewer side effects than aspirin, but more than acetaminophen. It is a good choice for those who have aspirin-caused stomach problems. It is less toxic than the other two at high doses, but is more expensive.

When taking aspirin, you will decrease stomach lining irritation and bleeding by crushing the tablets and mixing them in juice, milk, or water before swallowing them. With all of these analgesics, be cognizant that they should be taken as directed. If greater doses are needed over a prolonged period (more than ten days in a row), seek medical aid. Last of all, protect small children by using safety-cap containers stored out of their reach.

COUGH AND COLD PRODUCTS

If you have experienced the sneeze that is followed by a chill through your body, and then shortly thereafter have developed a sore throat, runny nose, drippy eyes, and a cough, be assured that you have something in common with virtually everyone else: the common cold. The common cold is caused by a virus that changes strains as fast as some folks change their mind and therefore it has been impossible to develop a vaccine to cure the cold. The best that can be done is to treat the symptoms. The common cold will run its course in a week if you don't treat it with medicines, and it lasts about seven days if you do! What medicines will do—on the positive side—is allow you to feel less uncomfortable during your waking hours and

Table 11.3   A Comparison of Aspirin, Acetaminophen, and Ibuprofen

	Aspirin	Acetaminophen	Ibuprofen
Indicated use	Pain, fever, inflammation	Pain, fever	Pain, fever, inflammation
Allergic reactions, side effects	Allergic reactions of itching, rash, choking. Common side effects of upset stomach, ringing of ears. About 40% have some gastral bleeding. Can lead to ulcers or anemia.	Fewer than aspirin. Rare cases of skin rash and painful urination. High dose over long time may damage liver or kidneys.	Fewer than aspirin. Can cause skin rash, itching, G.I. upset, stomach distress, dizziness. May interfere with antihypertensive and diuretic drugs.
Contra-indication	Pregnant women in last trimester; children under 16 with chicken pox or flu (risk of Reye's Syndrome); those known to be allergic to aspirin; those with ulcers, gout, or stomach bleeding.	Alcoholics; people with liver or kidney disease or kidney infection.	People with gout, ulcers, or aspirin allergy; children under 14; pregnant women in last trimester.
Used in Treating:	Sprains, simple headaches, arthritis, broken bones, rheumatism, rheumatic fever. May help prevent heart attack.	Reduce pain, fever, in those who react poorly to aspirin. Does not affect blood clotting, so is safe after oral surgery.	Relief of joint pain, fever, inflammation of arthritis, toothaches, aches, and fever of cold. Excellent for menstrual cramps. Reduces blood clotting.

perhaps to sleep better at night. What they will not do is cure the cold. And on the negative side, cold and cough medicines depress natural reflexes like coughing and sneezing, thus allowing mucus buildup in the air passageways, especially those of the lungs, that may become an ideal breeding ground for bacteria. This may help to explain the chest cold that sometimes follows a head cold.

Commercial cough and cold remedies can be listed in five different categories: the cough suppressants; the antihistamines that dry up the runny nose and watery eyes; the anticholinergics, which also dry up eyes and nose; the nasal decongestants that open nasal passageways; and the expectorants, which encourage removal of mucus from air passageways in the lungs and throat. These five categories might be further honed down to two: cough suppressants and decongestants.

Cough suppressants exist mainly in the form of cough syrup, many times in combination with an expectorant and decongestant. The FDA panel reviewing these drugs warned that combination products are a waste of money if a cough is not accompanied by other symptoms (see Table 11.4).

Table 11.4 Cough and Cold Preparations*

Action	Mechanism	Active Ingredient	Brand Name (Examples)	Drawbacks
Suppressant (antitussive)	Inhibits cough reflex in medulla	Dextromethorphan, codeine, or diphenhydramine	Benylin, Congesperin, Pertussin 8 Hour, Romilar 8 hour, St. Joseph's Children's	Can suppress productive cough, leads to risk of infection of lungs due to mucus buildup
Expectorant	Helps loosen and thin mucus and other secretions	Usually guaifenesin	Anti-Tuss, Robitussin Expectorant	Question about effectiveness, still under FDA review
Combinations	Clear or prevent runny nose and sinus congestion; loosen mucus and other secretions; inhibit coughing	Dextromethorphan or codeine (suppressant); guaifenesin (expectorant); phenylephrine HCl, ephedrine, or phenylpropanolamine (decongestant); doxylamine, chlorpheniramine maleate (antihistamine); acetaminophen (pain reliever); alcohol; other.	Cheracol, Cheracol D, Coricidin, Dristan Cough Formula, Consotuss, Anti-Tuss DM, Halls Cough Syrup, Quiet-Nite Liquid, NyQuil Liquid, Romilar III, Robitussin DM and PE, Sudafed Cough Syrup, Triaminic DM, Vicks 44, 44D, and 44M, Robitussin CF	As a group, these combinations are not endorsed by the FDA. May contain less-than-effective doses of ingredients; combinations may be counterproductive and/or unsafe.

*Buying Guide, 1985; Moore, 1983.

Cough preparations with codeine were found safe and effective, as were preparations with dextromethorphan. The narcotic cough suppressants may become habit-forming; history shows that before strict laws on the marketing of codeine were passed, heroin or morphine addicts unable to get their choice drug would resort to taking cough syrup with codeine.

Taking a cough suppressant may prolong a cold because the natural mechanism for clearing the throat and lungs is depressed, but if the cough is a dry, hacking one, a product that soothes the throat may be helpful. It is particularly dangerous to disregard a sore throat, since streptococcal infection can result in rheumatic fever or other autoimmune disease.

Decongestants work by reducing the swelling of nasal tissues and the volume of serum lost from those tissues. Most decongestants in cold remedies are not effective at the doses recommended. Decongestants applied directly to the nasal passageway (usually by spray) are generally more effective than those taken orally, but the rebound effect here endangers the cold victim and he or she may actually become dependent on nose drops or nasal inhalants. This occurs because even though there is an initial shrinkage of tissue, once the medication is taken there is an engorgement of the tissue that surpasses the original stuffiness—hence more decongestant is needed. Labeling should indicate that one should not use the product for more than three days in a row. These products must also warn that persons with diabetes, heart disease, hypertension, or thyroid disease should not use the decongestant.

Whenever a cough or cold product is purchased, the consumer should be aware that (1) the preparation will not cure a cold; (2) it may have adverse effects, especially if it has a combination of ingredients; (3) it should be taken only as directed; and (4) the product should not be taken at all by some persons (Hecht, 1976).

Physical and mental fatigue or depression decreases the ability of the immune system to fight disease. A person so weakened is more likely to succumb to the common cold virus. If you recognize the symptoms of your cold and act immediately to counteract them with rest, good nutrition, and relaxation, you stand a better chance of staving off the consequences of a cold.

STIMULANTS AND ANTIOBESITY PREPARATIONS

A section of Chapter 7 was dedicated to showing that antiobesity preparations containing various amphetamines, while pharmacologically effective in curbing appetite, were not effective in long-term weight control. One can hardly expect nonprescription commercial preparations to be more effective! The "active" ingredients of these drugs range from caffeine and methylcellulose to various combinations of natural plants.

Antiobesity preparations can be divided into the following categories:

1. *Bulk preparations*. These add bulk to the gastrointestinal tract for the purpose of producing a sensation of being full. The active ingredient is usually methylcellulose, a nonabsorbable cellulose that is supposed to swell in the stomach. Popular examples of this type of preparation are Melozets, containing methylcellulose, flour, and sugar; Metamucil, containing dextrose, psyllium, and muccilloid; and Reducets, containing methylcellulose.

2. *Low-calorie foods and artificial sweeteners.* These are sold as drugs in drugstores and as food in supermarkets, but probably should best be classified as a food. A popular example from the past is Metrecal, which contains dry milk, soy flour, sugar, starch, dried yeast, corn oil, coconut oil, and vitamins. A similar product on market shelves today is Sego.

3. *Benzocaine preparations.* These are substances that act as local anesthetics to diminish response and sensitivity of the stomach. Examples of this type are Shape Up, containing benzocaine and sodium carboxymethylcellulose; and Slim Mint, which contains benzocaine, methylcellulose, and dextrose.

4. *Glucose preparations.* These substances use glucose to stimulate the satiety centers of the hypothalamus, thus reducing physiological hunger. Examples here are Ayds, which contain corn syrup, vegetable oil, vitamins, and sweetened condensed whole milk; and Proslim, which contains soy isolate, sucrose, dextrose, and powdered milk.

5. *Appetite suppressants that work on the central nervous system.* The active ingredient in most of these products is caffeine (a derivative of xanthine), which is indigenous to coffee, tea, and many soft drinks (especially the colas): or phenylpropanolamine (see Table 11.5). Caffeine does produce some stimulation of the CNS, and in most individuals will result in slight wakefulness, restlessness, and mild excitement. The diuretic action of caffeine may promote dehydration.

Phenylpropanolamine is a CNS stimulant, and in high doses its stimulating effect can be significant enough to contribute to appetite suppression. High doses can elevate mood and increase confidence, but can also have the potential to cause headaches, anxiety, irritability, apprehension, insomnia, agitation, and psychosis. Caffeine toxicity may also occur due to high doses, especially when it is taken in combination with phenylpropanolamine. Many people respond to amounts of caffeine in excess of 1,000 milligrams per day with behavioral symptoms that mimic anxiety neurosis.

Phenylpropanolamine toxicity may become more evident in the United States due to its CNS stimulating effect which has been ''black-marketized'' as various street drugs (Cohen, 1980). It has appeared at drug paraphernalia shops and on the street as ''Coco Snow,'' ''Pseudocaine,'' and capsules that look like popular am-

Table 11.5   **Examples of OTC Appetite Suppressants**

Brand Name	Caffeine	Phenylpropanolamine
Anorexin	100 mg	25 mg
Appedrine	100 mg	25 mg
Dex-A-Diet II	200 mg	75 mg
Dexatrim	200 mg	50 mg
Pro-Dax		75 mg
Prolamine	140 mg	35 mg

phetamines. As discussed in Chapter 6, the dangers of street drug look-alikes have been apparent since the 1950s and 1960s.

To reiterate the advice given in Chapter 7 regarding weight management: the most effective way to lose weight and maintain that lower weight is to change one's life style to include more physical exercise, moderate intake of a variety of nutritious foods, and an effective stress management program.

NONPRESCRIPTION DRUGS AS PART OF THE DRUG CULTURE

Over-the-counter medicines have been called ineffectual, innocuous, or mildly helpful. While most authorities agree that if taken as directed they do little harm, it has been pointed out that ineffectiveness often leads to overmedication and crossmedication, and may be a legal path to drug misuse and abuse.

Indirectly, nonprescription drugs may contribute to an even more serious social problem. The existence of so many drugs in the home, the ever-increasing reliance on chemicals as cure-alls, and the massive amounts of advertising are suspected to be related to the youthful drug scene of today. Advertising in general and drug advertising in particular are seen as having a significant influence on illegal drug use. The typical advertisement is composed of three parts: the first stage presents the problem or pain, the second stage brings on the pill, and the third stage shows orgiastic ecstasy, with everyone living happily ever after. The message of illegal drugs is in essence the same as that of OTC drugs: quick, easy escape or pleasure, immediate relief and gratification, instant solution to all problems. The relationship between OTC drug use and that of illegal psychoactive drugs has been found in several studies. One of the most publicized studies, conducted in New England, demonstrated an association between (1) student use of popular OTC analgesics and the use of illegal psychoactive agents, and (2) maternal use of OTC analgesics and the use of illegal psychoactive agents by their children (Estes & Johnson, 1971). It may be that the same factors that contribute to the overuse of OTC analgesics also permeate the use of illegal psychotropic drugs, but it is even more likely that the students who use these drugs have developed a pattern of seeking a chemical resolution to their pain and problems. More studies of this nature are currently being conducted, but empirical evidence and knowledge of the American drug scene would tend to make the results predictable.

REFERENCES

"Buying guide: over-the-counter cough syrups." *University of California, Berkeley Wellness Letter* 1(4):3, 1985.

"Buying guide: pain relievers." *University of California, Berkeley Wellness Letter* 1(2):3, 1984.

Cohen, Sidney. "Over-the-counter medicines. psychophysiological reactions." *Drug Abuse and Alcoholism Newsletter* 9(7):4, 1980.

DHEW, Food and Drug Administration. "Over-the-counter drugs." *Federal Register* 40(56):12902–12944, 1975a.

DHEW, Food and Drug Administration. "Over-the-counter sleep aid drug products." *Federal Register* 40(236):57292–57329, 1975b.

Dipalma, J. R., ed. *Drills Pharmacology in Medicine*. New York: McGraw-Hill, 1981.

Estes, J. W., and M. Johnson. "Relationships among medical and nonmedical uses of pharmacologically active agents." *Clinical Pharmacology and Therapeutics* 12(6):883–888, 1971.

Flowers, R. J., et al. "Analgesics—antipyretics and anti-inflammatory agents," in A. G. Gilman et al., eds. *Goodman and Gilman's the Pharmacological Basis of Therapeutics*. New York: Macmillan, 1980.

Food and Drug Administration (FDA). "A new standard for antacids." *FDA Consumer,* July/Aug. 1974.

Greenblatt, D. J., et al. "Psychotropic drug use in the Boston area." *Archives of General Psychiatry* 32:518–521, 1975.

Hecht, A. "The common cold: relief but no cure." *FDA Consumer,* September 1976.

Moore, D. F. "Over-the counter drugs," in G. Bennett et al., eds. *Substance Abuse: Pharmacologic, Developmental, and Clinical Perspectives*. New York: Wiley, 1983.

Rickels, K., and P. Hesbacher. "OTC daytime sedatives." *JAMA* 223:29–33, 1973.

Solomon, F., et al. "Sleeping pills, insomnia and medical practice." *New England Journal of Medicine* 300(14):802–808, 1979.

SUGGESTED READINGS

Armstrong, J. B. "Overmedicated society." *Canadian Medical Association Journal* 112(4): 413, 1975.

Babb, R. R. "Constipation and laxative abuse." *Western Journal of Medicine* 122(1): 93–96, 1975.

Beek, C. R. "Laxatives: what does 'regular' mean?" *FDA Consumer,* May 1975.

Graedon, J. *The People's Pharmacy*. New York: St. Martin's Press, 1976.

Griffith, H. W. *Prescription and Nonprescription Drugs*. Tucson, Ariz.: H. P. Books, 1983.

Handbook of Non-Prescription Drugs. Washington, D.C.: American Pharmaceutical Association, 1977.

Kaufman, Joel, et al. *OTC Pills That Don't Work*. New York: Pantheon, 1983.

Schaffer, C. B., and M. W. Pauli. "Psychotic reaction caused by proprietary oral diet agents." *American Journal of Psychiatry* 137(10):1256–1257, 1980.

Zimmerman, D. R. *The Essential Guide to Nonprescription Drugs*. New York: Harper & Row, 1983.

CHAPTER 12

STEMMING THE TIDE

Self-Test: ALTERNATIVES TO DRUG TAKING

On an individual level, stemming the tide of drug use comes from the willingness to use a variety of outlets other than drugs in order to meet basic needs. This questionnaire has been developed to show the options you choose in various stressful situations. Place a check next to any of the ways that you use or would be willing to try in each situation given here (Centers for Disease Control, 1983, pp. 182–185).

1. You are facing a boring evening or weekend at home and you feel very lonely.

_____ Go to a movie   _____ Work on a hobby or project

_____ Read a book   _____ Watch television

_____ Smoke some marijuana   _____ Take a short trip

_____ Go out shopping   _____ Go out to eat

_____ Have an alcoholic drink   _____ Call a friend

_____ Other(s)_____

2. You are at a party where you know very few people and you are feeling uncomfortable.

_____ Take a stimulating drug   _____ Have a few drinks

_____ Introduce yourself to a stranger _____ Start a party game

_____ Talk to someone you know

_____ Have something to eat   _____ Find something to read

_____ Sit down and watch the people at the party

_____ Pick out a record or tape you'd like to hear

_____ Leave the party briefly to take a walk

_____ Other(s)_____

3. You are feeling particularly discouraged because of a series of recent setbacks.

_____ Become involved in charity work

_____ See a therapist or counselor

_____ Relax with an alcoholic beverage

_____ Join a club or organization

_____ Watch some interesting television programs

_____ Go to a sports event

_____ Take a drug to feel better

_____ Give your house a thorough cleaning

_____ Start a new hobby

_____ Try biofeedback training

_____ Other(s)_____

Self-Test: ALTERNATIVES TO DRUG TAKING (continued)

4. You are feeling quite anxious about an upcoming event that will affect your future.

_____ Use a drug that has a calming effect
_____ Begin using a deep relaxation technique
_____ Plan an outing with family or friends
_____ Spend some time exercising
_____ Busy yourself with housekeeping or home repairs
_____ Relax with an alcoholic beverage
_____ Talk to someone about your feelings
_____ Read an absorbing novel or book
_____ Spend a day in the park
_____ Call a radio talk show
_____ Other(s)_____

5. You are feeling angry and frustrated as the result of an argument with a close friend.

_____ Release your anger in a vigorous activity
_____ Pour yourself a stiff drink
_____ Go for a long walk by youself
_____ Get involved in a craft or hobby
_____ Visit a few friends
_____ Practice meditation
_____ Sit quietly and think through your feelings
_____ Go to the movies
_____ Take a tranquilizing drug
_____ Plan and cook a special meal
_____ Other(s)_____

SCORING: If you have chosen three or more alternatives to taking drugs in each of these situations, it would appear that you have developed a healthier coping style than those who consistently choose drug taking.

The history of drug use in the United States shows periods of high activity followed by periods of lower activity, somewhat like the ebb and flow of the ocean waves. The ocean is always there. The waves become smaller and larger depending upon many atmospheric factors. The decade of the 1980s has been described as a "tidal wave'' of illicit drugs as they flood across the United States, Western Europe, and much of the Third World. According to government officials, the newest wave of drug traffic and drug taking adds up to the worst drug crisis the world has ever faced, felt even more forcefully than the drug crisis seen in the 1960s. Southwest Asia's "Golden Crescent" (Afghanistan, Pakistan, Iran) has taken over from Turkey and Mexico as the major supplier of heroin. There have been bumper crops of opium in Burma, Thailand, and Laos. As a result, heroin addiction is rising faster in Western Europe than it did during the 1960s. In the United States, a cocaine glut is forcing down prices of that drug, making it now available to the average citizen. Even officials who in the past were willing to collect their money and look the other way while Third World producers put drugs out on the market have also become alarmed. Their concern stems at least partially from the new practice of paying for cocaine with the exchange of man-made pharmaceuticals manufactured legally in Europe and North America. For these Third World nations, the drug problem has come home, and they are finding that they do not have the experience or expertise to deal with their new problem.

It has been estimated that illicit drugs generate between $40 and $80 billion in worldwide sales. In Colombia alone, cocaine and marijuana generate $2 billion a year, which is about 10 percent of the country's economy. In the United States, the cost of drug abuse is conservatively estimated at $25 billion per year, and that drug abuse adversely affects the lives of a large proportion of the population. Parents are particularly frightened at the incidence of drug taking that appears to be starting at younger and younger ages, dipping into the junior high and elementary schools of the nation. For these reasons and many others, a counteraction has been launched by private and government officials to try to stem the rising tide of drug abuse in this country. This chapter highlights the government initiatives set forth in the 1980s and also the programs shown to be effective by education and counseling.

GOVERNMENT INITIATIVES

The government has embarked on an aggressive campaign to reduce the availability of illicit drugs through diplomatic initiatives, vigorous law enforcement, measures to enhance prevention education, and aid to research and treatment activities. This initiative, entitled "A Federal Strategy for Prevention of Drug Abuse and Drug Trafficking" (1982), set the tone and direction for the government's overall effort to reduce drug abuse during the 1980s. The following is a brief description of the five main aspects of the Strategy.

Diplomatic Initiatives

As drug abuse is a major national and international issue, the United States, in assisting the governments of producer and transit nations, insists that these governments gain control over the cultivation, production, and distribution of illicit drugs (as is their responsibility under international treaties). Since 90 percent of the illicit drugs in the United States are produced in foreign countries, the ultimate goal of the international program is to reduce the availability of illicit drugs to this country. Within this goal, a top priority is crop control at the source through destruction of illicit crops in the fields and reducing licit production to remain within legitimate needs. A second priority is to stop the transportation of illicit drugs as close to their source as possible.

The Strategy recognizes that the international illicit drug control program can be only as effective as the national programs of the governments with which the United States negotiates and collaborates. The diplomatic challenge is to raise international consciousness of the illicit drug issue so that acceptance of national responsibility becomes an international reality, evidenced in increased action by affected governments—producer nations, transit nations, and consumer nations. Therefore, the strategy of the United States is a multifaceted policy and program approach addressing all of the international aspects of the drug abuse problem, including:

- Encouraging and assisting governments of producer countries to undertake crop control programs.
- Developing innovative mutual assistance treaties with foreign governments directed at facilitating judicial action against the drug trade, at seizing assets derived from drug trafficking, and at preventing banking procedures that conceal illicit drug transactions.
- Encouraging other nations to support international narcotics control programs which would include development assistance linked with crop control and cooperative law enforcement efforts.
- Encouraging international development banks to incorporate clauses in their loan agreements prohibiting the use of development assistance to enhance the growing of illicit drug crops.
- Curtailing the diversion from licit international commerce of pharmaceuticals and chemicals essential to the manufacture of illicit drugs.
- Increasing the effectiveness of international organizations involved in international drug control.

Some further description of the three spearheads mentioned here (crop control, development assistance, and enforcement assistance) may enhance the understanding of United States diplomacy in the international drug problem.

Crop control can take several forms: chemical eradication (used in Mexico for opium and cannabis control); manual eradication (used in Burma and Colombia to control opium poppy and coca leaf cultivation, respectively); and government ban on cultivation. The United States assigns its highest priority to crop control, but recognizes that comprehensive crop control agreements may not be possible in all areas. For instance, current political situations make it difficult for the United States to deal directly with some host governments. In addition, illicit drug production generally occurs in remote areas that are often beyond the effective control of the central government. The economic self-interest of the people who have traditionally cultivated these crops outweighs their consideration of the problems created by their harvests.

For a government to achieve control of illicit drug production it must be aware of the national and international effects of their domestic drug production, and have the political will and capability to enforce control policies. These conditions, which were critical to the success of the control programs in Turkey and Mexico, are not universally present in other producer countries.

The United States, then, seeks to heighten the awareness of the governments of drug producer countries, and then to encourage the governments to demonstrate their commitment to crop control through scheduled reductions in cultivation and production. The United States attempts to bolster political willingness through bilateral assistance programs, multilateral programs, and diplomatic efforts directed through other governments and/or international organizations.

As far as *development assistance* is concerned, the social, political, and economic consequences of change must be considered in developing a drug control program. While law enforcement and technological assistance may greatly improve a nation's ability to destroy illicit crops or interdict drug shipments, production in some areas is likely to continue unless the people involved are offered reasonable economic alternatives, such as income replacement programs that include crop substitution.

It is the United States policy that drug-related development assistance agreements, planned with the full involvement of host governments, should be conditioned upon concurrent agreements to reduce illicit drug production and evidence of the host government's commitment.

Strong *enforcement and control measures* by the host government in all drug source and transit countries are emphasized, as the United States cooperates with foreign drug control agencies by collecting and sharing intelligence on illicit drug production and trafficking. The United States also gives bilateral assistance for equipment, as well as training and technical services designed to strengthen foreign drug control programs. The United States supports and participates in international regional organizations concerned with drug control.

Drug Law Enforcement

The second point in the Administration's five-point program is reducing the availability of illicit drugs in the United States by disrupting key trafficking networks; intercepting illicit drugs en route to the United States; and cooperating with all levels of law enforcement officials and prosecutors to achieve the highest possible rate of conviction for drug traffickers, the seizure of their assets, and the ultimate destruction of their criminal organizations.

Federal efforts to stop the flow of drugs continue to be directed at seizing illegal shipments before they are smuggled into the United States. This is accomplished through the efforts of the Coast Guard on the high seas and by the United States Customs Service and Border Patrol along borders and at ports of entry. The Drug Enforcement Administration (DEA), responsible for developing interdiction intelligence, participates in joint operations along the borders and subsequent investigation of drug trafficking inside the country.

Domestic drug law enforcement is directed not only at the importation of drugs but also at the manufacture, distribution, and sale of illegal drugs within the United States. This includes the investigation, prosecution, and incarceration of drug offenders, as well as the seizure and forfeiture of contraband, profits derived from illegal activities, and drug-related assets. Domestic drug law enforcement seeks to expand the ongoing drug eradication efforts throughout the United States, such as the eradication of the cannabis plant by appropriate means; halting the flow of pharmaceutical drugs from legitimate uses into the illicit drug traffic; and bringing to bear the full range of federal, state, and local government resources against illicit drugs and the activities associated with the organizaiton or conspiracy behind drug trafficking.

Detoxification and Treatment

The federal government provides limited funds, on a matching basis with the states, to treat drug abusers, stimulating a national treatment capability far beyond that which federal resources alone can provide. Treatment programs have been directed at overcoming the physical problems of drug dependence and providing psychological and social counseling to help the individual drug abuser get along without drugs.

Specifically, the thrust of the federal detoxification and treatment strategy is to:

- Make visible the national network of drug treatment programs and established referral systems.
- Continue the evolution of successful drug treatment delivery services, with emphasis on encouraging the states to make their own decisions regarding the allocation of available funds.
- Seek less expensive, yet effective, treatment alternatives.
- Integrate drug treatment services into the general health and mental health care system to provide improved accessibility, acceptability, and use of mental health services; improved early case finding, referral, coordination, follow-up, and preventive/educational efforts; improved efficiency and reduced costs of the total health care delivery system; improved citizen participation in, and concern with, the care of the mentally ill; and creation of a unique training setting in primary health and mental health care.
- Encourage private industry, religious groups, private organizations, and state agencies to work together to support treatment programs.
- Promote drug-free treatment programs.

Research

The federal intervention strategy supports the development of new knowledge through basic and applied research, epidemiological surveys, and the transfer of that knowledge in an understandable and timely way to health care professionals, educators, law enforcement officials, and the public. The objectives of the research strategy are:

- Producing accurate, current, and clearly written information about drugs and alcohol and making this information widely available in a credible form to be used in education and prevention efforts.
- Developing an effective system to monitor the composition and potency of illicit drugs.

- Continuing to support longitudinal and epidemiological research to expand knowledge of alcohol and drug use patterns, risk factors, and the long-term health effects of alcohol and drugs.
- Giving priority to research into the development of chemical agents that will block or change the expected physiological effects of the drug.
- Emphasizing basic research into drug action, effect, and sites of action that ultimately produce biological and psychological effects.
- Studying the effectiveness of prevention and treament approaches.

The following activities are a few examples of government research involvement.

- The study of brain receptor mechanisms such as those identified for naturally occurring opiatelike peptides.
- The effects of alcohol consumption on neurotransmitters and their receptors.
- The basic biological and behavioral processes affected by marijuana.
- Determining the abuse properties of drugs and estimating the reinforcing potential of drugs.
- Examining the biological and behavioral factors that may predispose some individuals to drug abuse and tend to make others resistant.

Education and Prevention

Major drug abuse prevention efforts during the past decade have demonstrated that there is no quick-and-easy solution to the complex problem of drug and alcohol abuse, so government strategy builds on prevention efforts that have a demonstrated potential for success, and remains flexible in responding to the problems of drug and alcohol abuse needs of each community. Since the people closest to the potential drug user can provide the most effective prevention effort, local groups have instituted many promising approaches to drug and alcohol prevention, including decision making, peer support, confrontation, and family, school, and community involvement.

The education and prevention strategy is based on the following premises:

- Drug and alcohol use must be addressed in the context of a range of problems that threaten young people and their families such as health hazards, unemployment, and alienation from community authority.
- Since school-age children are especially vulnerable to drug and alcohol use, the major thrust of education and prevention efforts must be directed to school-age children and their families.
- Parents and parent groups must be involved in education and prevention, as they are especially effective in preventing the use of drugs by school-age children. The Parent Movement is an outstanding example of the effectiveness that is possible when concerned citizens gather to address mutual problems.
- Accurate and credible information about the effects of drugs and alcohol must be readily available.
- The proper role of the federal government is to provide leadership, encouragement, and support.

In the private sector physicians, pharmacists, and other health care officials are asked to work with health care facilities, private organizations, and the legal system to find ways to reduce the dangers of inappropriate use of prescription drugs. In addition, commercial manufacturers are discouraged from glamorizing products by outright or subtle association with the drug culture.

EDUCATIONAL INTERVENTION

The key to controlling drug trafficking and drug abuse is to reduce the demand for drugs; therefore, prevention and education should be the main focuses. The United States has seen that costly law enforcement programs have done little to keep illicit drugs out of the country, to divert the interest and attention of young people from the "glamor" of the drug culture, or to arrest the chronic use of drugs in the adult population.

In current psychotherapies and psychosocial theory it is believed that to cure a problem, the cause should be treated rather than merely the symptoms. While drug abuse exists, both treatments are probably necessary, but prevention of drug abuse in school-age children and treatment of adult drug dependents may best be approached by filling the "voids" the drugs are asked to fill by drug takers. To encourage healthy behavior, personal needs must be met by appropriately healthy means. However, many people have not been educated regarding the choice of healthy outlets or have made a habit of reverting to unhealthy means. Examples of this are the cigarette smoker who needs a cigarette to calm down (rather than using a relaxation technique), or the shy youngster who finds that alcohol helps to diminish social awkwardness and uses the drug rather than learn positive social skills.

A psychosocial model of drug-taking behavior, such as the one presented in Figure 12.1, shows the progressive steps of drug taking along with appropriate intervention points that can stop progress toward drug abuse.

As pointed out in Chapter 2, drug-taking behavior is due to many psychosocial factors; therefore, appropriate intervention must be directed at those factors if the drive to diminish drug taking is to be successful. On a continuum of "least serious" to "most serious" regarding damage to the drug taker's physical, biochemical, and psychological being and also difficulty of rehabilitation, these factors are:

Curiosity
Spiritual search
Pleasure-boredom
Peer influence/social alienation
Lack of identity/apathy/psychic alienation

It appears that self-efficacy, or the conviction that one can successfully execute a behavior in order to produce a desired outcome, is related to non-drug taking (Eraker, 1986). Put in another way, those who have a strong sense of self-esteem, self-confidence, or self-actualization have less association with drugs because, rather than look to drugs as answers to their needs, they have fulfilled their needs in a growth-oriented fashion. It appears that education and counseling programs that work toward the end of establishing greater self-esteem in students and clients are appropriate preventive and interventive plans of action to fight drug abuse.

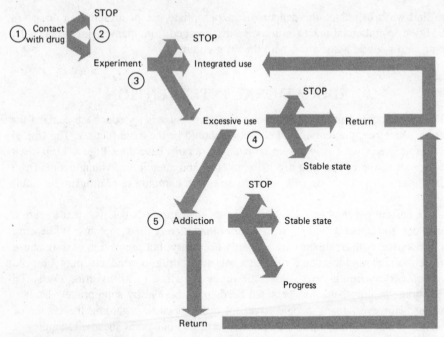

Fig. 12.1   Pathway to excessive drug use showing possible intervention points (numbered).

Ideally, an educational program offered by parents, school, and other institutions should be presented at each of the intervention points shown in Figure 12.1. The program should be multidimensional, graded for age and ability, and evaluated by empirical means so that success or failure can be noted. The programs should include cognitive and behavioral information and the practice of carryover skills. The following sections discuss some examples and merits of cognitive training, behavorial techniques, and various skills that have been successfully used to help prevent or discourage drug abuse.

The Cognitive Approach

Cognitive training includes factual information regarding drugs of abuse so that students know the potential physical, emotional, and societal hazards that accompany the use of these drugs. Cognitive training also includes rational therapies such as those promoted by Albert Ellis (1971) and William Glasser (1975), and other more recent techniques based on their earlier work (e.g., Kreigel & Kreigel, 1984; McKay & Davis, 1981). These therapies ask a person to become aware of thoughts, feelings, and actions in various settings, evaluate whether they are irrational or rational, and then execute future behavior based on what is actually there. Management of anger, an emotion that has been poorly studied but contributes to health impairment (both physical and mental) and disruption of personal relationships, can be approached in cognitive therapy. Novaco has used Stress Innoculation as a method to help individuals understand and manage their anger and stress (1978).

The common elements in the cognitive approaches, whether they are aimed at interpersonal communication, sports performance, or other forms of stress alleviation, include:

1. Recognizing thoughts, feelings, and reactions to stressful situations.
2. Identifying what the reaction was based on.
3. Rehearsing future situations based on rational beliefs and information rather than on irrational fears.
4. Performing cognitively correct behaviors.

Behavior training may be included in some systems, but may be better explained as a separate entity under the auspices of behavioral approaches.

The Behavioral Approach

Behavioral approaches should be included in all drug intervention programs. These approaches may take the form of behavior modification or may stem from other psychotherapy theory such as Neurolinguistic Programming or transpersonal psychology. However, regardless of the approach, these basic elements usually are included:

1. Assertiveness training
2. Journaling, diary-keeping, or self-monitoring
3. Affirming positive resource states
4. Contracting
5. Decision making

Each of these elements aims at behavior change toward greater self-efficacy.

Assertiveness training helps to develop the ability to express honest feelings with ease and comfort and to take advantage of personal rights without denying others of theirs. These learned behaviors are dependent upon autonomy, which in turn is based upon good self-concept and self-confidence (Chenevert, 1983; Shainess, 1984). Successful assertiveness training programs give students the opportunity to practice assertiveness skills in class by role playing their own uncomfortable life situations and allowing rehearsal of new skills outside the classroom with guaranteed support from within. Assertiveness and self-esteem feed on each other in a positive feedback cycle.

Journaling, diary-keeping, and self-monitoring are integral parts of self-discovery, which is necessary before behavior change can occur. There are highly developed schools of journaling (e.g., Proghoff, 1980) that can promote rapid emotional growth, and all three vehicles promote self-awareness and give direction to new behavior. Behavior modification programs always ask the individual to do some kind of self-monitoring, whether the program be smoking cessation, weight reduction, or any other kind of behavior change (Stuart & Davis, 1978).

Using *affirmations* has been referred to as psychological seeding—implanting positive attributes and behaviors in the mind to replace old, negative thoughts. The affirmation is a verbal or written description of a desired attribute or behavior stated in the present tense, as if the result has already been achieved; e.g., "I am an assertive person." This affirmation is then used to create reality.

Since all individuals have succeeded at something in their lives, it is also possible to have students reclaim (relive) such a time and use it as a positive resource state to help them toward other successes. Through theory of projection (seeing in others what is unclaimed in the self), people can also affirm for themselves what they admire in others. Another form of affirming positive behavior is seen in the mental imagery technique that is being studied in the fight against cancer (Simonton et al., 1978) and other diseases (Goleman, 1984).

Two simple forms of doing affirmations are stating out loud or writing down one desired state (in the present tense) ten times upon arising and/or going to sleep at night. Sondra Ray (1982) gives a number of specific examples of affirmation techniques, as do Hay (1984), Houston (1982), and Zdenek (1983).

The helper or buddy system, which provides ready support for wanted behaviors, works on the theory of positive feedback or reward. When individuals are going through the same training, i.e., having similar behavior problems, the buddy system is employed to help both maintain desired behaviors. Techniques might include the freedom to call each other at any hour of the day or night if needed, getting together socially, or sharing personal feelings. The helper system may involve two trainees, but many times it is a nontrainee significant other who is the helper for the person undergoing behavior change. It is useful for the individual to supply a written request list citing specific areas of help desired from a helper. Such examples would be: "Please do not nag, scold, or preach about my desired behavior change." "Please remind me when I use victim language," or "Please be supportive of me when I feel weak and want to succumb to my old, unwanted behavior."

Contracting is another technique for reinforcing behavior change. Many smoking cessation and other drug behavior change programs ask the client to sign a personalized contract including these items: (1) a statement claiming willingness to make a behavior change, (2) definite time guidelines of when that change will occur, and (3) visible proof(s) that the behavior is in fact changing in the desired direction. These contracts are usually signed by witnesses or in some way made public in order to reinforce the commitment. Contracting theory and use are further outlined in Ostrander and Schroeder (1978).

Formal training in *decision making* can aid in not only the initial decision to change drug-taking behavior but also in other areas of one's life that are causing stress and which may be at the root of unwanted behavior (Leventhal & Cleary, 1981). Training in decision making many times includes the other methods that have been discussed in this section, such as cognitive techniques, assertiveness, and so forth.

Skill Training

A potential strategy in the fight against drug abuse is providing attractive alternatives to the use of drugs. If the desire to change one's consciousness must be met, it can be met through safe, constructive, and creative means which also enhance self-esteem and self-actualization. These means include meditation and other related techniques, such as biofeedback training, yoga, autogenic training, and neuromuscular relaxation. All are positive approaches to reaching an expanded state of consciousness and which, when compared to taking drugs, are less dangerous, more controllable, active and creative, requiring and promoting self-control and self-discipline. These qualities can serve as both means and ends. This section on skill training describes five mind-control skills.

Meditation. Meditation appears to be the most simple, most direct, and most popular approach to mind control, body control, and self-transcendence. The term *meditation* usually refers to a specific technique but should be considered a state of mind, the same state of mind that can be induced by other popular techniques.

Modern meditative practices represent a mixture of philosophies and techniques descended from ancient Yoga and Zen Buddhism. As time passed, slight variations in philosophy and/or technique led to the development of numerous forms of meditation, and today's marketplace of meditative disciplines is indeed plentiful. Regardless of their ancestry, all the meditative techniques have at least two phases, which in general include a quiet body and a quiet mind. One cannot relax or quiet the mind if the brain is being bombarded with the stimulation of tense muscles and hyperactive glands. Thus, elaborate exercises, postures, and other rituals were developed in an attempt to slow the body activities to a point where the mind would also be allowed to become quiet. The primary goal is to reduce what is referred to as the "surface chatter" of the mind . . . the constant thinking in the form of planning, remembering, and fantasizing that seems to occupy our every waking moment and keeps us implanted in our ego consciousness. As the ego chatter diminishes, so do the ego defenses. Anxiety is reduced; thus arousal is reduced as both the body and the mind achieve the quiet and peace natural to the ego- or self-transcendent state of consciousness.

Research on meditation has shown that during meditation the activity of most physical systems is reduced; thus unlike drugs, meditation does seem to induce physical relaxation. At the same time, the meditator is in complete control of the experience and has control over emotions, feelings, and memories. Although meditation is a passive *state of mind,* it is an active *process* that takes thought, preparation, and practice.

Common to all meditation are concentration and the closely related techniques of contemplation and mental repetition. Concentration demands control over the mind's tendency to daydream and flip from one ego-related thought to another. The technique of meditation includes a myriad of ways to help learn concentration. The most widely used is the verbal or mental repetition of a word or sound called a *mantra.* A mantra can be a single word such as "om" (a Sanskrit word meaning to be "whole" or "one"), considered to be the universal mantra, or a phrase from the teachings of ancient Yoga masters. Herbert Benson (1975), who Westernized meditation in his work, *Relaxation Response,* simply uses the word "one." Benson deritualized meditation, thus giving a technique to those who felt uncomfortable with Eastern philosophy and rituals.

Biofeedback Training. One problem with meditation is the subjectiveness of the process. Most students simply take for granted that if they follow the instructions given them, they are in fact meditating, but many express doubt of obtaining an altered state. When compared with the drug experience the signs are subtle. Occasionally there is visual imagery and a sense of detachment from the body, but most physical sensations are confined to a heaviness or numbness in the limbs and an extreme sense of relaxation and calm. Electroencephalographic studies of experienced meditators do show that during meditation, slowed brain-wave states are induced. While some researchers contend that the presence of slowed brain waves does not necessarily indicate a meditative state, it has been generally established that tranquil states are most often related to slowed brain wave states (Table 12.1).

The purpose of biofeedback is to heighten awareness of body function. Biofeedback is best understood as an educational tool that provides information about behavior or performance. A gross example of a biofeedback instrument is the bathroom scale. It gives feedback information on the success or failure of a weight-loss program. More sophisticated biofeedback instrumentation can detect the amount of tension in muscles, the temperature of the skin, the activity of the brain, blood pressure, or other biological signals that are usually not readily apparent. Biofeedback magnifies the subtle signals of the body so that they become more noticeable, and change can be charted.

Researchers and clinicians are using EEG biofeedback to train individuals to produce and maintain slow brain-wave states at will. The motivation varies from the reduction of stress, to getting high, to increasing creativity. The benefits are similar to those of meditation, that is, a production of an altered state of consciousness, an interaction with the interior self, increased self-awareness, and increased self-control. Like meditation, the individual actively produces the state at will and can terminate it instantly, while remaining close to normal thinking consciousness. Unlike meditation, however, the individual knows for sure that an altered brain state does exist. Biofeedback is only a learning tool, though. One learns to produce the

Table 12.1   States of Consciousness as Determined by Brain Waves, and Feelings Often Associated with Each State*

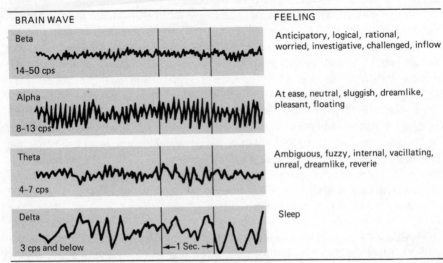

BRAIN WAVE	FEELING
Beta 14–50 cps	Anticipatory, logical, rational, worried, investigative, challenged, inflow
Alpha 8–13 cps	At ease, neutral, sluggish, dreamlike, pleasant, floating
Theta 4–7 cps	Ambiguous, fuzzy, internal, vacillating, unreal, dreamlike, reverie
Delta 3 cps and below ←1 Sec.→	Sleep

*Benson, 1975.

state and sense its presence, and to reproduce it without the instrument. The sensing is thus transferred to an autosensory system. A drawback to biofeedback is that good instrumentation is expensive. What is available for less than $500 is totally inadequate. Yet, biofeedback has become so popular that those interested can usually search out a research project, counseling center, or clinic that may offer training.

It is extremely difficult to produce a tranquil, altered state of consciousness if the brain is being bombarded with stimuli. For example, if muscles are tense, feedback heightens activity of the reticular activating system and cortex activity is increased, further tensing the muscles and creating a positive feedback system, which makes relaxation difficult. Slowed brain waves may be impossible if such alpha-blocking activity is not reduced. Research has shown that the alpha state is associated with (and perhaps responsible for) reduced activity of the autonomic nervous system, and results in the diminished arousal of most systems including voluntary muscle tension. Biofeedback training of other systems such as muscles, temperature control, and respiration can likewise be techniques for controlling states of consciousness.

As in meditation, brain-wave biofeedback depends on the art of passive concentration so that alertness may be maintained, but that concentration itself does not induce tension and anxiety. To achieve full relaxation, one cannot be apprehensive; one must void the mind of memories, anticipation, and awareness of pain. Focusing on the internal self in general enhances one's awareness of self and enables one to better recognize the influence of thought and feelings and physical reactions. One begins to see the mind and body as a unit, which is a goal of biofeedback.

Yoga. The word *yoga* is derived from the Sanskrit root meaning "union" or "reunion," and is a method of physical, mental, and spiritual development based on the philosophies of Lord Krishna. Knowledge was passed from enlightened master to student, generation after generation for thousands of years before the first written record appeared around 200 B.C. in Patangali's Sutras. Since then thousands of books have been written describing the many types of yoga called *paths,* which have developed into spiritual schools and in many instances have become distinctly separate schools. Raja yoga or Royal yoga, the path to self-realization and enlightenment, is very similar to the meditative practice described earlier. The most popular path in the Western world is Hatha Yoga, which uses positions and exercises to promote physical and mental harmony. Most yoga practice starts with Hatha yoga, for it is said to provide the body with the health and endurance needed to learn more advanced forms of yoga. Hatha yoga is practiced for its own rewards, which include strength, flexibility, and the reduction of muscle tension; it calms the body in preparation for quiet altered states of consciousness.

Autogenic Training. "Auto-genesis" (self-generating) describes a variety of mind-directed techniques; however, the term *autogenic* has become synonymous with a technique associated with self-directed mental images. This describes a simple yet advanced technique centering on a conditioned pattern of responses that become associated with particular thoughts. Recall those moments when you allow your mind to run away with you and fantasize a tragic event. You get chills and the hair rises on the back of your neck. This represents a conditioned physiological response to that particular association. The opposite is true and also produces a dramatic physiological response. If you imagine yourself in your favorite relaxation spot, perhaps sitting on a quiet beach with the sun warming your body or fishing your favorite stream, a quieting response is physiologically triggered. The technique of autogenic training helps condition through self-generated recall of previous experiences. In other words, you talk to your body and tell it to assume a previously conditioned state of consciousness.

Neuromuscular Relaxation.   The technique of neuromuscular relaxation utilizes a series of subtle exercises in which specific muscles are first contracted and then relaxed. It requires intense but passive concentration on the activity itself, but more important, on the feeling of muscle tension. To fully relax the muscles one must be free of apprehension, and void the mind of memories, anticipations, and awareness of pain. The primary end is the reduction of muscle tension, and since reduced muscle tension diminishes stimulation of the brain, the secondary result is a focus of attention away from ego consciousness.

TO STEM THE TIDE

The professionals engaged in drug education and treatment continually petition for greater interest and funding, and parents continue to fear and to show concern that their children will be exposed to drug taking and dependency. If prevention is, indeed, worth a pound of cure, all institutions in the country will awaken to the need to continue to study the drug abuse problem, to better utilize proven means of intervention, and to disseminate information about successful programs. Only at that time will the spiral of drug abuse diminish to an all-time low.

REFERENCES

A Federal Strategy for Prevention of Drug Abuse and Drug Trafficking. Office of Policy Development, The White House, 1982.

Benson, Herbert. *The Relaxation Response.* New York: Avon Books, 1975.

Centers for Disease Control. *An Evaluation Handbook for Health Education Programs in Alcohol and Substance Abuse.* Washington, D.C.: Dept. of Health and Human Services, 1983.

Chenevert, Melodie. *STAT: Special Techniques in Assertiveness Training.* St. Louis, Mo.: Mosby, 1983.

Ellis, A., and R. Harper. *A Guide to Rational Living.* Hollywood, Calif.: Wilshire, 1971.

Eraker, Stephen A. "Smoking behavior cessation techniques and the health decision model." *JAMA,* 1986.

Glasser, William. *Reality Therapy.* New York: Harper & Row, 1975.

Goleman, Daniel. "Herbert Benson on the faith factor." *American Health* 3(3):48–53, 1984.

Hay, Louise L. *Heal Your Body.* Farmingdale, N.Y.: Coleman Publishing, 1984.

Houston, Jean. *The Possible Human.* Los Angeles: J. P. Tarcher, 1982.

Kriegel, Robert J., and Marilyn H. Kriegel. *C Zone: Peak Performance Under Pressure.* New York: Doubleday, 1984.

Leventhal, H., and P. Cleary "Review of the research and theory in behavioral risk modification." *Psychology Bulletin* 88:370–379, 1981.

Novaco, R. W. "Anger and coping with stress," in J. Foreyt and D. Rathzen, eds. *Cognitive Behavior Therapy*. New York: Plenum Press, 1978.

Ostrander, Sheila, and Lynn Schroeder (with Nancy Ostrander). *Superlearning*. New York: Delta, 1978.

Proghoff, Ira. *The Practice of Process Meditation*. New York: Dialogue House, 1980.

Ray, Sondra. *I Deserve Love*. Millbrae, Calif.: Les Femmes, 1982.

Shainess, Natalie, *Sweet Suffering: Woman as Victim*. New York: Bobbs-Merrill, 1984.

Simonton, O. Carl, S. Matthews-Simonton, and James Creighton. *Getting Well Again*. Los Angeles: J. P. Tarcher, 1978.

Stuart, R., and B. Davis. *Slim Chance in a Fat World*. Champaign, Ill.: Research Press, 1978.

Zdenek, Marilee. *The Right-Brain Experience*. New York: McGraw-Hill, 1983.

SUGGESTED READINGS

Brown, B. B. *Stress and the Art of Biofeedback*. New York: Harper & Row, 1977.

Buss, A. H. *Self-Consciousness and Social Anxiety*. San Francisco: W. H. Freeman, 1980.

Dickson, A. *A Woman in Your Own Right*. London: Quartet Books, 1982.

Everly, G. S., and D. A. Girdano. *The Stress Mess Solution*. Bowie, Md.: Robert Brady, 1980.

Girdano, D. A., and G. S. Everly. *Controlling Stress and Tension: A Holistic Approach*. 2nd ed. Englewood Cliffs, N.J.: Prentice-Hall, 1985.

Goldfried, M. R., and C. Robins. "On the facilitation of self-efficacy." *Cognitive Therapy and Research* 6:361–380, 1982.

Gottlieb, B. H., ed. *Social Networks and Social Support*. Beverly Hills, Calif.: Sage, 1981.

Grieger, R., and J. Boyd. *Rational-Emotive Therapy: A Skills-Based Approach*. New York: VanNostrand Reinhold, 1980.

Karoly, P., and F. H. Kaufer, eds. *Self-Management and Behavior Change: From Theory to Practice*. New York: Pergamon Press, 1982.

Mahoney, M. J. *Self-Change: Strategies for Solving Personal Problems*. New York: Norton, 1979.

McKay, M., M. Davis, and P. Fanning. *Thoughts and Feelings: The Art of Cognitive Stress Intervention*. Richmond, Calif.: New Harbinger, 1981.

Meichenbaum, D. *Cognitive Behavior Modification: An Integrative Approach*. New York: Plenum, 1977.

Moon, J. R., and R. M. Eisler. "Anger control: an experimental comparison of three behavioral treatments." *Behavior Therapy* 14:493–505, 1983.

Nezu, A., and T. J. D'Zurilla. "An experimental evaluation of the decision-making process in social problem solving." *Cognitive Therapy and Research* 3:269–277, 1979.

Mishria, R. *Yoga*. New York, Lancer Books, 1959.

Pelletier, K. R. *Mind as Healer: Mind as Slayer*. New York: Delta, 1977.

Peplau, L. A., and D. Perlman, eds. *Loneliness: A Sourcebook of Current Theory, Research and Therapy*. New York: Wiley, 1982.

Robbins, J., and D. Fisher. *Tranquility Without Pills*. New York: Wyden, 1972.

INDEX